TRUE
STORIES OF
WORLD WAR II

Edited by Robin Cross

LUME BOOKS

LUME BOOKS

First published by Michael O'Mara Books Limited in 1994

Copyright © Robin Cross 1994, 1995

This edition published in 2023 by Lume Books

The right of Robin Cross to be identified as the author of this work has been asserted by them in accordance with the Copyright, Design and Patents Act, 1988.

www.lumebooks.co.uk

CONTENTS

INTRODUCTION

The stories gathered here may read like high adventure, but to those who experienced battle it was both frightening and bewildering. What therefore is it like to be in the front line of battle? What is it like to engage in hand-to-hand fighting, to suffer bombardment, to test one's own courage at the sharp end where battles are won and lost? In World War II, mighty political and technical forces were harnessed but, at the end of the day, defeat was suffered and victory secured by the soldiers on the ground.

These eyewitness accounts bear testimony to the many faces of soldiering in the greatest conflict in human history. The reality of war with its strange combination of tedium, tension and terror is vividly evoked from sniping duels in the ruins of Stalingrad to the bitter battles fought for tiny islands in the Pacific Ocean, and the clash of armour in Normandy.

For some the war was a great adventure. For the émigré Vladimir Peniakoff it meant a chance to form his own 'private army' and wage personal war against the Third Reich. 'Popski', as Peniakoff was affectionately known, was an obvious 'hero' but many amazing exploits were undertaken by men (and women) who never thought of themselves as heroes and who would have hated to be so described.

There are, indeed, many examples of heroism in these pages, but they also show the other faces of war: muddle and confusion; the struggle to survive in inhuman conditions; the waste of young lives and the strange lottery which decided who lived and who died.

This anthology covers the major theatres of the war on land from a soldier's-eye view: Bill Maudlin's description of how his beloved infantrymen scratched home comforts from the wreckage as they fought their way up the Italian peninsula and Ken Tout bouncing his tank through the killing grounds of the Normandy bocage.

These are their stories which speak with an immediacy that bridges the gap of half a century between us and those titanic events. From generals to GIs, these are the true voices of men at war.

1

DUNKIRK TO WAKE ISLAND

World War II, the effects of which are still working themselves out in the mid-1990s, began on 1 September 1939, when Germany invaded Poland. Two days later Britain and France declared war on Germany. Poland fell in six weeks, and was partitioned between Germany and the Soviet Union. The following eight months saw an uneasy lull on the Western Front known as the 'Phoney War', which came to an abrupt end in April 1940 when Germany invaded Denmark and Norway. On 10 May Hitler unleashed an offensive in the West which bundled the British Expeditionary Force (BEF) out of France. Bombardier J.E. Bowman was serving in the 22nd Field Regiment with the British 4th Infantry Division when the storm broke and the retreat began.

By the 22nd the defence of the River Escaut[1] had to be discontinued. Amiens, seventy miles to the south had fallen and the German tanks were at Boulogne, threatening the Channel ports. The effort to outflank us from the north went on relentlessly, with more concentrated attacks on the Belgians.

The BEF was placed on half rations, but it did not seem to make much difference. It wasn't all that unusual to see a squeaking piglet or two being hoisted into the cooks' wagon.

---

[1] The line to which the Allied armies in Belgium completed their withdrawal on 19 May. German advances to the south quickly made this line untenable.

The cooks were admirable providers, assiduous for our well-being, and worked better under pressure.

There was hostile shelling at Avelghem and Escanaffles and once more we put down fire on the bridge. Hostile air-burst ranging is reported for the first time, possibly, probably, by 88mm guns.

At about three o'clock in the afternoon the main German attack had developed and the 6th Black Watch of 12 Infantry Brigade had been pushed back on Castor Bridge. Two of the companies had to fight their way out.

We manhandled the Gun into a private garden, up the narrow drive, over the tiny lawn at the back and forward into a flower-bed with the summer flowers just forming. There was no sign of life. The occupants had either fled or were hiding. If they were at home they got a big shock when the first round went off, for the blast cracked a few windows. One bright, new, yellow shell followed another, rammed into the rifling and then up and away over the garden fence. The rest of the Troop were belting away in other gardens up the road and the air was filled with the sound of rotating projectiles, whirring away in their trajectories.

We pulled out, very hastily, just as it was getting dark. It was very lively, there were shell-bursts quite near and the small arms were rattling away too close for my liking. We sped away after the others, the fourth gun in the Troop, so it was harder for us to keep up and particularly difficult to catch up. We took a wrong turning. In a narrow road at the bottom of a hill with steep banks on either side we ran into the Black Watch who were withdrawing and dragging their wounded with them. They were slipping and sliding down the steep slope. I was half out of the tractor, about to give the order to unlimber in order to turn round, when Driver Burbanks, shouting for me to stay, did an impossible about turn, mounting a yard up each bank as he did so and saving us a valuable two or three minutes. Again, it was little short of a miracle that we found the right road and joined the Troop[2], for we had gone a few miles out of our way.

By 02.30 hrs on the 23rd the whole Division was across the Courtrai Canal. The infantry had marched another twenty-three miles. We were now north-west of Roncq in support of 12 Infantry Brigade, on a defence line erected during the winter by the BEF. I am as certain as I can be that no gun positions, previously prepared by us, were ever occupied by our Battery. On this day there was no firing. The enemy were busy catching up with us. In the afternoon of the 24th they arrived and shelled Lauwe and Haluin. Our own ammunition was now restricted.

This was the day when news finally got to us that we were in a very tight spot indeed and that we were edging our way to the coast. It was a good thing that we had no crystal ball in which to peer; and that the gauntlet that we would have to run when we got to the sea was hidden from us.

The day before, leading units of 1st Panzer[3] had passed Calais. Now they were only fifteen miles from Dunkirk. The British assessment was that Dunkirk would fall the next day, the 25th. Then a curious decision was made, the reasons for which have been speculated upon and discussed ever since. Herr Hitler decreed that the determined columns threatening Dunkirk should halt. Everyone sat back in amazement, wondering what the next trick was to be pulled out of the bag.

---

[2] Bowman's regiment had two batteries, each containing three guns troops and twelve guns.

[3] A German armoured division which was part of General Guderian's XIX Corps.

None came. We, unknowing, had been reprieved for a vital few more days. It was still far from a happy situation, however, for Dunkirk was overlooked by enemy guns from vantage points on high ground.

To the north the German infantry and guns were concentrating on the Belgians whose morale was deteriorating steadily. It would appear that they had given up.

From now on the adrenalin flowed faster. An atmosphere charged with anxiety and foreboding had crept in. Our primitive instincts of stealth and cunning became more pronounced in our struggle for survival.

Our Troop went to a 'rover' position at Werwicq on the 25th, with the wagon lines north of the river at Comines. The refugees were appearing in droves on the north side of the river, struggling to keep ahead of the fighting. They were not allowed across the bridge. What was left of a medium battery stayed with us for the night, but drew out next morning to join 4th Medium Battery RA. By the evening the BEF was almost enclosed, with eight French divisions.

On the morning of the 26th we came back to rejoin the Battery and pointed our guns northward. Massed columns of German troops of all arms, with a lot of horse-drawn transport could be seen moving along the Weleghem-Menin road. I wondered at the time why we did not blow them off it. Now I know that our ammunition was in short supply. The OP[4] was shelled by an enemy field battery.

From this point decisions changed almost hourly. Recce parties went out to find positions, only to find that they were already occupied by the 'mediums'. Other places were found

---

[4] Observation Post.

for us west of Ploegsteerte. There was an OP at Messines, an FOP (Forward Observation Post) at Warneton. Some trucks were abandoned (by orders from above I presume) but some left by other units but still in working order were commandeered. They should have been destroyed. From now onwards, wrecked vehicles were to be seen wherever we travelled.

Now it was revealed that King Leopold of the Belgians had surrendered and his army with him. To say that 3rd Division was in ever graver danger of being outflanked would be to understate the crisis. The Belgians had left bridges intact, just walked away from them as it were. They were blown by 3rd Division's sappers, just as the German recce patrols appeared.

Our own recce parties were reconnoitring positions and laying wire near Elverdinghe, north-west of Ypres. The OP was to have been at Brielen, a little over to the east. The wire was ordered to be cut, the recce party redirected to join the Regimental Column at Woesten, north of Elverdinghe on the Furnes road. In the late afternoon or early evening of the 28th, we were rolling our way northwards on the main road to Furnes.

The 3rd Division and the 50th were to hold the line of the Yser Canal, and were to fall back to an intricate plan, once the 2nd, 4th and 44th Divisions had withdrawn to what was to become known as the Dunkirk perimeter. Obviously the whole front was becoming compressed and the roads more and more congested.

The Colonel of the 12th Lancers of 3rd Division had the foresight to realize that the bridges over the Yser at Dixmude and at Nieuport would not only be undefended but would still be whole. He sent parties of his regiment to these places, accompanied by sappers of the Royal Monmouthshire RE, who blew the bridges. Had it not been for forethought such as this, and there must have been many such examples, we should never have got out.

The whole of the route from Louvain must have been spattered with wrecked bridges.

There was this village in which we hesitated and halted, running into the Hun, under shell fire and pointing the wrong way. Our infantry were busily engaged kicking open doors, lobbing grenades through windows and protecting each other as they darted from cover to cover. It must have been the village of Woesten, an intermediate point to which the 2nd Battalion, Royal Ulster Rifles of 3rd Division had just withdrawn. I understand that their Regimental History records that the events of the following day were to be one of their most disagreeable experiences.

This was no place for us so we did not waste much time unhooking Gun and limber, turning the tractor (with great difficulty – there was congestion), and hooking up again. Through debris, past sagging walls and burning interiors we edged along, as if on a conducted tour. Through a broken window I glimpsed a body hanging by the neck, swaying from a low beam. Summary justice was meted out in these parts. We crept along, up a corridor with enemy troops very close on one side, and not very far away on the other. Through Dickebusch and Vlamegtinghe, which is about half-way between Ypres and Poperinghe, with Passchendaele some ten miles over to the east, we made our slow journey. Veterans of the First World War were familiar with these names and so was my mother, for these were Flanders' fields where the poppies blew 'between the crosses, row on row'. More had come to join them, a new

8

generation. It was a blessing that my mother could not see us, but she and many another would be aware of our dilemma and would be sorely troubled on this night and on a few more nights to come.

At 02.00 hours on the 29th, the column halted at Furnes. Enemy patrols arrived at Dixmude a few hours later. Lord Gort had been told to evacuate as many as possible and about seven thousand troops had got away.

Not far from our final position we were in hiding under trees which lined the road. Sgt. Artificer Bickle was resting under a hedge, manipulating his primus stove, brewing up as casually as if he were on some Victorian picnic. He invited me to take tea with him, whilst overhead, flying low, contemptuous of our presence, wave after wave of heavy enemy bombers throbbed onwards, intent on spreading more suffering and devastation.

It was here that he gave me his book of Kipling's *Barrack-Room Ballads*, signed H.V. Bickle, Jubbulpore 1935. Of all my books, with the exception of those given me by my family over the years, it is the one I treasure most. He must have foreseen the grim struggle for survival which lay ahead for us, but he remained non-committal.

2nd corps, consisting of 3rd and 4th Divisions were assigned to hold the left or eastern flank of the Dunkirk perimeter. This they were to do until the night of 31st May/1st June.

We were in action early in the morning in our last position north of Oost-Dunkerque, on either side of the road to Nieuport. It became very lively. The OP was on a bridge at Nieuport until heavy hostile shelling forced the occupants to move to a house on the front at Nieuport-Bains. Under the direction of these persistent, harassed people at the OP, the Battery shelled Nieuport. The Belgians had failed to blow two more bridges. One Troop of 18prs. of 60th Field Regiment RA, joined us.

When the Battery had taken up position in a large clearing, surrounded by trees which gave us some air cover but did not interfere with our field of fire, I still did not know where I was. The English Channel was over there beyond the dunes and there was this place called Dunkirk further up the road which was becoming something of a talking point.

We dug slit-trenches and gun-pits in the soft, sandy soil. At least here was one place where we could dig in, for not only was the ground suitable but we stayed here two or three days, which was quite a change for us.

We recorded and fired on targets and dropped into our routine. Very few civilians showed themselves, none if they were wise, and there was a rumour here that Fifth Columnists were lurking about. Bullets were certainly being fired, for single rounds could be heard swishing through foliage, sometimes fraying branches. The sharpshooters must have been banging away haphazardly or have been very bad shots, for as far as I know, no one was hit by missiles. Gunner L——, his courageous spirit made even better with wine, took an anti-tank rifle with him into the lower branches of a tree, mouthing a string of indecipherable Gaelic curses with the word 'bastard' frequently interpolated. The anti-tank rifle was a big cumbersome weapon on the lines of an elephant gun. No one ever discovered what L——'s target had been. Had it been real or was it some wild Scottish wraith summoned by his wine-fevered brain?

At his one and only shot, L—— was propelled from the tree by the powerful recoil and was brought hastily to the ground, shaken but with no limbs broken. We laughed a lot as we dusted him down. I was glad to have been at Woolwich with him.

The Command Post had its troubles. Heavy shelling caused it to be moved. The one hostile observation balloon was reported, but there is no evidence to suggest that we did anything about it. Signal wires were being cut by shell fire and also by saboteurs, for those lines laid along the roadside suffered most. 'A' and 'C' Troops took two guns each from 'B' Troop. I remember them coming in on the left of my Gun.

We were not short of ammunition now. On the 30th two guns from each Troop were destroyed by their own gunners. More rounds were distributed to us, the ones who were left.

A sergeant of one of the guns which had joined us was sitting on the trail having a bite to eat when he dropped over dead. A small shell splinter from a shell exploding at what was thought to be a safe distance had pierced a vital part and killed him immediately.

By this date 100,000 French and British troops had already been evacuated. At night two officers and sixty ORs 'left for home'. I have always been under the impression that the married men and those under a certain age were chosen. There must have been few who were younger than I, yet I remained. As for being married, I must confess that I wouldn't have shied away from the matrimonial knot just then, provided that I could have obtained a lightning divorce. Nor would consummation have been insisted on in my *mariage de convenance*. I was too worn out.

It appears that embarkation points had been set up. I am told by one of the officers in charge of the party which had just left that the Regiment's column was split up at Bray Dunes, between La Panne and Dunkirk, not far from where I was, by an air attack just after dawn. People had to make their own way in groups or individually.

Here was I still, however, on this night of 30/31st May, with Sergeant-Major Prior and one or two others, including Driver Dodds.

Round the Gun the shells and cartridges were stacked. I was not unmindful of the fact that if they were hit we would be distributed over a wide area.

The Sergeant-Major, back at his former role as No. 1, took over as No. 2 as well and rammed the shells and also operated the breech. I brought up the ammunition, loaded, layed and fired the Gun. Doubtless the lean and nimble Sergeant-Major brought up a few rounds between whiles. We had quite a time of it, the Sergeant-Major and I, for although the firing was by no means continuous we indulged in short, hectic bursts of energy. Our frenetic movements, had anyone been there to see, must have appeared like an old film which had been speeded up. Appropriate tunes should have been played on the honky-tonk piano, but we had our own accompaniment.

Deeply engaged in one of our lonely, vociferous escapades, with the Sergeant-Major and I throwing ourselves about in slavish fashion and the Gun rearing back and belching, we both registered a very short whistle followed by an ominous dull thud which seemed to come from under the Gun. We exchanged quick looks of alarm.

Of course, this happened in the small hours when the body's resistance is said to be at a low ebb. We, the unwashed and smoke blackened, were still very much awake, in our begrimed uniforms which we had worn night and day for three weeks.

There was just one redeeming feature. It had seldom rained.

Between times I sprawled on the mound of shells, regardless of the danger, and pulled on a cigarette, concealing the glow of its tip as only soldiers can. I could have sunk a pint or two, but no alcohol had passed my lips during the campaign. We got a long break for two or three hours before dawn, so I settled down in a slit-trench and ate two tins of bacon, which was rolled in greaseproof paper. They were delicious – an outstanding gourmet's delight. There was no shortage. I could have had a hundred such tins, for who was left to eat them? Afterwards I chain-smoked my way into a cylindrical tin of Players Export.

My eardrums were still buzzing, but then, I was accustomed to it. It went with the job.

At dawn the Sergeant-Major and I looked under the Gun. In the centre, between the wheels was a hole in the ground, clearly visible. We could only conclude that a large projectile had burrowed its way in and failed to go off.

On the 31st the shelling and air attacks continued, and intensified as the day wore on.

It was a strange atmosphere, for although we were not 'stonked'[5] in the strictest sense it was as well to be watchful, for things flew about with no set pattern and at no set time. Sometimes simultaneous explosions accompanied great clouds of dust and smoke which flew up in a line a hundred yards or so in front of the Gun. I did not investigate, but there seemed to be nothing just there to shoot at. This thunderous group of giant hammer strokes would occur periodically. One of my mates did have a look, but all he got was a severe wound in the back. The last I saw of him was when I helped to lift him into

---

[5] British military slang for a heavy artillery bombardment.

13

a 15 cwt truck which was brought into use as an ambulance. He arrived home safely and made a good recovery.

Others were not so fortunate. A cook walking through the clearing to collect wood for his fire caught a piece of metal in his chest. The fragment spun his woollen vest into the cavity it made. A young officer was machine-gunned from the air and was found wounded in his truck.

We fired off more ammunition from our great pile, but there was still some left when, towards evening, we were ordered to destroy the guns.

There must be few gunners who have had to undertake this drastic task. It is a shameful thing and is only done when all else has failed. Little did I know that mass destruction was taking place everywhere. Vehicles, weapons, equipment and stores were being smashed and wrecked so that they would be useless to the enemy, who was now right on top of us.

Sergeant-Major Prior and I went to each gun in turn.

The Sergeant-Major says that 'Tiffy' Bickle was present, and there is every reason to believe that he was, for he was the obvious person most qualified to supervise such drastic action, even though he would resent it most strongly. I personally cannot recollect his being there, but the occasion was, to say the least, tense, and I have discovered from other researchers that the mind tends to distort or to bypass some details.

The procedure is set out in the 'Gun Drill for Q.F. 25pr.', in Appendix IV under 'Disablement'. 'The extent of disablement ordered will depend on the time available and the probability of recapture. To destroy the gun. Place an HE shell in the muzzle. Load with HE. Fire the gun from under cover by means of a length of rope or telephone wire attached to the firing lever.'

The defiant death-cry of the Gun was in keeping with His arrogant nature. He went out with a very big bang. His last round had been fired and I, His Personal Bodyguard, had destroyed Him.

Neither I nor the Sergeant-Major looked back or spoke as we climbed into the remaining vehicle which was to take us to the beach; nor did we talk much about it afterwards. There was firing all round us. Shell bursts, mortar fire and bullets from light weapons were closing in. It really was time to go.

I had removed the Dial-sight and Telescopic Sight. These I took with me. I placed the stiff leather cover of the Dial-sight between my legs, tucked well into the lower part of my body as I sat in the tractor. My intention was to save not only the valuable instrument but to protect those parts which were to me even more valuable.

It appears that we were not quite the last of our Battery to leave. Almost the final entry in the War Diary reads:

May 31 1900hrs. Destroyed most transport and all guns exc. I see, under 2/Lt. Babington, which remained in action until 2400 hrs....

Everyone who was at Dunkirk will have his own personal story. There are as many tales as there were people. This is mine. It cannot be verified, nor can it be queried except by those who question its truthfulness, for I travelled alone for much of the time.

On alighting from the Quad, it was just getting dark. We walked down a narrow street, presumably leaving the driver to wreck this, our last tractor.

Three things happened to me in very rapid succession, convincing me that I had been dumped in a very unhealthy spot indeed. I had been given no indication at all of what to expect, but in all fairness, I don't think many in authority would have anticipated such a violent greeting either.

With no warning at all there was a brilliant flame and a tremendous crash. It took me a few seconds to collect myself and even then it was difficult to assess what I saw. I was sprawled out alongside what looked like a naked woman. There had been no preliminary love-play. Here it was, laid out on a plate. The earth had really moved for me.

On further inspection, more figures were revealed, some with fragments of flimsy clothing attached. The figures were not made of flesh or bone. I had been blown through the glass window of a shop specializing in ladies' underwear. I stood up and dusted myself, stumbled over a dummy, said 'F ... ' and found the Dial-sight.

Launched once more on my journey, I followed other cautious wayfarers until I came to what I took to be the edge of a beach.

The earth moved again, but this time I was very, very conscious of it. I seemed to be part of and surrounded by a kaleidoscope of coloured lights. There were green, yellow, many colours, but purple predominated. I was deafened temporarily by the explosion. I think it must have been a big shell which had burst almost on top of me for there was no sound of aircraft. It had buried itself deep in the sand before it burst.

My ears hurt, my eyes had gone out of focus but I could still walk, even if I did stagger about at first.

As I walked over the sand I could see the light reflected on what I took to be the sea. Now that I was more orientated and my eyes had readjusted themselves, I observed a great glow over to the left which was Dunkirk. There were flashes all round, even out to sea, the unmistakable flashes of guns. Over the horizon, way out to sea, these glows came and went. Express trains passed high overhead and there were great 'crumps' inland. I assumed that the Navy's battle-wagons were sitting way out to sea, firing their big stuff at Jerry.

By the water's edge was a long queue of men waiting patiently. There was some sort of pier or pontoon stretching out into the sea but I could not see any boats. No one spoke. We just stood and waited on that night of 31st May, staring silently out to sea, each one of us aware of the menace which surrounded us, each one intent on his own preservation.

It is only recently that I have discovered that this structure, seen only by me in the darkness, was indeed a causeway which the sappers had constructed on two columns of lorries which they had driven into the sea. The idea was to run a shuttle service of small boats to and from this pier to the destroyers and whatever other vessels had collected a mile or so out to sea. At the start of the evacuation from this point there were only fifteen small boats and the journey out took over an hour. Three squadrons of bombers had attacked at dusk, before I got there, or did I catch the tail-end of it, and the 'Fourth Division' account states that a medium gun had ranged on the area. It concludes: 'The embarkation began at nine at night; four hours later not more than four hundred men of the Division had been embarked.'

To my mind, there was not just one medium gun. Quite a few cannons had their muzzles pointing in our direction, and there were plenty of free samples being distributed, courtesy of Krupps ammunition works in Essen, to show for it.

Nothing was fair in these encounters. Out of the blue there came a salvo of high velocity shells firing air-bursts. I thought they were 88 mm. The fragments whistled and screamed down on us, clearly visible like fire-flies in the darkness. The shells burst above our heads with ear-splitting force. I knew at once that this 'stonk' was prerecorded. Jerry was putting down harassing fire on a target on which he had ranged accurately during the daylight. We had done the same thing to the Hun many times in the past weeks. I was getting some of my own medicine, and it was not nice. As a fellow artilleryman I could not help but admit his accuracy, but I did not stay to appreciate it.

I turned and ran as fast as I could, ducking instinctively as I went. Of course, others had the same idea. A soldier running in a crazy uncontrolled fashion in front of me, let something fall. I caught it as it fell and shouted, 'Hey mate, you've dropped something.' Indeed he had, but he never returned to retrieve it. It was his arm, severed at the shoulder. I got rid of it. It was no use to either of us.

'Bloody hell,' I said to myself, 'let's get out of here.' It was not a very articulate statement, but it had a great feeling behind it.

On the edge of the dunes was a beach hut, still undamaged, from which came signs of activity. I looked inside and wonder of wonders, on all that beach, in all that turmoil here were a few of our chaps brewing up. Among them was Bombardier Anstee, huge and brawny, possibly more formidable than Bombardier Earle, and the ubiquitous Sergeant-Artificer

Bickle. Anstee had left the Battery the evening before, but had only got this far.

'What are you on, you little bleeder?' quoth Anstee. He didn't get up to give me a characteristic nudge, the nearest he ever came to affectionate greeting. I was glad, for it would have knocked me over. Instead he proffered a mug of char. Like Sergeant-Artificer Bickle, wherever Anstee was there was a pint of hot, sweet tea with plenty of tinned milk.

I kipped down with them for the night. If the events of the last hour or so could be considered as a sort of hors-d'oeuvre, an introduction to the main course, I was not very keen on sampling the rest of the menu.

But it had to be sampled. Either we went on and faced what there was to face or we would be taken prisoner, possibly shot in the process. I did not relish the thought of being stuck away in a prisoner-of-war camp for the duration. If we stayed where we were and waited for Jerry we would be shot at anyway. Our backs were really up against the wall. England was only a few miles across the Channel, but apparently it was inaccessible.

Sergeant-Artificer Bickle had me up and about just after dawn.

'Bombardier Bowman,' he said, 'come down to the beach with me ek dum. There is an anti-aircraft gun which, with a little repair, we can turn on the Hun.'

My heart sank right down to the soles of my boots. I was not very happy as it was, and being a night owl I was even less happy when I was expected to peck about on dangerous beaches just after sunrise.

'Christ,' I thought, 'this Kiplingesque gesture is going a bit too far.'

I obeyed his order and went out with him to inspect his bloody cannon, hoping that it had been blown away. My attitude may not have been in the best tradition of the Regiment, but he had caught me at a bad time. ·

We arrived at our objective, a strange looking, small anti-aircraft gun of foreign extraction. It was smaller than a Bofors and stood out in splendid isolation. 'This is where you hand in your dinner-pail, Bombardier Bowman. Open up with this bloody thing and we'll be stonked by the whole f ... g German Air Force.'

I was reminded of Lord Cardigan's comment before the Charge of the Light Brigade.

'Lord Cardigan saluted once more, wheeled his horse and rode over to his second-in-command, Lord George Paget, remarking aloud to himself as he did so, "Well here goes the last of the Brudenells." '

He survived, against tremendous odds but I didn't think that there was much chance for us.

The expert artificer cast his professional eye over his discovery. Everything seemed to be in order. There was ammunition. But on closer examination the firing pin was missing. Without tools and material there was no way of making or even improvising such a fundamental part.

My cold perspiration subsided. The opportunity of earning a posthumous VC was gone and I was reprieved. My friend walked disconsolately back to the dunes. I never saw him again. By that one act alone, unrewarding though it had proved, he had earned his place in Valhalla.

It was a beautiful morning, with the sunlight reflecting on the water, but there were few I think who would appreciate it. All along the water's edge were ragged lines of khaki-clad figures, stretching out into the sea. One or two groups were struggling with rowing boats. Apart from these I could see no other vessels of any kind, apart from one intrepid naval vessel standing at a distance offshore. It was either a frigate or a destroyer. As I looked an explosion seemed to take place and the ship sank with no fuss whatsoever. The bows tilted right up out of the water, then the hull went down vertically until it disappeared. Only a few seconds seemed to have elapsed from beginning to end. I saw no survivors, no wreckage. Where that brave ship had been there was only the smooth glistening surface of the sea.

As I was still blinking in disbelief at what I had seen, or thought I had seen, the Messerschmitts came in flying low, one following the other at a safe distance and firing their machine-guns as they came. Everyone in sight flung himself to the ground like a puppet jerked on a string. The heart raced and the adrenalin really flowed. Lying stretched out in the sand and trying to burrow into it, I tilted my head a little and saw the sardonic leer of the pilot, his head encased in a black flying helmet.

The bullets spat into the sand in straight lines. One hit the ground between my body and my left arm with a great smack, just below the armpit. I watched the line of bullets spit along. One hit the water-bottle of the man two or three yards in front of me and another hit him in the shoulder. The fellow further along was not so lucky for he looked as if he had been stitched by a giant sewing machine. Bullets had gone up the middle of his back and the last one had taken off the top of his head. Blood spewed out of the stitches. Discarded equipment littered the beach and all along there were rifles sticking up in the sand with tin hats on top to show where the owner had been hastily buried.

I saw no future at all in staying in this area, so on to the road I went, by the beach huts and bungalows. Fortuitously, I met Driver Dodds, the same who had driven us to the beach. He was at the wheel of a 15 cwt truck now. Where he had acquired it or where he had got the petrol from were twin mysteries. Driver Dodds had unrevealed properties. One of them was a cheerful optimism in a very tight corner, the other was resourcefulness of a very high quality. Dodds considered it would be a good idea to take a gentle morning drive into Dunkirk, for he thought we should have a better chance of getting a lift home. There was a lot of sense in what he said so I climbed aboard, with a couple of others. The driver leant back in his seat as he drove, passing the time of day and making pleasant small-talk about the scenery, seemingly oblivious to the fact that there were shells, bombs and hostile aircraft all conspiring to kill us. Furthermore, as we drew near to Dunkirk there were increasing signs of destruction, unpleasant sounds and much smoke and fire.

It goes without saying that I was tired. I was also so dirty that no self-respecting tramp would have come within sniffing distance. My socks felt as if they had been soaked in treacle. No longer was I a milk-faced boy, for three weeks the sun had shone and for the whole time I had been exposed to it. I took off my steel-helmet and wiped the sweat off my face and brow. There was a great dent in the helmet where something very solid had tried to penetrate.

I still had the Dial-sight. Having brought it so far I was absolutely adamant about hanging on to it.

Driver Dodds, he with the compass grafted into his brain, did not think it prudent to drive any further when bits of masonry started to fall on the bonnet of his truck. Nor did I. We decided to ditch it and put it out of action. Very warily we made our way through empty streets where walls were bulging dangerously and threatening to fall on us and where fires burnt unattended. The only movement was from hunted folk such as ourselves. Once we stopped for cover in a big cellar which was filled mainly with civilians. They made us welcome but we could not stay. Time was running out for us. Eventually, having threaded our way over mounds of rubble and round wrecked and burnt out trucks, taking whatever shelter we could get when the whistle of a bomb told us it was close, we came to the Mole at Dunkirk. It was getting on for late afternoon on 1st June.

At the approach to the pier, on the left-hand side were sitting two brass-hats eating their haversack rations. I could tell by the red tabs on their collars and by the elaborate braided insignia on their hats that they were military men of high rank.

I went on to the pier unheeded, walking cautiously over planks which had been laid over great gaping holes caused by explosions. Drifts of smoke hung about and there was the stink of cordite. A guarded, watchful atmosphere surrounded the pier, common to places which are under surveillance by an enemy.

Bodies were lying to one side, motionless under greatcoats or groundsheets. Round them flies buzzed and hovered, attracted to the blood.

A boat was moored to the pier, making steam. Wounded men were being taken aboard and some of them were in a sorry state. Faces were hidden in blood-stained bandages, legs which had been hastily tended with field dressings showed savage, raw gashes from which blood oozed. Men with abdominal wounds groaned and writhed, or just lay back, their faces drawn and waxen.

I became devious. Here was a ship and given the slightest chance I would sail in her. I mingled with the troops, a motley lot representing several regiments, who were carrying the stretchers on board. As I helped with one stretcher after another my own clothing became blood-stained.

The vessel was almost full and I could see that she was preparing to cast off. When my last burden had been put down I promptly got lost in the crowd. As we slid away from the jetty Jerry had one final go at us. We suffered a near miss from a bomb, but there was no apparent damage and we slipped out of the harbour and into the gathering darkness.

In a cubby-hole below decks a sailor in a blue jersey and trousers was curled up asleep. There was room for one more so I edged in quietly beside him with my few possessions and fell into a deep sleep.

I must have awakened when the engine stopped throbbing. There were signs of movement on board and the ship was stationary. Nudging my companion who had not moved an inch I said, 'Hey mate, we must be in Blighty.'

There was no response so I examined him more closely. I found that he was ice-cold and rigid, but there was no outward sign of injury. Afterwards, when I thought about it, for my reaction at the time was vague, I considered that there must be few people who had crossed the Channel, unaware that they had a corpse for a bedfellow.

There is always a certain type of chap who can come up with the answer. Up on the deck, leaning on the rail I asked the bloke next to me where we were and what was holding us up. We were standing off Dover Harbour, he said, waiting for the boom to be lowered so that we could enter and dock. I understood that the boom was a chain which was raised underwater to stop submarines from getting in, but I never checked the authenticity of his information.

The white cliffs were there all right and just down the road was Shorncliffe Barracks where it had all started nine months before. It seemed a lot longer than that and I felt a lot older.

The catalogue of British disasters in the opening two years of the war was mitigated by victory over the Luftwaffe in the Battle of Britain and the Italians in North Africa. In the desert war things got tougher for the British Eighth Army after the arrival of the Afrika Korps, commanded by General Erwin Rommel, in February 1941. The flavour of the tank battles fought in this phase of the struggle is vividly caught by Robert Crisp, who commanded a 'Honey' tank, the name conferred by British crews on the American Stuart M3 light tank. It earned the nickname because of its excellent handling qualities, reliability and ease of maintenance.

The order went through all the intercoms from commander to crew: 'Driver, advance. Speed up. Gunner, load both guns.' The Honeys positively leapt over the top of the ridge and plunged down the steady incline to the Trigh.[1] I knew my driver, who was getting used to this sort of thing, would have his foot hard down on the accelerator, straining his eyes through the narrow slit before him to avoid the sudden outcrops of rock or the slit trenches that littered this oft-contested terrain. On each side the Honeys were up level with me. That was good. My wrist-

---

[1] The Trigh Capuzzo, the main east-west track in Cyrenaica, the eastern province of the Italian colony of Libya, and the scene of much bitter fighting in the desert war.

watch showed 1 o'clock as I gripped hard on the edge of the cupola and pressed back against the side to ride the bucking tank.

We were half-way down the slope and going like bats out of hell in the bright sunlight before the Jerries realized what was happening. Then the familiar pattern of alarm and confusion and panic-flight away from us at right angles to the road. There was no slackening of speed, and within another minute we had hit the soft sand of the well-worn desert highway and become absorbed into the cloud of dust and that frightened herd of vehicles stampeding blindly northwards.

I had the same intention in my mind as on a previous occasion – to go right through them, turn about and cut off as many as possible, shooting up everything that tried to get past. I put the mike close to my lips and told my tank commanders briefly to start shooting. My own gunner pulled the trigger immediately and within seconds the dust was full of the criss-cross pattern of tracers drawing red lines through the yellow cloud and puncturing the fleeing dark shapes with deadly points. From the turret tops we let go with tommy-guns and revolvers, and every now and again the whip-crack of the 37-mm interjected the staccato chatter of the Brownings. I could still see a Honey or two racing alongside, but what was happening beyond the narrow limits of vision I could only guess. And my guess was that the whole squadron was there. Another minute perhaps, I thought, and then I would give the order to turn about.

Suddenly, through the dust, I saw the flat plane of the ground disappear into space. I yelled like mad at the driver to halt. He had seen the danger only a fraction of a second after I had, and jerked back on the brakes even while I was shouting at him.

The tracks locked fast and tore up sand, rock and scrub in a brief and frantic tussle to stop the momentum of the tank. We skidded to a violent stop with the front sprockets hanging over a sharp drop that started the descent of a steep escarpment.

The first thing I saw, through popping eyes, ten yards in front and below me, was a motor-cycle combination lying on its side with three German soldiers standing stiffly at attention in a row beside it, their backs towards me and their hands stretched high above their heads. I rejected immediately a quick impulse to shoot them. While my mind was still trying to absorb this apparition I became aware of the astonishing scene at the foot of the escarpment, where it levelled out into a broad wadi. Vehicles of all shapes and sizes were everywhere – some upright and still moving away as fast as they could; others stationary and bewildered; many lying on their sides or backs with wheels poking grotesquely upwards. Dark figures of men darted wildly about.

Even as I watched, a great lorry went plunging down the escarpment out of control; it struck some outcrop and leapt high into the air, somersaulting to the bottom in a fantastic avalanche of earth, rock and scrub and odd-shaped bundles of men integrated with jagged pieces of wood and metal. The concentration of transport in the wadi below was a wonderful target. I said quickly into the mouthpiece: 'Both guns. Mens and vehicles. Fire with everything you've got.'

The bullets went zipping inches above the heads of the three immovable figures in front of the tank. They never twitched a muscle. When the 37-mm cannon suddenly went off they jumped involuntarily, but none of them turned their heads or gave any indication that I could see of fear or curiosity. They just stood there, three backs and three pairs of arms while the tracers went streaming in flat, straight lines into the dusty turmoil below. I wondered idly where the rest of the Honeys were, and if they were having as good a time as mine was.

Suddenly there was a fearful bang, and simultaneously I was drenched from head to foot in an astonishing cascade of cold water. For a moment or two I was physically and mentally paralysed. I just could not believe that anything like that could happen. Then realisation came swiftly and terribly … the water tins on the back of the tank had been hit. It could mean only one thing. As I looked backwards I was already giving the order to the gunner to traverse the turret as fast as he bloody well could. In one comprehensive flash I saw it all, and the fear leapt up in me. Not fifty yards away a 50-mm anti-tank gun pointed straight at the Honey, pointed straight between my eyes. Beyond it were other guns and then as the dust drifted over the scarp the sight I had dreaded most – a number of motionless Honeys and the huddled figures of black-bereted men crouched on the sand or stretched out in the agony of death.

It took less than a second for the whole scene and its awful meaning to register in my mind. I could see the German gunners lamming the next shell into the breech as the turret whirled. I yelled: 'On. Machine gun. Fire.' In the same moment I saw the puff of smoke from the anti-tank gun and felt and heard the strike on the armour-plating. Quickly I looked down into the turret. A foot or two below me the gunner was staring at his hand, over which a dark red stain was slowly spreading. Then he gave a scream and fell grovelling on the floor. In the top right hand corner of the turret a jagged hole gaped, and through it, like some macabre peepshow, I could see the gun being reloaded. I knew that in another few seconds I would be dead, but something well beyond reason or sanity impelled my muscles and actions.

I leaned down and pulled the trigger, and kept my finger there until the gun jammed. God knows where the bullets went. Twice I felt the Honey shudder and the second time more water came pouring in. When the Browning stopped and my mind leapt about searching for some way to stay alive I suddenly saw the slim chance. If the tank would move at all, and we could drop over the edge of the escarpment, we would be out of sight of those blasted anti-tank guns. I could see them framed in that jagged hole, the gunners working feverishly, their faces strained and vicious. I said urgently into the mike: 'Driver, advance. Over the edge. Quick!'

Nothing. I thought: 'My God, Whaley's had it. We've all had it,' and screamed down into the turret: 'Driver, advance. For Christ's sake advance!' Then I saw what had happened. In falling, the gunner had jerked back on the intercom leads to the driver's earphones. The cords had tightened round his neck, pulling him backwards over the driving seat and half-strangling him. He wrestled frantically with his earphones and ripped them off. He didn't need them to hear my panic bellowing.

I felt the gears engage, and for a split second the world stood still. Then the engine revved, and the Honey heaved forward and dropped with a violent crash over the escarpment. In the turret we were hurled about like corks, and then the bouncing stopped and we rode smoothly down the slope. We were out of sight of the guns on the top of the escarpment, and with a great rush of unbelief I knew we were going to get away with it. The three German motor-cyclists still stood motionless. The tank could not have missed them by more than a few inches, yet they still had their hands in the air. Down in the driving compartment Whaley was wrestling with the sticks to keep the tank on a diagonal course that would take him to the bottom of the slope away from the enemy. When the ground levelled out a bit I ordered him to turn right to run into a little wadi that offered a safe way out to the south. We were travelling with the turret back to front, and I prodded the operator with my foot as he bent over the prostrate gunner and indicated to him that I wanted the turret traversed back to the normal position. While he was turning the handle I could not resist a last backward look at those three men. Incredibly, they were still standing as we had left them. I began to think they had become literally petrified with fright and would stay there down the centuries in some miraculous monument.

So much had happened in a few minutes, or a few hours it might have been, and I had looked so closely into the valley of the shadow, that I found it difficult to return to reality. I just could not fully absorb our situation. I had to grip the hardness of the armour-plating and see the familiar figures of the tank crew to realize that we were still alive, and that we were going to stay alive. The gunner lay their groaning in pain and sobbing in fear. There was nothing much wrong with him, and I shouted at him roughly to pull himself together. My thoughts went out to the rest of the squadron. Where were they? What had happened to them? Were they all dead? It was something I had to find out.

We were chugging along casually through the deserted silence of the wadi. It was uncanny after the tumult and terror just behind us, and the thought kept on intruding that we were no longer on earth, that we were driving in some ghost tank on another level of existence ... that we were all dead. When I put the mouthpiece to my lips I was half-prepared to hear no voice come out. The unreality persisted when the Honey swung right in response to my order, and moved slowly up the slope of the crest. As soon as my eyes were above the lip of the escarpment we halted, and the full picture of horror burst out on me immediately.

Not much more than 500 yards away, like a projection on a cinema screen, lay the battlefield. My eyes lifted to the tall black columns, leaning slightly with the wind, and followed them down to the Honeys' gasping smoke. Four of my tanks were blazing infernos; three others just sat there, sad and abandoned. A line of anti-tank guns, with their crews still manning them expectantly, lined the edge of the drop. The whole scene was silhouetted sharply against the yellow clouds of dust which rose in a thick fog from the wadi below. I could see many men running about between guns and tanks and vehicles. My heart ached as I picked out the familiar bereted figures of our own troops, huddled in disconsolate groups or being shepherded singly by gesticulating Germans.

The year of 1941 was a grim one for the British. At the end of April about 16,000 British and New Zealand troops were landed on Crete following the evacuation of Greece. They were reinforced by 12,000 troops from Egypt. At the end of May the island fell after an airborne invasion launched by General Kurt Student's XI Fliegerkorps. About 18,000 troops were rescued, but nine British warships were sunk and seventeen severely damaged during the evacuation. Geoffrey Cox, a New Zealander who had been a newspaperman before the war, was responsible for producing a news sheet for the Crete garrison, a task that was soon overtaken by the German invasion and the Allied evacuation.

The climb began for us immediately, as we had to cross a ridge to get to the main road south, which began its serpentine, curling route from a point closer to Suda. When we reached it, and linked up with the main body of Force HQ troops, who had come on from Suda, it was already dark. Yet the white, dusty road was crowded as if with people coming away from a football match, long lines of troops taking advantage of the darkness to move free of air attack. Some were marching in organised units, but many were just streams of individuals, or small groups, trudging along in the darkness, or resting at the roadside, or curling up to sleep under the olive trees. Ellis Waterhouse was with the thirty or so men from Force HQ, clerks and signallers and drivers and men of the defence platoon. They were, like so many British troops of the time, for the most part small, stunted men, a product of the years of bad housing and inadequate food and hygiene. I feared that they would not have the stamina to keep up a good pace. So Waterhouse and I arranged to put three of the New Zealanders, who were all sturdy and very fit men, at the front of the column, and three at the rear, to set and sustain a reasonable pace. He marched at the front, I at the rear.

It was to prove a useful tactic, for it was essential to keep together and to keep marching as it got darker, and stragglers grew more numerous. Voices called anxiously in the darkness, 'Is this the way to the beach? Any water here, digger? Where the hell are you, Mac? For Christ's sake where are you, Mac?'

It was an overcast night, with no moon, and the darkness lay heavily over the road as it wound upwards through the olive trees. The black, jagged wall of the mountain rose ahead of us, very high against the sky. In front and behind were the shapes of men trudging onwards. In the ditches by the roadside, around every farmhouse and every well men were resting, talking little, the tips of their cigarettes moving dots of red in the dark.

At one bend a tank suddenly loomed up in the middle of the road. It was outlined by an eerie glare, which turned out to be an olive tree alight, with four or five others smouldering nearby. This must have been where they had machine-gunned the Australians that afternoon. Beyond was a staff car, burnt out.

Then, distantly, came the sound of a plane. We scattered to the roadside. The plane dropped a flare, a glaring, orange brown lump which descended slowly, lighting up hideously the olive trees and the roofs of a farmhouse and the road and dark shapes at the road edge as far as one could see before it guttered into darkness, and we could form up and move on again.

The Tommies were tiring now, and we had to make longer and longer halts. We had all been on short rations for over a week, and many — myself included — had scouring stomachs. After each halt it became more difficult to get the men onto their feet. Our tactic of having the fitter New Zealanders at the front and the rear was useful in keeping up the pace, but with every mile it became slower and slower.

At Stylos, the first village we reached, we came upon a barn serving as a dressing station. Trucks used as ambulances, marked with crude white crosses of torn cloth stretched across grey blankets, were crowded with wounded men. Others, their white bandages showing in the dark, sat or lay on the edge of the narrow street. The barn was packed inside from wall to wall with men lying on stretchers or blankets or sacks. I felt I had seen it all before, somewhere. Colonel Thwigg, the New Zealand officer in charge, later provided the comparison. 'It was like the scene of the wounded at Atlanta in *Gone With the Wind*.' And indeed it was – life imitating art with a vengeance.

Thwigg had another tale of Crete, which said much not only about the New Zealand troops of that time, but about soldiers of all time. About the fifth day of the battle an artillery private drove up to Thwigg's Advanced Dressing Station with a truck full of wounded. He said, 'My unit's all knocked to bits – can I stay with you and drive this truck as an ambulance?' It turned out that he had a friend wounded in the leg, and he had scrounged the truck from somewhere to bring him to the ADS, and had picked up the other wounded on the way.

He drove the truck right through the retreat, and though there were strict orders that only walking wounded were to be evacuated – all lying wounded being left to be taken prisoner – the man used to smuggle his friend aboard at each move. At this Stylos dressing station the Colonel said, 'You had better keep an eye on your cobber because I'm not in charge here anymore and they may shift the wounded to another hospital at any time.' The man replied, 'I've thought of that. I've moved my mate to that house over there and I've changed his dressing and found him some rations.' When they got down near the beach at Sphakia he put the wounded man in shelter in a cave, and then spent all day driving up and down the open road, despite the bombing and machine gunning, ferrying wounded down to places close to the beach.

Thwigg concluded, 'He must have carried his friend all the way to the beach, because the next time I saw them they were drinking cocoa together on the mess deck of the ship which evacuated them. The man who had done it all, who could not have been more than twenty-five or so, looked suddenly fifty years old.'

Dawn showed us to be moving along the edge of a wide valley, with the flat ridge of the pass high above us against the skyline, and the road curving and winding and doubling back and forth towards it for what seemed mile upon mile. All the way up it were the moving figures of men, climbing, halting, climbing slowly again. The daylight gave faces and uniforms and bodies to the dark shapes of the night, revealing them as walking wounded with bloody bandages, one man with a bandaged stump of an amputated hand; as sailors off boats in Suda; as airmen; as Cypriot muleteers; as detachments marching under officers or NCOs; as other men straggling in ragged lines or small groups. Every few yards a figure lay on the roadside in the sleep of the utterly exhausted. Now and then a lorry came along, jammed with wounded, with bandaged men clinging to every corner of it – and a few who looked shamefully fit also grabbing a ride.

All along the road were abandoned lorries and cars, some of which had been hit by aircraft fire, and burnt out, others abandoned for lack of petrol, or because of a breakdown. Some had gone off the road in the dark, tumbling hundreds of feet down to rock filled ravines. Gear spilled out from them – papers, web equipment, mess tins, a paybook, an abandoned steel helmet.

The Tommies in our small unit were close to exhaustion now. It was not surprising, as it was now five o'clock, and we had been on the road nine hours. Soon the planes would be over, and movement would be difficult. Waterhouse decided to halt at a place where olive trees offered shelter, to let the men sleep and rest, and to push on in the darkness of the next night. My New Zealanders were still in good shape, so we left the British party, and carried on on our own, our eyes always on the ridge above our heads. At one point there was a big open well close to the road. We joined the queue at it, and after twenty minutes or so were able to lower our waterbottles into it, and fill them, and drink. It was brackish water, with a brown stain but we drank it thankfully.

On the next stretch, seated on a rock by the roadside, was the surreal spectacle of a girl with blonde hair falling onto the shoulders of her khaki uniform bush shirt, and with her legs in ill-fitting khaki drill trousers. She looked like someone on her way home from a fancy dress party. It was Nicky of Fernleaf House.[1] Her face was crumpled with weariness but her smile was as dazzling as ever. With her was Ian Pirie, in a brand new khaki uniform at least one size too big, and with major's crowns on his shoulders. The admirable plane-potting major, his rifle by his side, was slumped in sleep. They were all close to exhaustion, worn out by the night's march. We chatted for a few moments, and moved on, leaving them to rest.

The climb up the final, interminable serpentine to the top of the pass was a nightmare of fatigue. We had hoped to make it before the planes came, but soon after seven o'clock one flew in a leisurely fashion overhead, the morning sun glinting on its wings, its black Luftwaffe crosses large and menacing. It machine-gunned the road in a desultory fashion. Yet it need hardly have bothered, for the sound of its engine, even in the distance, had been enough to send the lines of climbing men, robbed now of the support of discipline and often even of the presence of friends, scattering among the thorn bushes and the rocks. Just off the road a queue, several hundred strong, had formed at a big well. As the plane appeared the men in it

---

[1] The villa in which Cox had worked on his news sheet for the troops.

scattered, and then later tried to reform. But many men lost the places they had had, and sat brokenly on rocks nearby, too exhausted even to argue with those now ahead of them. Others, their nerves worn threadbare, shouted hysterically at anyone who continued on the road whilst the plane was still to be heard. Further up, near the summit, two shots were fired, almost certainly by bomb-happy fugitives trying to halt any movement which could attract aircraft.

At long, long last, about nine o'clock, one of what had proved a multitude of false summits proved to be a true summit, and we crested the ridge and looked southward down the other side of the range. We were astonished by what we saw. Instead of a repetition of the steep, pine-clad and olive-clad slopes through which we had been climbing, we were faced with a lush green bowl of fields and trees and white walled houses, encircled by hills. This was the Askifou Plain, a round, fertile plateau set like an oasis in these gaunt White Mountains. We could see the white road leading round the western edge of it, and then climbing away in a new set of hairpin bends into a new range to the south, the last range before the sea.

The sight of this Shangri-la brought an immediate lift to our spirits, the more so since it was so utterly unexpected. We strode off downhill towards the plain. There we reached a well with its lifting gear still in action, offering good clean cool water to drink and to wash in. Nearby was an orchard with long grass. It seemed sensible to get some sleep here, and to push on in the late afternoon, so that we could complete the journey in the dark, free from the planes which must surely be over in their scores at any time now. I needed rest, as for three days past my stomach had been scouring in a condition close to dysentry. Within a few minutes I was deeply asleep.

I woke with a jerk about an hour later, to hear Barry Michael talking in a low voice to one of the others. 'He's exhausted,' he said, in not unkindly tones. 'We could easily push on, but he's exhausted. Yet if we pushed on now we might get to the beach in time to get away tonight.'

I realised they were talking of me. I realised too that if they were fit enough to keep going, as their officer I must keep going too, however exhausted I felt. There was another factor too. There had been no planes overhead since we had crossed the pass. The roads, which I had expected to have been made impassable by enemy aircraft during the day, were remarkably open. So I pretended to sleep for another ten minutes, and then bestirred myself, looking around, and said, 'I think we should risk the planes and push on.' Barry Michael had meanwhile found a ration dump that provided, of all things, a tin of pineapple. We ate that as if it were ambrosia, and set off on the remaining twelve miles to the sea.

There were two ways southwards out of the Askifou Plain. One was by the main road which wound up over the final range, climbing back up to a height of some 2,500 feet in yet one more series of bends, before plunging down towards the sea. The other route, a dusty road no more than a track, led from the floor of the valley towards the mouth of the Imvrotiko Ravine, cleft like an axe-cut through the mountain wall. I opted for the second, not because I knew of its nature, but because it avoided the option of a further climb – and that on a road open to machine gun fire.

The first part of our route lay through a narrow valley, on either side of which hills covered with pine trees rose steeply. There, in mid-afternoon, enemy aircraft swooped on us, spraying the road and hillsides with machine gun fire. In rushing for cover, we split up, Michael and McIntyre climbing the hill on one side, and the others and myself on another. When the attack finished some ten minutes later I could find no sign of Michael and McIntyre, and after waiting for a while had no choice but to push on with the others. We came out onto a small plain – not much more than a large clearing – beyond which showed the narrowing entrance to the gorge. Here a New Zealand captain flanked by a couple of soldiers stopped us. 'This is a gathering point for New Zealanders,' he said. 'You'll not get off in a small party. They are taking only the fighting formations. What battalion are you from?'

I explained the men were from the 18th, but were now with me at Force HQ. 'The 18th are in the first gully to the left,' he said. At that moment the sound of returning planes could be heard. The captain moved smartly to the cover of a clump of rocks. I had to make an instant decision. 'You will have a better chance back with your battalion,' I said, and the four moved off quickly towards the side gully.

I plunged on into the narrow shaded entrance of the ravine alone, troubled by my decision. Had I thrust them on a course leading to a prison camp? That anxiety remained at the back of my mind until, ten days later, I was able to establish that all six of them had got safely off. But I needed now all my wits about me, for the path through the ravine was menacingly lonely and silent, as the sheer cliffs rising on either side grew taller and taller, and closed in ever more narrowly. What if it proved a blind alley, if I came to a barrier which would force me to climb the high walls on either side or retrace my steps? I dared not contemplate this possibility but strode on, sometimes at a half trot. It was well into the evening now. I hung ever more firmly onto the strap of my rifle, slung over my shoulder. At last, at about seven in the evening, the defile began to open out, and its walls to lean back, disclosing a magnificent display of purple rhododendrons. Then I rounded a bend to see the sea, deep blue in the late evening light, clear and serene, stretching to the horizon beyond which lay, distantly, Egypt and safety.

At the end of the ravine I came out into a village. Around its well sat a group of Cretan civilians. They eyed me warily – and eyed, all too interestedly, it seemed to me, the rifle I was carrying. I kept it slung over my shoulder as I drank, and filled my water bottle, and asked the way to Sphakia. They spoke swiftly among themselves before one pointed out a rough track leading westward. How far was Sphakia? Three, four kilometres, they said.

The light was going now, and I hurried as fast as I could, with the sea on my left and, towering above, on the right, high rocky slopes rising steeply towards pine covered heights. I had gone about two kilometres when I was faced by an officer in Marine uniform, his hand on the butt of his revolver. 'Where the hell do you think you are going?' he said. 'To Sphakia.' 'Well you can't,' he said. 'No one is to move on these slopes during the daylight. Do you want to bring every bloody German plane down on us? The orders are clear. No movement by day – and anyway no individuals are allowed into Sphakia, only formed units. I've a good mind to arrest you as a deserter.'

I protested I was from Freyberg's headquarters, and had orders to report there. He paused, weighing me up in case I was a Fifth Columnist or a German in disguise. Then he said, 'His headquarters aren't in Sphakia. They are in a cave up on the right hand side of that wadi' – and he pointed to a shallow gully running down from the slopes above us. I set out up it, and just as dark fell I came upon a group of caves set into the hillside, two with stone barricades set across the entrance. They looked like a setting for the legend of Cyclops. In one cave I found Robin Bell. In another were the General and Colonel Stewart. In a third, smaller cave were several British officers from Creforce, including three of the British Intelligence officers. They had come across by truck, and were well installed, with some rations and a bottle of sherry. I drank thankfully a glass of sherry, ate a couple of slices of bully beef – all my stomach would take aboard – and lay down on the cave floor to sleep, secure in the knowledge that no bomb or bullet could reach us in this natural anti-aircraft shelter.

I slept, however, only brokenly, for the night proved cold. My legs, in thin drill shorts, were bitterly cold. I regretted my overcoat, which indeed – he later stressed – kept Peter McIntyre warm on the hillside where he and Michael were spending their night.

In the spring of 1941 Rommel launched his first offensive in North Africa. His attack carried the Afrika Korps to the Egyptian border. In his rear the port of Tobruk on the Libyan coast, one of the best harbours in the Mediterranean, remained in Allied hands, held by the Australian 7th Division and threatening his flank. In April three German attempts to capture Tobruk were beaten back. The port then came under siege. Frank Rolleston, a Queenslander serving with 18th Brigade, has written of his impressions of daily life during the siege of Tobruk during the summer of 1941.

It was some two days after that the 18th Brigade moved up to the salient and Jack Dalton and myself formed part of what is known as the advance party, the purpose of such a party being that these soldiers will be able to have all the details of the particular position they are to take over explained to them, by the unit already in those positions. Also, since the changeover would take place at night, the advance party could guide their mates into their correct positions on the defence line and having been told all the various points about the area, there is no delay with explanations having to be made to the incoming unit.

For the first time I could have a good look at Hill 209 in daylight, and it was some two miles distant. Jack and I found out that the positions my company was to take over were behind the actual forward defences being some hundreds of yards back but still very much in the danger zone. Apparently some of the men were the survivors of the ill-fated attack on R.7 by the 2/43rd, for that was the battalion the 2/9th was to relieve, and I was talking to one chap who told me that he was one of the men who got right in near the R.7 and that he never worked his rifle so fast in all his life, although he was not in there very long.

He had the look of a man who was suffering from shock and his face was flushed as a man might be after several days in a drinking bout. As I recall it, he said that he had two brothers killed and one wounded in that attack, but although in later years I did ask some members of the 2/43rd if they knew of a case of four brothers being in that attack, I could find no one that could give me any information. I have often wondered since whether I misunderstood him, for it would be a bit unusual to have four brothers in the one company.

Jack and I found out that the defences we were to occupy were only miserable holes gouged out of the ground, and into the rock and I don't think they would be more than three feet deep with flimsy overhead protection, of no use at all against a direct hit, and serving only to keep the sun out. These holes were connected by crawl trenches, only about two feet deep, and I realised that we could be in for a rough time under heavy shell fire if the enemy had this position ranged, as I thought they would.

My worst fears were confirmed when the 2/43rd chaps told us that they had suffered losses in this position, and that every day it was shelled not only with high explosive shells, but shrapnel shells bursting in the air some 50 feet up. The 2/43rd fellows made no secret that they wanted to get out as soon as possible and when they were leaving once it got dark Jack said, 'Well goodbye, the best of luck'. One of the 2/43rd chaps said 'It's you fellows who are going to need the luck'.

Our men were to arrive the following night so Jack and I had to spend a day in this position on our own, and I suppose we were not taking the precautions to conceal ourselves as the 2/43rd fellows had told us, that although the position did get its share of machine gun bullets, this was mainly at night time and we were a bit careless, this being daylight.

Suddenly we heard the scream of approaching shells and Jack and I had no time to dive for a hole, but lay flat in the crawl trench. Next thing the salvo of shells fell right on the position, falling so close that the sand thrown up was falling on us, just as if we were under a tip load of dust.

The dust cleared away but before we could move, over came another lot, and again we were covered with flying dirt and sand, and when it cleared away Jack seemed still, so I grabbed his hand thinking he may have been hit. Deciding that we might be safer in one of the round deeper holes with light covering Jack and I moved into one of them. We could distinctly hear the enemy guns fire again and Jack said 'Here's another lot coming' and in seconds the shells arrived. Presently the shelling eased off and I said to Jack 'You know I was saying my prayers then' and Jack said 'So was I, and I feel sorry for anyone who has not got the consolation of a prayer at a time like that'. I remarked to Jack that I noticed a strange hissing noise when the shells were landing, and Jack said that he noticed the same thing, and was wondering if it was a fuse working. A few hours later we were telling a chap that was in another position nearby, and he said 'That hissing noise you heard was shrapnel pellets, from shells bursting in the air above you'. It appears that the enemy were mixing air burst shells, with the high explosive type which explode when they hit the ground, and as far as I could see the salient was the place they used this type, for in the other sectors the concrete posts gave better protection from air bursts.

That night our unit arrived to take over and Jack and I directed our men into their respective positions. However Jack had a bit of trouble for he picked a motor truck that was stopped and clear in the moonlight, as marker, and when he was not looking it moved off so that when he looked around and spotted a truck in a different place he thought that he was looking at the first truck. This caused some confusion and harsh words but things were sorted out after a while, which was just as well for machine gun bullets began to whistle and whine around that portion of the front just then.

Jack moved off to the section position held by his section, and in similar kind of layout of holes and crawl trenches to the one I was in. In fact the whole line of defences near this area consisted of this poor cover.

Things seemed fairly quiet during the night except that the bullets seemed to zip and whine around the position the whole night, and in fact before daylight I had a peculiar experience. 'Bluey' Williams decided that we had better send in an ammunition report to our company H.Q. before daylight, and asked me to go down to Coy H.Q. with such a report so they would know there what ammunition we might need.

I knew that there was an old 44 gallon drum lying where this Coy H.Q. was, and set off but soon realised that I must have missed it and circled around, and to my surprise came right back on the post I had left. In fact in the moonlight, one post looks the same as the other, and I was right on this post and went in asking for H.Q. before I realised it. What a fool I felt, and set off again determined to find Coy H.Q. and not a little scared for the air seemed full of whining bullets, and again I realised that somehow I had missed the place I was looking for.

Suddenly four men loomed up in the moonlight carrying a man on a stretcher, and they asked me if I knew where the front line was, as they had got slewed in the new surroundings, for they were 2/9th men and one of them had come up with my party to Tobruk.

I think they were looking for 'B' Company, and when I told them that the front line was just in front of us, one said 'No wonder we have been fired on'. I asked them how badly hit the man on the stretcher was and the chap I knew said 'He's dead, he got hit by a bullet just back there, and I listened for his heart beating, but it gave a kind of flutter and stopped.'

After directing them as well as I could, I decided to try and get back to my own post because bullets were flying around and I was on my own, and the Coy H.Q. seemed as elusive as ever. Besides seeing that fellow lying dead on the stretcher didn't exactly help things in my mind either. I recall that I did ask the men with him, his name, and they said it was Christie.

I did not have much trouble finding my way back to my post for it loomed up when I thought that I still had some distance to go, and I told 'Bluey' that I couldn't find the Coy H.Q. and he said he had got sick of waiting for me to come back and had sent someone else, who had apparently found the place alright. 'Bluey' gave me a pretty stiff lecture saying that if there had been an attack and the ammunition was needed, it could be serious.

Of course I knew that, but I had done my best. Later I found out where I had gone wrong was in looking for that 44 gallon drum to indicate the H.Q. because the drum had been there in the daylight, and someone had taken it away, so of course I walked right past the place I was looking for, as being more or less underground nothing was visible. Later I was talking to the fellow who was on sentry duty, but sitting in a hole, and he said I went past him quite close in the moonlight, but knowing I was one of the fellows in that area he did not bother saying anything.

I learnt two valuable lessons that night, from my experience with that drum, and Jack Dalton's experience with the truck that moved. The lesson learnt was never rely on anything for a marking point or guide if it is something that can be moved.

We found out that the Germans regularly worked our positions over daily with their artillery, and I could well understand why those 43rd chaps were glad to get out.

About the second day Doug Harvey and I were trying to deepen the shallow crawl trench when a shrapnel shell burst above us about 50 feet up, with a big cloud of black smoke, and a sheet of flame. As we went flat I heard Doug give a cry of pain, but thought he had hit his hip on the side of the crawl trench. However, he had been hit on the hip with the shrapnel, and blood was coming through his clothing.

I ripped the cloth away and tore my field dressing open and with the help of someone else got a rough kind of bandage on, while more shells burst around but none directly above. Doug was sent back and out of Tobruk, but was made 'B' class as a result of this wound, and I never saw him again. He had a sister that was in the army nursing sisters. Some two years afterwards Tom Beil told me that he struck him in a staging camp, and Doug asked about us and wanted to know if that *'big bloke'* (that was me) was still going strong.

Every night we had to go out on working parties or listening posts, and the enemy apparently nervous of another attack, would loose off machine gun fire at the slightest sound. One night when we were going out *'Bluey'* and I and a couple of others called in at a forward post and while he was talking to the N.C.O. in charge of the post, I took a look through a gap in the sandbags and the N.C.O. said to me 'I wouldn't do that if I were you. The Germans have got a machine gun trained on that spot you are looking through and send along a burst every now and then.'

I heard *'Bluey'* say 'How far is it to the enemy lines?' The N.C.O. said 'A little over 500 yards, and I bung a few mortar bombs over every now and then from this 2 inch mortar.' No doubt because he knew that our 2 inch mortar only had a range of about 500 yards, *'Bluey'* said 'But isn't it a bit far for the 2 inch mortar?' The N.C.O. replied, 'Yes, but I think some of them hit the target O.K.'

The Germans were certainly methodical in their shelling timetable, which was usually in the afternoon as a rule at the same time, and for about the same period. One day a shell scored a direct hit on the spot Jimmy Mercer was occupying in Jack Dalton's section position and although he was in the defence hole he was killed instantly. Section leader Sandy Powell, in the same hole suffered shell blast.

Later when it got dark, someone said there was some phosphorus glowing in the dark and that the Germans must be using phosphorus in their shells, as this was glowing where Jimmy Mercer's dugout had been blown up. Phosphorus like poison gas is I think outlawed in war, but it is also used for tracer bullets and tracer in anti-aircraft shells, and I really think that the shell which hit that dugout was an anti-aircraft shell, and that the phosphorus came from that part used for tracer.

Actually, the guns which were firing these air bursting shells were from the famous German 88 mm, a mobile gun that could be used for anti-aircraft, tanks, or for shelling infantry. A thing that had me puzzled was, why we seemed to be caught napping by these 88. shells for we had no warning until they exploded above us, and yet we could hear the other H.E. shells coming. Years later I was able to realise just why we could not hear these shells when in a book I saw some pictures or photos taken by the Germans, which showed that a 88 mm gun had been moved right up behind Hill 209, so that it was firing at us from only about two and a half miles. Thus it would be much closer than the enemy guns firing high explosive shells.

To explain what this means it must be remembered that I did say earlier that a shell fired from a distance and travelling at a speed less than the speed of sound will be heard by its screaming sound before it lands, but if the shell is travelling faster than the speed of sound, then the shell will hit its target before anyone is warned by the scream of the shell. The 88 is a high velocity gun, and at two to three miles would certainly outstrip the speed of sound.

This arrival without warning was nerve wracking, and again in Jack Dalton's section one day, a shell which was probably of this type, or since it exploded on or near the ground could have been H.E., caught Harry Elms and Merv Smith napping, completely blowing Elms leg off below the knee and breaking the handle of a shovel they were using trying to deepen the shallow dugouts.

Our stretcher bearer Harry Blundson, heedless of danger dashed across from my section, and as he did and when half way across, an air-burst shell exploded about 50 feet over head, without hitting him, and as I looked over another one burst, almost directly above my position, and I could see the sheet of flame shooting straight down at me, while the big cloud of black smoke drifted to one side in the wind.

A few minutes later the stretcher bearer and another man rushed over with Harry Elms on a stretcher, and down to the R.A.P. They said he was cheerful, but the next morning we were told that he had died.

In that section post, besides Jack Dalton, there was Jack Suthers who was in the tent with me in Brisbane, and also 'Darkie' Thomas. 'Darkie' was a good hearted fellow, who had admitted that he had been a wanderer all his life and had never settled down, spending his money as it came, and travelling with side shows around the various agricultural shows. However Jack Dalton said 'The first man to rush to Harry Elms aid was 'Darkie'. It would seem Jack must have been mistaken in the confusion, for 40 years later, the section leader, 'Sandy' Powell, an honest and truthful man assured me that he himself was the first to reach Harry Elms.

A few days afterwards Merv Smith, the chap who was with Harry Elms when he got hit, was hit in the neck by a bullet, near his section post. However the wound was not fatal, and he did rejoin the unit sometime later.

Actually we were really in a more dangerous position than the more forward posts for the dugouts were deeper there, whereas we had very shallow dugouts and no worthwhile overhead cover, although of course the forward posts received more attention from mortars, and had machine guns directed at their every move.

In fact some of those forward posts which were concrete could be worse than a lightly built post if a shell actually did land in the post, although of course in the salient our forward posts that were opposite the posts we had lost when the enemy pushed in from 209 were sandbagged dugouts and not concrete. R.8 on our left and S.8 on our right marked the start of our concrete posts on either side of the salient.

The reason I say that a concrete post could be most dangerous if a shell did penetrate and explode in the post is, because the concrete being solid will not absorb the blast like soil or sandbags, even though it might have a better chance of stopping the shell getting into the post in the first place.

One day a big shell landed in R.8, a position held by some of our 'C' company men, and it killed three men and wounded others. Two of those killed were a little fellow named Toy and another chap named Peter Laffin, who I think came from the Julia Creek area in Queensland and was a drover or cattleman. I was told that he was killed outright by the shell and that Doug Nolan whom I mentioned earlier suffered shell shock from the blast. Both Laffin and Nolan, and I think Toy, had been in the party that came to Tobruk with me and as I said earlier Doug

Nolan, discharged from the army because of the effects of that shell blast, was to die from a broken neck in a fall from a horse about 18 months later. I believe that Peter Laffin had a brother later, either missing or captured in Malaya, after the Japanese invasion. Only a few days before we moved up to the salient, I asked Peter how he was finding Tobruk, and he said 'Not really as bad as I thought I would.' That night as we were going out on patrol after that shell had landed in R.8 we stopped near a point for instructions, and the food truck had come up fairly close and just then they were bringing the bodies out, and carrying them past us. They appeared to be wrapped up in blankets.

One night 'Bluey' Williams, Harry Rashleigh, Augie Theurakauf and myself went out on a rather dangerous listening post which entailed getting fairly close to the enemy in the vicinity of R.7. This was not a very pleasant prospect for that chap from the 43rd who had survived the assault on that post, had told me that the whole area seemed to be full of booby traps and mines and that he really thought that by far the greater part of their casualties were from these.

We were also sending out a fighting patrol, and in due course we set off. As I recall it, 'Bluey' did not take his Thompson submachine gun with him, as I think Charlie Alder took it on the fighting patrol in place of the Bren gun he normally carried. These sub-machine guns fired a heavy .45 bullet usually contained in a drum type magazine of 50 bullets or a box type of 25.

The Germans were very 'jumpy' in this area for we later found that they had several killed in the attack by the 43rd and they kept sending up flares. Still we worked our way fairly close to their positions by crawling along the ground, hoping we wouldn't hit any trip wires or mines, and I think perhaps we got closer to the enemy than we intended. Feeling along the ground we suddenly discovered a signal wire which *'Bluey'* thought might connect two enemy posts, and was holding the wire when he suddenly whispered, 'Watch out, someone's pulling the other end of this wire.' However it was discovered that the wire had got caught in the equipment of one of our men so that the wire moved when he moved.

Suddenly the moon started to rise and light the place up and *'Bluey'* said, 'We better get out of here' and we had just started to move out when about half a mile away we heard the sound of firing, and *'Bluey'* whispered 'There's the Tommy gun' as we could hear the quick bursts. The enemy already alerted must have seen some movement for the next thing a machine gun opened up on us, forcing us to ground. There was none of this short bursts, the enemy appeared to be putting a whole belt or magazine through at us, and the bullets passed over us and alongside us with an angry 'Hiss, hiss, hiss, zing, zing, zing.' I could feel some of them driving into the soil alongside me, and lay so that I was facing the stream of bullets and with my tin hat on a slope thinking it might just deflect a bullet. Our only protection were the slight hollows in the ground, and the camel bush which was scattered all over the desert, a ferny weed about 18 inches high. Suddenly the firing stopped, almost at once we jumped up and ran, but immediately the machine gun opened fire again and down we went again. Again when it stopped firing we jumped up and ran, and after doing this for a couple more times, the gun did not re-open fire. Suddenly *'Bluey'* said, 'I think they got one of us because there's only three of us, and we will have to go back and find him.' Fortunately the missing man, Harry Rashleigh, came rushing along at that moment, for

52

it seems he had been a bit slow getting up and the machine gun had pinned him down temporarily.

Apparently the enemy had decided that they had either wiped us out or that we had got away for they ceased fire. Actually it was a miracle that we were not hit, for the bullets were very close, but there is an old saying that there is a lot more space than men for the bullets to hit as a rule.

We were taking a breather when gun flashes in the enemy territory denoted artillery fire, and next thing over came a salvo of shells bursting in a line some distance away. 'Bluey' said that the shells were moving closer to us and the only thing was to head back as close as possible to the enemy lines, which we did, and after about a quarter of an hour the shelling stopped. No doubt the enemy opposite, not knowing how many men were out there and fearing an attack, had called up artillery support.

When we judged it safe we moved back, and after going some distance encountered four men moving in the moonlight. Not being sure who they were, we split up, with two trying to approach them from either side, but when challenged it turned out they were from our fighting patrol, and one man was our platoon officer Lieutenant Lloyd Evans, who now took charge of the party. I think he was a bit slewed and uncertain, for as we approached our own wire, he said 'I want to be sure that this is our own wire'. However a knocked out German tank gave him his bearings, and we got through without incident, except that my clothing caught on some barbed wire, which I ripped free, for about that point the Germans could fire along our wire and I did not want to linger, for mines and booby traps were in that wire area as well.

The rest of our fighting patrol returned safely, and I found out that what had happened to them was that they came on a party of what may have been Italians, apparently putting in mines. Lieutenant Evans called out 'Surrender Jerry', whereon the answer was a burst of automatic fire from an enemy gun, which Charlie Alder instantly returned, and the gun stopped. There was some confused shooting and although our party was a bit separated I heard of no casualties. Jim Hamill believed the enemy Germans and that they were wiped out.

About this time we were started on the job of building a new defence post forward of our front line, and possibly there was more than one post being built. It was dangerous work, for the enemy flares at times were so continuous that the front was almost bathed in the glow of fading and new Hares for long periods, and the machine gun fire was most persistent. Since it was necessary to stand perfectly still while the flare was at its brightest work was at a slow rate.

We were told that the new defence position would be occupied by us as soon as we completed it, and I must say I was a bit concerned about this news, for the enemy were already mortaring the spot in daytime.

A few weeks previously, just before my arrival in Tobruk the enemy had dropped pamphlets to our men as follows;

AUSSIES

After Crete disaster Anzac troops are now being ruthlessly sacrificed by England in Tobrouch and Syria

Turkey has concluded pact of friendship with Germany. England will shortly be driven out of the Mediterranean. Offensive from Egypt to relieve you totally smashed.

YOU CANNOT ESCAPE

Our dive bombers are waiting to sink your transports. Think of your future and your people at home.

Come forward – show white flags and you will be out of danger.
SURRENDER!

Of course these had no effect at all on our men, and I am sure not a single man surrendered because of them. The pamphlets had high souvenir value and I did see one. It was rather amusing to note the wording 'Think of your future and your people at home' because actually we had thought of them, which was the reason we were in Tobruk to defend our homes and people from Hitler's barbaric rule. During the time I was in Tobruk I did not hear any talk of surrender or what we would do if the enemy broke through, for no one believed it would happen.

Tobruk was relieved during the Crusader offensive in 1941. It changed hands again in June 1942, when its garrison of British, Indian and South African troops surrendered after a fresh assault by Rommel.

On 22 June 1941 Germany invaded the Soviet Union. The Red Air Force was almost wiped out on the ground. In a series of colossal encirclements millions of Russian soldiers were taken prisoner. On 4 July the SS division 'Das Reich', part of Guderian's Panzer Group Centre, crossed the River Berezina. Serving with the division's artillery regiment was Oberscharführer Roman Geiger.

Ushakova, lying on a long ridge, was a typical small Russian village running on a general line west to south-east. Some 200 metres outside the village there was a single, large tree visible from a very long way away. This was, if I remember correctly, known as Point 306.

Our No 8 battery of the division's 2nd Artillery Regiment, took up position some 2 to 3 kms to the south-west of Ushakova, in support of infantry from our own division as well as from army units. The OP was manned by Untersturmführer Kindl, a signaller and a telephonist. It was the second day [in that position] and the Russians had been attacking without pause. Shellfire regularly cut the telephone line and over the radio Kindl asked for protection for the OP. Untersturmfürher Schuelke ordered me, 'Geiger, take a machine-gun and go forward to protect the OP and the infantry in Ushakova.'

My No 1 on the gun, Hasenkopf, took two boxes of ammunition and I carried the gun and we followed the telephone line. Although I did know from map coordinates where the OP was located, following the wire would bring us to the spot more quickly. We moved through the village which was under Russian artillery fire and infantry fire. The OP had been set up some 50 metres to the right of the large tree. Kindl waved to us and pointed out the position we were to take up in a ditch about 30 metres to his right. The 'Black Sow', an 18 cm Russian gun, began firing at the big tree on the ridge. Far away we could hear the soft thump as the gun fired, then 15 to 20 seconds later there would be a rushing sound and then a frightful explosion. The rate of fire was about one round every three or four minutes. The next shot landed about 10 metres from us. Then the Russian infantry began an attack. With the sun at my back I had good observation in an easterly direction and fired short bursts at them. But there was a small area of dead ground which I could not cover and the Russians worked their way forward through this until they were about 50 metres away. I could see their brown helmets shining in the sunlight. They got no farther forward than that. Kindl left the OP together with the wireless operator as it was impossible to give clear fire orders over the radio. He shouted out to me, 'Do a good job, Geiger', as I flung the first egg grenades. By this time the fire of the 'Black Sow', was being laid on the village itself and shells had begun to explode in the first houses. Once again that whistling sound was followed by a crashing explosion. Then there would be a pillar of smoke and when that had cleared away, there was nothing to be seen. Some houses were burning like tinder boxes. Untersturmführer Kindl was hit during the bombardment and lost a leg. He died on the way to the RAP.[1] The signaller was killed immediately. I kept the Russians back with short bursts of fire and by throwing grenades. Our right flank was covered by marshy ground, so we had nothing to fear from that sector.

Ushakova was now completely alight. There was the sound of rifle and machine-gun fire and shouts of 'Ooooorah!' as the Russians stormed the village. It was time for me and my No 1 to get out. To our right and to our rear there was a piece of swampy, meadow land. We made our way back through this firing bursts of fire from the machine-gun and throwing grenades. Just as we were nearing the battery area we saw the last prime mover drive off towing its gun and disappearing in a cloud of dust. The battery had had to move because its position had become too dangerous. As we two made our way back to our unit we realized that there were wounded men lying in the side-cars of motor cycles.

As a result of the furious Russian assaults our front line had collapsed. Then I saw an armoured car flying the 'Reich' pennant. In the vehicle was our divisional commander,

---

[1] Regimental Aid Post.

Obergruppenführer Hausser. I reported to him and he looked through his binoculars in the direction of Ushakova. It did not look all that good. Over the radio he ordered up the Stukas. That was comforting. An hour later, by which time Hasenkopf and I had reached the battery positions, the Stukas were on their way. Seven of them swung round in a great curve and gathered over the signal flares that were being fired to indicate targets. Less than a kilometre in front of our positions dive-bombers screamed down out of the sky with their sirens howling and plastered the enemy with bombs. It was frightening to think of that rain of fire. We supported the Stukas with all the shells we could fire off. For the rest of the day we were stood down but on the following day we went in with panzer and SPs and recaptured Ushakova.

In the Soviet Union the Germans had been brought to a halt and then driven back in December 1941. In the summer of 1942 Hitler launched a fresh drive in the south, aimed at the oilfields of the Caucasus mountains and Stalingrad, an industrial city on the Volga where General Paulus' Sixth Army was to become locked in a bitter battle which would lead to its eventual entombment. The ruined city was a hunting ground for snipers. By November 1942 the ascendancy of the Soviet snipers over their German opposite numbers had become so pronounced that the head of the German army's sniper school at Zossen, SS Standartenführer Heinz Thorwald, was despatched to restore the balance. A crack Soviet sniper was assigned to deal with Thorwald.

The arrival of the Nazi sniper set us a new task: we had to find him, study his habits and methods, and patiently await the right moment for one, and only one, well-aimed shot.

In our dug-out at nights we had furious arguments about the forthcoming duel. Every sniper put forward his speculations and guesses arising from his day's observation of the enemy's forward positions. All sorts of different proposals and 'baits' were discussed. But the art of the sniper is distinguished by the fact that whatever experience a lot of people may have, the outcome of an engagement is decided by one sniper. He meets the enemy face to face, and every time he has to create, to invent, to operate differently. There can be no blue-print for a sniper; a blue-print would be suicide.

I knew the style of the Nazi snipers by their fire and camouflage and without any difficulty could tell the experienced snipers from the novices, the cowards from the stubborn, determined enemies. But the character of the head of the school was still a mystery for me. Our day-by-day observations told us nothing definite. It was difficult to decide on which sector he was operating. He presumably altered his position frequently and was looking for me as carefully as I for him. Then something happened. My friend Morozov was killed, and Sheykin wounded, by a rifle with telescopic sights. Morozov and Sheykin were considered experienced snipers; they had often emerged victorious from the most difficult skirmishes with the enemy. Now there was no doubt. They had come up against the Nazi 'super-sniper' I was looking for. At dawn I went out with Nikolay Kulikov to the same positions as our comrades had occupied the previous day. Inspecting the enemy's forward positions, which we had spent many days studying and knew well, I found nothing new. The day was drawing to a close. Then above a German entrenchment unexpectedly appeared a helmet, moving slowly along a trench. Should I shoot? No! It was a trick: the helmet somehow or other moved unevenly and was presumably being held up by someone helping the sniper, while he waited for me to fire.

'Where can he be hiding?' asked Kulikov, when we left the ambush under cover of darkness. By the patience which the enemy had shown during the day I guessed that the sniper from Berlin was here. Special vigilance was needed.

A second day passed. Whose nerves would be stronger? Who would outwit whom?

Nikolay Kulikov, a true comrade, was also fascinated by this duel. He had no doubt that the enemy was there in front of us, and he was anxious that we should succeed. On the third day, the political instructor, Danilov, also came with us to the ambush. The day dawned as usual: the light increased and minute by minute the enemy's positions could be distinguished more clearly. Battle started close by, shells hissed over us, but, glued to our telescopic sights, we kept our eyes on what was happening ahead of us.

'There he is! I'll point him out to you!' suddenly said the political instructor, excitedly. He barely, literally for one second, but carelessly, raised himself above the parapet, but that was enough for the German to hit and wound him. That sort of firing, of course, could only come from an experienced sniper.

For a long time I examined the enemy positions, but could not detect his hiding place. From the speed with which he had fired I came to the conclusion that the sniper was somewhere directly ahead of us. I continued to watch. To the left was a tank, out of action, and on the right was a pill-box. Where was he? In the tank? No, an experienced sniper would not take up position there. In the pill-box, perhaps? Not there either – the embrasure was closed. Between the tank and the pill-box, on a stretch of level ground, lay a sheet of iron and a small pile of broken bricks. It had been lying there a long time and we had grown accustomed to its being there. I put myself in the enemy's position and thought – where better for a sniper? One had only to make a firing slit under the sheet of metal, and then creep up to it during the night.

Yes, he was certainly there, under the sheet of metal in no-man's-land. I thought I would make sure. I put a mitten on the end of a small plank and raised it. The Nazi fell for it. I carefully let the plank down in the same position as I had raised it and examined the bullet-hole. It had gone straight through from the front; that meant that the Nazi was under the sheet of metal.

'There's our viper!' came the quiet voice of Nikolay Kulikov from his hide-out next to mine.

Now came the question of luring even a part of his head into my sights. It was useless trying to do this straight away. Time was needed. But I had been able to study the German's temperament. He was not going to leave the successful position he had found. We were therefore going to have to change our position.

We worked by night. We were in position by dawn. The Germans were firing on the Volga ferries. It grew light quickly and with day-break the battle developed with new intensity. But neither the rumble of guns nor the bursting of shells and bombs nor anything else could distract us from the job in hand.

The sun rose. Kulikov took a blind shot; we had to rouse the sniper's curiosity. We had decided to spend the morning waiting, as we might have been given away by the sun on our telescopic sights. After lunch our rifles were in the shade and the sun was shining directly on to the German's position. At the edge of the sheet of metal something was glittering: an odd bit of glass or telescopic sights? Kulikov carefully, as only the most experienced can do, began to raise his helmet. The German fired. For a fraction of a second Kulikov rose and screamed. The German believed that he had finally got the Soviet sniper he had been hunting for four days, and half raised his head from beneath the sheet of metal. That was what I had been banking on. I took careful aim. The German's head fell back, and the telescopic sights of his rifle lay motionless, glistening in the sun, until night fell …

On 7 December 1941 the Japanese entered the war, launching a devastating surprise attack on the great American naval base at Pearl Harbor on the Hawaiian island of Oahu. Neither the Americans nor the colonial powers in the Pacific – the British and the Dutch – were in any way prepared to stem the tide of Japanese conquest. For six months the Japanese ran riot, carving out a huge Pacific empire. By April 1942 the islands of Guam and Wake, the Philippines, French Indo-China, Burma, Thailand, Malaya and the Dutch East Indies, three-quarters of New Guinea and Papua, the Bismarck Archipelago and a substantial part of the Gilbert and Solomon Islands were in Japanese hands. To the north, they threatened the Aleutians and the approaches to Alaska; in the west they were encamped on the borders of India; to the south they menaced Australia.

In December 1941 the tiny atoll of Wake, lying some 2,000 miles west of the Hawaiian islands, was held by 525 US Marines under the overall command of Commander W. Scott Cunningham. Their atoll was the objective of a strong Japanese naval task force. On 8 December Wake came under heavy air attack. Three days later the Japanese task force launched an assault which was beaten off with heavy losses. Cunningham takes up the story.

The telephone roused me about three o'clock on the morning of the eleventh. I stumbled out into the hallway of the cottage, trying to fight off the stupor of sleep into which I had fallen, and reached for the receiver.

'Cunningham.'

'Captain, this is Gunner Hamas at the battalion command post.

I came awake fast. Elmer Greey's head appeared in his doorway and he watched me inquiringly.

'Major Devereux[1] reports ships sighted on the horizon.' For all his formality, John Hamas's voice was crackling with excitement. 'He requests permission to illuminate with searchlights.'

Ships on the horizon! The softening-up process was over, then, and they were moving in for the kill. And what could six old five-inch guns do against the batteries of longer-range weapons they were sure to have?

Our only hope was to ambush them. We must lie silent and dark until they steamed in so close our guns would be effective, and then we must hit them with everything we had.

'No,' I said flatly. 'Don't use the searchlights. And don't commence firing until further orders.'

I slammed down the phone and began dressing. Greey and Keene came into my room to learn the news, and I told them to notify Putnam's command post and any other points they could raise. Then I set off at a run for my truck outside.

It was a perfect tropical night. A half moon was coming up over the ocean and the air was cool and soft. The roar of the surf had a hypnotic, almost soothing quality about it. The

---

[1] Major James P. Devereux, commander of ground troops on Wake.

former bird sanctuary lay peaceful and serene before me as I turned on my blued-out lights and began the ride down the pockmarked coral road to the communications center. I might have been a vacationer on some island paradise, setting out before dawn for a day's fishing.

Could the ships be friendly?

There was a remote chance, of course. Pearl had sent no word of approaching help, but that might have been for reasons of security, or there could have been a breakdown in communications.

But I didn't really believe it. Any help for Wake would have been too far away when war began to reach us by now, or we would surely have heard of it somehow. One way or another we would have heard. Almost beyond doubt this was the enemy, arriving in force to follow through on the work done by the bombers during the past three days. And I was damned if I was going to show my hand too soon. Let them come in believing we were off guard or helpless!

Wake Island's stunted rats were out in force tonight. I swung the wheel sharply to avoid a pair of them ambling peacefully across the coral, and turned off a minute later at the magazine. Inside, the dimly lighted room hummed with activity. Radio men hung over their equipment; the talker exchanged words in low tones with someone on the telephone; a decoding officer stood by to translate messages arriving or going out.

It had been Wesley Platt, the strong-point commander on Wilkes, who had first got word of the ships from one of his lookouts. He had passed it on to the battalion command post, and Gunner Hamas hurried to awaken Devereux. Platt wanted to turn on his battery of searchlights for a better look. Devereux had gone out onto the beach to scan the horizon himself, confirmed the presence of some objects a number of miles away, and passed on the news, and the request, to me. And now, as we waited, the alert and the warning to keep the lights dark and the guns silent had gone the rounds. At Peacock Point, at Kuku and Toki, men waited in the dim moonlight for the order to open fire, or dug their foxholes deeper against the shelling that might begin at any moment. At the airstrip, the planes were ready but silent.

So Wake lay, inactive but alert, as the tiny specks on the horizon grew larger.

Three-thirty … four o'clock …

I was scared, plenty scared, though I tried not to show it. My muscles ached from tension.

Four-thirty …

'They're getting closer. An awful lot of 'em.'

Five o'clock.

The advance ships in the task force were only about four miles off Peacock Point now.

BOOM!

We could hear it above the surface. The invaders had opened fire.

Still our guns remained silent, our searchlights dark.

A column of Japanese ships moved parallel to Wake's southern shore, advancing from Peacock Point toward Wilkes. Then it turned toward the atoll, moved in closer, turned again, and began steaming back toward Peacock. Other ships advanced toward Wilkes. The guns continued to sound, with increasing frequency.

The telephone talker motioned to me. I grabbed the phone.

'Captain?' It was Hamas again. 'Lieutenant McAlister reports a destroyer, range four-six-hundred, off Kuku Point.

Lieutenant Barninger has ships in his sights off Peacock. Major Devereux ordered me to notify you.'

I took a deep breath and looked at my watch. It was 6:15. The long silence was over.

'What are we waiting for, John?' I yelled. 'Cut loose at them!'

And as Gunner Hamas relayed the order to the batteries around the atoll, I could hear the five-inchers open up.

It was a sweet, wonderful, glorious shoot-up.

Barninger's guns opened up on Peacock and hit a light cruiser[2] on the second salvo. She turned and began to run; the guns scored twice more before she got out of range.

McAlister opened on Wilkes. He had a problem – his fire control equipment was virtually worthless after the bombing of the day before – but that didn't interfere with the work of Battery L. Nothing could bother Battery L this moonlit morning. Battery L was red hot. Three ships were in sight; the guns chose one and let fire. Dead on target! As the crews cheered, it blew up before their eyes and sank.

Another ship; another hit.

Another, perhaps a transport, and another hit.

And yet another, this one a light cruiser from its silhouette, and, by God, another hit!

And now the guns on Peale had their chance to get into the fight. They had been waiting for something to come within range, and the Japs obliged. Three ships slipped on past Wilkes and turned north toward Toki Point, and Kessler's men at Battery B opened up.

---

[2] This was the *Yubari*, flagship of the task force's commander, Rear Admiral Kajioka.

They hit the leading ship. The enemy let loose a hail of fire in answer, and the communications lines between the fire control equipment and the guns were shattered. Battery B kept on firing anyhow.

And then, only forty-five minutes after our first gun had sounded, it was all over – at least, so far as the shore batteries were concerned. The task force sent out to take possession of Wake had had enough, and was running for cover.

But it was not all over for the Japs. As the invader retreated out of range behind a heavy smoke screen, Paul Putnam's[3] impatient flyers moved in for their share of the banquet.

They had gone aloft when we opened fire. After discovering, with some amazement, that no planes accompanied the invaders, they had circled beyond range of our own guns and bided their time. Now they struck.

Putnam was up there himself, with Elrod, Freuler and Tharin, and thanks to Freuler's hard work in the brief days of peace, the little Wildcats carried their lethal cargo of bombs that didn't properly fit the bomb racks. It was the first chance they had had to use them, and they made them good.

The Japs threw up all the antiaircraft fire they could, but the Wildcats kept attacking. They bombed and strafed two light cruisers, knocking out the torpedo battery of one and the radio shack of the other. Freuler set a fierce gasoline fire raging on a transport.

As they expended their bombs and machine gun belts, they came roaring back to the airstrip for more, time after time. Two other pilots, Kinney and Hamilton, got their turns. The fleet

---

[3] Major Paul A. Putnam, commander of the twelve-strong squadron of Grumman Wildcat fighters based on Wake. Most of his aircraft were destroyed in the first Japanese air attack.

continued to race for home, and the four little fighters continued to harass them. And it was Hank Elrod, apparently, who scored the greatest victory from the air. He dropped a bomb on a destroyer; minutes later Kinney sent his plane screaming down toward the same ship just in time to see it blow up in his face.

And that was that. The Japs limped away over the horizon and were gone. We had sunk at least two ships and scored hits on maybe half a dozen others. And we had suffered no casualties.

Not until after the war would we know exactly what we had accomplished, or the size of the fleet Japan had sent out to scoop up the remains of Wake's defenders. Rear Admiral Sadamichi Kajioka, commander of the enemy's 6th Destroyer Squadron, had been on that light cruiser Barninger's men hit when the firing opened at Peacock Point; it was the *Yubari*, flagship of a force numbering two other light cruisers, six destroyers, two patrol boats and two medium transports, with a pair of submarines out ahead to run interference.

Rear Admiral Kuninori Marumo had commanded the other two light cruisers, *Tenryu* and *Tatsuta*. There were 450 landing troops in the patrol boats – two old converted destroyers – and a force of garrison troops in the transports.

Despite a heavy sea, they were already beginning to put their troops into small boats when our fire opened. As Admiral Kajioka pulled his battered flagship out of range, the destroyer *Hayate* was sunk by Battery L on Wilkes, which then scored hits on the destroyer *Oite*, one of the transports, and one of Admiral Marumo's light cruisers. It was the destroyer *Yayoi* that had been hit by Kessler's men on Peale, and the destroyer *Kisaragi* that Elrod had sunk from the air.

Having lost two destroyers and at least five hundred men, and with five or six of his remaining ships damaged. Admiral Kajioka withdrew to Kwajalein in the Marshalls. It was, as a Japanese authority would write after the war, 'one of the most humiliating defeats our Navy had ever suffered.'

And it was more. It was the first authentic victory of the war for our forces. The *Hayate* and *Kisaragi* were the first enemy ships to be sunk by U. S. naval forces since the fighting had begun. The fact that little Wake Island had turned back an invasion fleet would be an incalculable boost to the morale of a nation dazed by the destruction at Pearl Harbor.

We did not know all this on the morning of December 11, but we knew enough to celebrate. And in less than two weeks we would see further proof of the shocking surprise we had given the Japanese. They had been so confident of taking the atoll that they had laid out all their plans for its administration; the copies of an Imperial Rescript issued to us after our capture were dated December 11.

If we had been confident on Wednesday, we were delirious now. At the airstrip, where I went after the shore guns ceased firing, sweating members of the ground crews shouted and pounded one another on the back. Even the loss of two planes – Elrod's fuel line had been cut, and he had to crash-land on the beach, and Freuler nursed his plane back with an engine hopelessly wrecked by enemy flak – could not dampen our spirits. We would wish desperately for those planes in the remaining days of the defense, but now we couldn't be bothered. We had turned back the enemy force. We had beaten off an invasion. And we had suffered no casualties!

I went down to the defense battalion command post on the southern shore to congratulate Devereux on his men's performance, and then a group of us headed happily for the nearby Marine Officers' Club. There was a little beer left, though the refrigerator was not working, and we felt entitled to a celebration.

It was like a fraternity picnic. War whoops of joy split the air; warm beer was sprayed on late arrivals without regard to rank; already the memories that would last a lifetime – a tragically short lifetime for some – were being recalled, relived, and even embroidered.

Big John Hamas pushed his way through the crowd to the corner where I sat on an empty ammo box, drinking my beer in sleepy, relaxed, triumphant peace.

'Captain,' he gloated, 'you told us to cut loose at them, and boy, did we cut loose at the sons of bitches!'

I grinned at him happily. He stood there a moment, towering over me, and then he set down his beer can with an air of finality. 'Well,' he said, 'the celebration's over for me … sir. Got to round up my civilians and get some more ammunition over to Wilkes.' Gunner Hamas was not one to rest too long on his laurels.

I had work of my own to do, the proudest task of my Navy career: report the good news to Pearl Harbor. At that point we were not sure just how many ships, or what kind, we had actually sunk. But we knew beyond doubt that two had gone down – we thought they were a destroyer and a cruiser – and I decided to stick to the positive facts rather than make any claims we couldn't support. I drove back to my command post, dashed off the message, handed it to one of the decoding officers, and looked at my watch. Only 8:45. I would have sworn the day was half gone already.

Word of our victory brought a response that was all we could have desired, aside from a promise of reinforcements. Back came a commendation from Pearl saying we had performed our duties 'in accordance with the highest traditions of the Naval Service.'

I read it to Putnam, Devereux and the others as soon as I had a chance, but there was some unavoidable delay. At nine o'clock the Japanese bombers arrived for a fourth raid. And now we had only two planes left to fight them off.

This time there were seventeen of them, coming in from the northeast, and for the first time in four raids I found myself protected by concrete and steel. The unfinished magazine that formed my communications center and command post had its disadvantages – there was no door, for example – but after the plywood at Camp Two, the brush near Camp One, and the foxhole at the airstrip it was a comforting sensation to look up and find a solid roof over my head.

The magazine brought us through the raid without a scratch, though I promised myself we would lay in a supply of sandbags to protect the entrance hereafter, and when I went on my routine post-raid inspection I found the same was true of the entire atoll. No one had been hurt, and on top of that, Lieutenant Davidson in one of the two Wildcats had shot down two more bombers. On this day of victory nothing could stop us.

Gunner Hamas had come as close as anybody to getting killed this time. With a crew of six civilian volunteers he had loaded a truck with shells, powder, detonators and hand grenades for John McAlister's battery on Kuku Point, and they had driven down to the boat landing only minutes before the bombers were sighted. There Kirby Ludwick, the sailor in charge of the boat crews, took the truck aboard one of the launches and set out across the channel.

They had just cleared the landing when the bombers swept in. Hamas and Ludwick looked at each other and agreed without saying a word that they had a job to do. The battery needed the supplies more now than ever. So on across the channel Ludwick guided the boat with its load of explosives, and all hands crossed their fingers and waited for a bomb.

They made it all right – we all led charmed lives that day – and Hamas's crew of civilians abandoned him, with his blessing, to stay on Wilkes and help out wherever McAlister needed them.

Bryghte Godbold's three-inch battery at Toki Point on Peale had attracted a large part of the enemy's fire. Again, no damage had been done, but it was clear Battery D might be wise to take a leaf from Battery E's book and move while there was time. So, late in the afternoon, the job was begun. Two hundred and fifty civilians pitched in to help move the battery almost the entire length of Peale, from Toki Point to a spot near the bridge.

Meanwhile, Pearl Harbor had given me a small assignment for the day: locate a confidential publication relating to direction finders, which had been in the possession of Pan American and report its destruction. It was easy enough to report *that*. Not only that publication but all others at Pan American's headquarters, and the headquarters itself for that matter, had been destroyed. The Japs had saved me the trouble.

But we had another job to do, along with the usual repairs, and it was one that could wait no longer. Our dead must be cared for.

They had remained in the big refrigerator until now, those who had not been buried where they fell, and I did not dare wait any longer to pay final honor to them and give them as decent a burial as possible.

We did the best we could. A civilian dragline operator scooped out a long trench, and a handful of us stood in reverent silence while the bodies of the dead were laid into it. A firing squad gave a last salute and a bulldozer covered the grave. There was no chaplain on Wake, but one of the contractor's employees, a lay preacher named John O'Neal from Worland, Wyoming, said a short prayer.

I gave orders that in the future our dead would be buried where they fell or in the closest practical space. There would be no more mass burials – and, I confidently hoped, there would be no need for them.

We had lost twenty-six officers and men of the fighter squadron, two sailors, and three enlisted men of the defence battalion. And how many civilians were dead? Thirty-five, perhaps, or forty or even more, counting those whose bodies had not been found.

It was a sad note on which to end the day. I tried to shake off my feeling of depression, to regain the spirit of victorious confidence we had all shared earlier, to remember the battered task force and the two bombers shot down by Lieutenant Davidson.

And then somebody was running toward me through the dusk, shouting something I could not hear above the surf, and I stopped stiffly and strained my ears to hear.

It was something about Lieutenant Kliewer, and now as the man came closer I could hear.

Kliewer had sunk a Jap sub.

He had found it basking on the surface as he flew the dusk patrol, and he had torn into it with bombs and machine guns. He had gone so low that fragments from the explosions hit his plane, and he had stayed to see the sub disappear below the surface and an oil slick appear where it had been.

Pearl wanted us to conduct unrestricted warfare, did they? Well, we had done it today. Surface ships, bombers, and now a submarine. If they'd just give us enough time we'd lick the whole Japanese Navy by ourselves.

I went back to my cottage thinking the hell with the dangers of a night raid, threw open the window to the soft breezes and the soothing sound of the surf, and slept like a baby.

Wake finally fell after the Japanese attacked again with overwhelming force on 23 December. An American relief force, including the carrier Saratoga, *was only 500 miles away. The gallant defenders of Wake had destroyed two modern warships and twenty-one aircraft and inflicted 1,175 casualties; 120 Americans died in the fight for the atoll.*

2

FROM DIEPPE TO THE PROKHOROVKA

Adolf Hitler sealed Germany's fate four days after Pearl Harbor by declaring war on the United States. From that moment the Soviet leader, Josef Stalin, lost no opportunity to urge his British and American allies to open a 'Second Front' in northern Europe. The Dieppe raid of August 1942, launched against a heavily defended sector of the French coast, had the principal aim of soothing Soviet impatience about the Allies' plans to return to liberate Western Europe. It was also intended to provide battle experience for the troops involved, 2nd Canadian Division and Nos. 3 and 4 Commandos.

Essentially a 'reconnaissance in force', the operation was a disaster and a timely warning of the dangers of a premature invasion of Hitler's 'Fortress Europe'. Nevertheless, it taught the Allies a number of useful lessons which were eventually incorporated into the plans for the invasion of Normandy in June 1944. The second-in-command of 3 Commando at Dieppe was Peter Young.

After Vaagso[1] one of the first jobs I was given was to go round various units and select volunteers to replace our casualties. By

---

[1] Vaagso is an island off the Norwegian coast. On 12 December 1941, the port of South Vaagso was raided by a British force supported by naval gunfire. There were heavy British casualties but the main targets were destroyed. After the raid German strength in Norway was increased and by 1944 was over 350,000.

this time Home Forces had clamped down on recruiting for the Commandos and the units I was allowed to visit were all Young Soldiers' Battalions. No. 6 Troop had always consisted for the most part of old soldiers, reservists with pre-war training and previous battle experience at Dunkirk, and I was a bit dubious about taking men of eighteen and twenty. As it turned out, these young soldiers were to have nearly eighteen months' training before operating in Sicily and Italy, where they did very well. Young soldiers will follow their commanders out of the innocence of their hearts.

Soon after this I was asked by John Durnford-Slater whether I would like to go to Combined Operations Headquarters and serve for a time on the planning staff. This sounded interesting, and early in March 1942 I joined the staff at Richmond Terrace, Whitehall, as a major. I worked directly under Robert Henriques, who had been Brigade Major of the Special Service Brigade, and Charles Haydon, now a major-general, was the head of our branch.

Our job was to select suitable targets, submit appreciations and outline plans, and when these were approved by the Chief of Combined Operations, Lord Mountbatten, to work out the details of the raid. At this time the scope of any raid was governed by two main factors: the range of fighter cover, then not more than seventy-five miles; and the availability of landing-craft, which were still in very short supply.

During the months that I spent at C.O.H.Q. the most important raid was that on St. Nazaire. The cover plan was beautifully simple; the officers and men detailed for demolition parties from various Commandos were assembled and trained on the pretext that they were doing a demolition course. At the end of the course, instead of dispersing, the students went off on the raid.

This operation, which was carried out by 2 Commando, was a desperate venture, involving as it did a six-mile run up the mouth of the Loire under the fire of many batteries.

After this operation I asked Charles Haydon if I could return to 3 Commando. By this time Sandy Ronald had left to become Second-in-Command of 6 Commando, and Jack Churchill had succeeded to the command of 2 Commando. And so I became Second-in-Command of 3 Commando, which I now rejoined at Largs.

Jack Churchill once told me that it was the Second-in-Command's duty to sit and wait until the Commanding Officer got bumped off. However that may be, I found that John Durnford-Slater liked to leave a great deal of the training to me, an arrangement which suited me down to the ground. Besides the normal training, to a very great extent he allowed me to select and train N.C.O.s. In this way I got to know all the officers and very nearly all the N.C.O.s and men, which was to prove invaluable to me later on.

I thoroughly enjoyed my new job. John is the most reasonable of men unless he has finally made up his mind. This, rightly or wrongly, was my opinion of him long before I became his Second-in-Command and I acted upon it throughout. It seemed to work. At any rate, in all the time that I was associated with John Durnford-Slater I do not remember having a single row with him, although we once had a near miss.

By this time, of the twenty-seven officers in the Commando only six had joined when it was formed: the Colonel, myself, Charley Head, Joe Smale, Bill Bradley and John Pooley. We had lost two of the best at Vaagso, several had gone to the Middle East with Layforce, a few had been promoted; others willingly or unwillingly had gone back to their own regiments.

To be honest, at least half of those who had left the unit had done so for the unit's good. John Durnford-Slater gave his followers a lot of rope and was an unusually sweet-tempered Commanding Officer, but once he had decided that someone was useless or crooked or had 'had it', that man was out.

In the summer of 1942 we left Largs for the last time and moved to Seaford, where once more we went into 'civvy billets'. The town was rather too small for the whole Commando, and so 5 Troop was billeted at Alfriston. The move to Sussex made a great change in the life of the Commando because we now found ourselves in a countryside teeming with troops, whereas in Ayrshire we had been able to train, and to a great extent to shoot, almost where we pleased.

The planning for Dieppe had begun as long ago as April when I had been on the planning staff at C.O.H.Q. Dieppe was selected because it would not be one of the invasion ports whenever it was finally decided to launch the Second Front. It was within the range of fighter cover. It also had obvious disadvantages. The whole coast for some miles on either side of the town is a wall of chalk cliffs, like those between Newhaven and Brighton, and this limited the number of suitable landing beaches. The planners had to decide whether to land several miles from the town, which meant crossing small rivers on the way, or to land on the waterfront of the town in the teeth of the garrison. A landing at Dieppe itself would call for the maximum of fire support from the Navy and the Royal Air Force.

Three Commandos were allotted to the force. Nos. 3 and 4 Commandos were to silence the two coast defence batteries on either flank of the port, while No. 40, the first of the Royal Marine Commandos, was to attack shipping in the harbour and to be available as a floating reserve. The main assault was to be made by the 2nd Canadian Division.

The task of 3 Commando was to land in two groups at two beaches, near the village of Berneval, 'Yellow 1', and near Belleville-sur-Mer, 'Yellow 2'. The Colonel was to land on Yellow 1 with the main body of the Commando, while I was to land on Yellow 2 with 3 and 4 Troops and a 3-inch mortar section. The two groups were then to move inland and together destroy Goebbels Battery of 5.9-inch guns, 450 yards inland on the outskirts of Berneval, between the village and the cliffs. The Colonel, with the general layout of the battery and its neighbourhood clearly in mind, was able to organise thorough rehearsals which were carried out on the downs behind Alfriston.

In July the raid was postponed for a month, which gave rise to the usual rumours that the whole show was off, but towards the middle of August it became obvious that it was really going to happen. First of all a detachment of U.S. Rangers arrived and later some Fusiliers-Marins – these last to act as guides.

The force embarked on the evening of 18th August and sailed from Southampton, Portsmouth, Shoreham and Newhaven about 9 p.m. No. 3 Commando sailed from Newhaven in a flotilla known as Group 5, consisting of twenty Eurekas.[2] These unarmoured landing-craft – designed, not for a seventy-mile channel crossing but only for a run of five to ten miles – each

[2] Landing-craft Personnel (Large).

carried about eighteen fully-equipped soldiers. We were escorted by a steam gunboat, a motor launch, and a larger landing-craft carrying 4 Troop. The Colonel and Commander E. B. Wyburd, R.N., were leading the flotilla in the steam gunboat, so as to ensure that we did not lose our way. The Eurekas sailed in four waves five abreast, and I was in the starboard craft of the first wave, which was commanded by Lieutenant Buckee, R.N.V.R., and the soldiers with me were the H.Q.s of my Group and of 3 Troop.

At first everyone was chiefly interested in watching the rest of the force moving out to sea, but after a time we tried to get some sleep; it was very uncomfortable and cramped in the landing-craft and I doubt if anyone dozed for more than a few minutes. About midnight we opened some tins of self-heating soup. It was tepid.

At 3.47 a.m., when we were still about an hour's run from the coast, a star shell went up on our port bow illuminating the group.

Immediately a heavy fire was opened up on us; 3- and 4-inch guns, ack-ack guns and machine-guns poured a stream of shells and tracer into the flotilla, while further star shells lit the sky. It was by far the most unpleasant moment of my life.

Five enemy craft were converging on us. It seemed impossible that our wooden landing-craft could survive for more than a few minutes. The tracer seemed to come swooping straight at us. In a few minutes we would be dead and there was absolutely nothing we could do about it. We crawled upon the face of the ocean, and always nearer to the deadly line of enemy ships. It was certainly very frightening – far more so than any land battle I ever saw before or since. I began to ram a clip into my Garand rifle. There wasn't much else to do. In the dark I found it unfamiliar. I wished I had stuck to my old Lee Enfield. Craft and Clark were at my side. I sensed that they were as unhappy as I was – which comforted me to some extent.

I was in the stern of the craft, where I had been trying to sleep; there was more room there. Now I wanted to speak to Buckee urgently. He was up forward beside the steersman. It was impossible to get to him through the soldiers crouched beneath the awning. I climbed up on to the narrow deck and ran along the side. We were still heading towards the Germans and every second brought us nearer the muzzles of their guns. I suggested to Buckee that it might be better to take some sort of avoiding action, but he replied that we were to follow the steam gunboat, which was navigating, so long as she was in action. Commander Wyburd had decided beforehand that, should he meet the enemy at sea, he would continue on his course and fight his way through, for he felt quite rightly that any alteration in course or speed would so disorganise the group that an orderly landing would become impossible. In any case, the destroyers *Slazak* (Polish) and H.M.S. *Brocklesby* were to give support to the landing-craft in the event of their being attacked by German ships. We ploughed on towards the Germans for what seemed a very long time; it has been estimated as ten minutes, but can scarcely have been as much; at the end of that time the gunboat, hit many times, reeled out of action, crossing our bows. Once more I urged Buckee to alter course and he now turned off 90 degrees to starboard.

Those of the landing-craft which escaped owed their survival to Wyburd's gallantry in keeping the gunboat on her original course, for the majority of the German gunners took his ship for their target. All his guns were put out of action, his wireless equipment was hit and about forty per cent of those on board were wounded.

On the other hand, we in the landing-craft now found ourselves far too near to the German ships and attracting a great deal of fire. The canopy of our craft was full of holes, but the men crouching down below were not hit. We made the best speed we could for several minutes and at last found ourselves out of range; behind us tracer could still be seen but no sound reached us.

The destroyers, meanwhile, were pursuing some project of their own.

As soon as we were clear we looked about to see where the rest of the group was, only to find that we were now alone. This did not disturb us very much; Buckee had little doubt that some of the other craft would be able to find their way to the beaches even without the gunboat to navigate. We turned towards the shore and started looking for Yellow 2. It was not difficult to estimate its rough position, as a light some miles away to starboard was evidently the Dieppe Lighthouse. We could now see the cliffs quite clearly and a black patch which Buckee said was the gully at Yellow 2. I thought it was Yellow 1, but Buckee insisted that he was right.

'There you are,' he said, 'there's your beach.'

'What do we do now?' I asked, rather pointlessly.

'My orders,' he replied, 'are to land even if there's only one boat.'

Not to be outdone, I said: 'Those are my orders, too: we are to land whatever happens, even if we have to swim.'

Buckee offered to land with his sailors to swell our party, but I persuaded him to remain with the craft. We arranged that if he should come under heavy fire from the cliffs he would leave us and that we would try to make our way to Dieppe and join the Canadians when the time came to withdraw. He was making directly for Yellow 2, but, fearing that there would be machine-guns in the gully, I asked him to run in about fifty yards to the right. We came in five minutes early, for it was getting light all too quickly, and touched down about 4.50 a.m.

We crossed the narrow beach, reached the foot of the cliff, turned to the left and approached the gully. The narrow cleft in the cliffs was completely choked with coils of wire with a rabbit-wire fence on the outside some ten feet high in front of it. I asked John Selwyn to tell his men to bring a Bangalore torpedo and blow a hole in the fence and was told that they had not got one in this particular boat. I said that we had better get to work with wire-cutters, but he said he had not brought any. I was vexed with Selwyn. I started to climb up the left-hand side of the gully, which looked the easier, but almost immediately lost my balance and fell back on top of Selwyn, who suggested that we were not doing much good and that it might be better to get back in the craft.

Similar thoughts were passing through my own mind at that moment, but being, I suppose, contrary by nature it needed only this to make me determined to carry on. I gave a sort of surly growl by way of reply and started climbing the other side of the cleft. When about twelve feet from the ground, my Garand rifle slipped off my shoulder and into the crook of my right arm, swinging me away from the wire. I thought to myself, 'If I fall off now I shall never get up,' but by some miracle I managed to keep my foothold and cling on with one hand. From this point the cliff became rather less steep and I reached the top, standing on the pegs with which the Germans had secured the wire, which served as a rope. The barbs were very close together but fairly blunt and this, though it cut my hands, was not as unpleasant as it sounds. On reaching the top, I could see the back of a notice-board which turned out to have the words 'Achtung Minen' written on it.

The men seemed to take a very long time coming up the cliff, though Driver Cunningham collected their toggle ropes and made a rope to help them up the worst bit. As we reached the top Hopkins pointed out some landing-craft running in on Yellow 1, five of them. Later on a small ship ran in and beached between Yellow 1 and Yellow 2. This was the German-armed tanker *Franz*, damaged by one of our motor launches.

By about 5.10 a.m. my whole party had reached the top and I led them into a small wood nearby and organised them into three groups under Selwyn, Ruxton – a recently joined subaltern – and myself. Some of the soldiers did not look particularly pleased at the turn of events, so I gave them a pep talk, telling them that if a party of nineteen could do any good it would be something to tell their children about. They looked a bit dubious. We had an odd assortment of arms; there was one Bren, six Thompson guns, ten rifles including my Garand, which had been given to me by the U.S. Rangers, a 3-inch mortar, which we had failed to get up the cliff, and a 2-inch mortar.

I now sent out scouts and started advancing through the cornfields towards the road which runs along parallel with the coast about a thousand yards inland. Looking out across the fields towards the battery we could make out absolutely nothing, though during our advance six Hurricanes came over and attacked it and were fired at by a light ack-ack gun. When we reached the road I took a careful look at the approach to the village through my field-glasses, expecting that there would be a German post at the entrance to the village. A French youth of about sixteen was passing on a bicycle when some of the men grabbed him. Though terrified, he was friendly and told me that he was trying to escape inland to avoid the fighting and that there were two hundred Germans in the battery. It was obvious that he would not betray our presence, and when I told him he could go on his way he swiftly leant forward, kissed me on the cheek, leapt on his bogwheel and pedalled for the hinterland! Ruxton advanced with his group while the rest of us covered him. He soon signalled that the coast was clear and we all arrived at the edge of the village just as the battery fired its first round. We cut some telephone wires at this point and then pushed on. In an orchard to the right of the road a French peasant woman sat calmly milking a cow.

To move through the gardens at the back of the houses would have taken too long so we went up the main street. Here we met some Frenchmen wheeling a wounded woman along on a hand barrow; she had been hit during the attack by the Hurricanes soon after dawn. The guns were still firing slowly, so the sooner we reached the battery the better; I gave the order to double and we ran down the street at a pretty good pace. I questioned several inhabitants, hoping to hear that some of the men who had landed at Yellow 1 had also reached the village, but there was no news of them and no sign of firing from that direction. We saw quite a number of the inhabitants, some of whom were members of the local fire brigade in their brass helmets; one of the houses in the village was on fire. The people very wisely kept out of the way, though several of them waved to us, and all those we spoke to were distinctly friendly.

When we came abreast of the church we were suddenly fired on by a German machine-gun post at the corner of the road about sixty yards ahead of us. Ruxton opened fire on two Germans whom we saw cross the road and get into position in a hedge. They fired their rifles at him, but he stood his ground and returned their fire with his Thompson sub-machine gun. Selwyn joined him and opened up as well; then Abbott came up and got the Bren into action. Selwyn put Lance-Corporal Bennett behind the church and engaged this enemy post with our 2-inch mortar; the German machine-gun ceased fire.

I cannot think why we had no casualties at this point, for our party must have been an easy enough target. While this shooting was going on another group pushed on into the churchyard and engaged the enemy from there. The Germans' fire was mostly high and one burst dislodged a shower of tiles from a roof which descended on Abbott, the Bren-gunner.

The doubling had done the men good. They had now got their blood up and quite recovered their spirits. They were beginning to enjoy themselves. I re-formed them behind the church, with the intention of placing the Bren and some snipers in the tower, while the rest of us held the area. It seemed certain that the belfry would overlook the gun positions, and I had visions of picking off the German gunners one by one as they served their pieces. Unfortunately, when I went inside to look for the steps leading up the tower, I could find none. The church, a lovely medieval one, vanished in the pre- D-Day bombing, but I was told several years later by the town clerk that the steps began ten feet above ground level and were reached by a ladder which had been removed. Moreover, the view from the belfry was obscured by a row of tall trees, so perhaps it was as well that I was forced to alter my plan.

We now tried to advance on the battery through the orchards at the north-west end of the village, hoping to outflank any post which might be guarding the tracks entering the battery from the rear. We passed a slit trench and the under-carriage of an aeroplane which had been camouflaged and rigged up to look like a small gun, but then came under fire again from riflemen whom we could not see. They did not hit anybody and probably could not see us very well. Next a machine-gun opened up on us, firing three bursts, but there were so many hedges that we could not locate this either. There seemed to me to be no future in advancing blind through these orchards against a hidden enemy, and it suddenly occurred to me that we might be better off in the cornfields.

We assembled again at the edge of the village and I set Selwyn's group to the flank of the guns, with orders to get within two hundred yards and snipe them. As he moved, my own group fired at the left-hand gun and continued to shoot while Ruxton led his men out to support Selwyn. My group then joined the other two. All three parties were fired at by small arms as we dashed to take up our new position, apparently by sentry groups posted along the edge of the orchards, but once again nobody was hit. The left-hand gun, which we imagined we could see clearly, and at which we had fired a certain amount, now turned out to be a dummy!

Once we were in among the crops I formed the men into two lines in extended order, with a good distance between each man and with the second line firing between the intervals in the first line. We now opened a hot fire at the smoke and flashes around the gun positions. Groups of riflemen were still firing at us from the battery position, but they were not marksmen.

All this time the guns went on shooting at a slow rate; possibly only one gun was in action, trying to find the range. Certainly there were no salvoes, and some of us estimated that the total number of rounds fired was no more than fifteen or twenty, though there must have been more. It seemed that the gun detachments were firing on their own account and that the observation post was not doing its job properly, possibly because we had cut their telephone wires, but more likely because of the enormous smoke-screen off Dieppe. The cloud of smoke there was very thick indeed and we ourselves could see none of the ships. To confuse the gunners the R.A.F. had dropped smoke on the battery and there was still a great deal hanging about. No doubt this air attack had upset them.

We had to fire from the kneeling position, because of the height of the corn, taking snap shots and moving about, so as to offer the most difficult possible target to the enemy, but we were almost exactly at right angles to the enemy gun-line and any bullet that whistled over No. 4 gun would give a good fright to the crew of No. 1 as well – at least so we hoped. I am very far from claiming that we caused many casualties, and indeed it was very difficult to see anyone to get a shot at. It was harassing fire, more or less controlled. The guns were about twenty to thirty yards apart and surrounded by concrete walls.

After a time, at about eight o'clock, we had our reward. There was a sudden explosion about one hundred and fifty yards to our front, an orange flash, and a cloud of black smoke. A shell screamed past overhead and plunged into a valley about a mile behind us. The Germans had turned their left-hand gun round and were firing it at us. Fortunately we were too close to be damaged, for the guns, not being designed to fire at point-blank range, could not be depressed sufficiently to hit us. It was nevertheless an unusual experience and for a moment I wondered what was happening. Indeed one of the soldiers came up to me and said indignantly:

'Sir! We're being mortared!' An odd deduction when a 6-inch gun was firing at us! The Germans in the Varengeville Battery used mortars against 4 Commando, but at Berneval it seems they had none, which was just as well for us. Fifteen feet of standing corn is said to stop a bullet, but I doubt if it is much protection against a mortar bomb. Selwyn told me afterwards that one of our motor launches, having taken us for the enemy, was also firing at us about this time and one of the men was hit in the ear, our first casualty. Every time the gun fired we gave it a volley of small arms, aimed at the black-and-yellow fumes which appeared. They fired four rounds at us, at the same slow rate as before, and then gave it up.

Suddenly two Messerschmitts came swooping up from our rear and flew over the battery without attacking us. Neither side seemed to know who we belonged to. We had come ashore with about a hundred rounds per rifleman. Firing rapidly it would be easy to spend that much ammunition in ten minutes, so we had to be very sparing; we were continually telling the men to fire slowly so as to keep up a steady whine over the heads of the gunners. The posts in the orchard continued to fire at us without respite, but without success. We kept all our fire for the big guns.

Coast defence guns firing at a normal rate should be able to fire one or two rounds a minute, for the operation of reloading, though complicated, should not take more than about thirty seconds. We spent approximately an hour and a half in the cornfield and during that time I do not believe the battery got off more than twenty or thirty rounds, including the four aimed at us.

The shortage of ammunition was now becoming acute, and as time went by it was becoming increasingly probable that

German reinforcements, including perhaps armour, would intervene. I did not care for the idea of meeting tanks in the middle of the cornfield, so I thinned out my line and sent Selwyn to form a small bridgehead round the beach, telling him that if the landing-craft was still there he was to fire three white Very lights.

So far we had paid no attention to the German observation-post which clearly deserved a visit. While the remainder of the party withdrew towards the beach, Ruxton with Abbott, Craft and Clark came with me to a point on the cliff from which we had a good view of this pillbox. Ruxton saw two Germans standing on the roof and fired a burst at them with the Bren, at a range of about four hundred yards. They disappeared and fire was returned immediately. Ruxton continued to engage the enemy post. Clark now reported seeing three white Very lights from the beach and we wriggled back into a small valley and began to make our way back to the boat. A group of riflemen were following us, at a respectful distance, and someone else was sniping from the Dieppe side of the gully. A few of the men covered our withdrawal, firing back at the German riflemen.

Captain Selwyn now withdrew his party and embarked, while the rest of us covered their withdrawal from the top of the cliff. The landing-craft had been under fire from the observation-post for some time. Riflemen had reached the cliffs about three hundred yards to the east, and the solitary sniper was still plugging away from the west. Three men waiting on the beach to cover Ruxton and myself down the cliff were cursed at by the sailors for their slowness and told to get into the boat.

Once aboard, they engaged the cliff-tops with the stripped Lewis gun belonging to the craft, scoring several hits. One German dropped his rifle down the cliff.

By this time Ruxton and myself, with Abbott our Bren-gunner, had crossed the beach and were wading out to the landing-craft. It was like those dreams you have of trying desperately to walk and making no progress. Eventually we laid hold of the lifelines and were towed out to sea. About three hundred yards out the craft hove to and we were dragged aboard. Quite a number of shots hit the craft at this point, and a sailor a yard away from me was severely wounded in the thigh. The battery fired a few shells at us but pretty wide of the mark. A bullet hit the smoke canister in the stern and we began to give out quite a respectable smoke-screen.

Shortly afterwards we fell in with the motor launch and transferred to her. We then returned to Newhaven, being unsuccessfully attacked on the voyage by a JU.88 at 10.45 a.m. and entertained nobly on whisky, cocoa, and rum so that I felt distinctly warm, if somewhat tight, on arriving at Newhaven.

There was no news of the rest of the Commando when we reached Newhaven, and in the afternoon I went up to London to report at C.O.H.Q. Having been on the planning staff there at the time of the St. Nazaire raid, I knew with what anxiety we had waited for any authentic information and how many days it had taken to reach us. I had an interview with Lord Louis Mountbatten and with General Haydon and was told to return for the conference which was to be held next day. I asked permission to reappear in my battledress which was rather the worse for wear, and Lord Louis replied: 'What the hell, there is a war on.'

I then went home to Oxshott and slept the night in my own bed.

Few of the 100,000 German soldiers who surrendered at Stalingrad on 31 January 1943 saw their homes again. From the beginning of the war on the Eastern Front the Wehrmacht had been merciless with the millions of Russian troops who had fallen into its hands. The Russians repaid them in kind. One man who did come back from Stalingrad was the unknown author of a report published by the German War Graves Commission.

After our last bits and pieces had been plundered, haversacks and blankets stolen, medals and badges ripped from our coats with curses and imprecations, the thousands of those who had been assembled were driven out on the march by an enemy who knew no mercy … Towards evening we reached the ruins of a place named Yersevko and stayed overnight there encamped on the snow. In the morning we headed for Dubovka. We left behind in Yersevko thousands of our comrades; German soldiers who had died on a steppe where there was neither food nor shelter.

Our second march day took the column of misery and dying to Dubovka on the Volga. En route we were attacked and robbed by civilians who stole anything we had with us. Boots were taken from the soldiers' feet so that they had to march bare-footed through the snow. Thousands died that day. They sank, helpless, to the ground right and left of the road and died in the snow which soon covered them. During the evening of 4th February 1943, we reached Dubovka. There was no POW camp there, only a simple, guarded, Collecting Point. There were no shelters, cookhouses, sanitary arrangements or anything else. Outside the town there were the ruins of a monastery, a large sheep pen and, in another place, a former Red Army troop camp consisting of earthen huts. There was no heating material. The only drinking water was a frozen puddle near a blown-up water pump. The Red Army left us to our own devices. Some supplies of raw salt fish and dry bread were issued. In the camp there was spotted typhus. Soon everybody was infected. In the camp there was starvation, cholera, dysentery, paratyphus and hunger delusions. Soon there were more dead than living. We never saw any Russian personnel. After twelve days we survivors were driven away from the heaps of dead to the gates of the monastery; first of all the rank and file and then, a day later, the officers. Two columns left this place of the dead. We left behind 17,000 dead comrades. The survivors, perhaps two to three thousand in number, marched southwards for two days, driven through the ruins of the city of Stalingrad. Whoever was too weak to go any farther was shot by the guards at the rear of the column, supervised by Soviet officers.

After 120 kilometres we reached Beketovka. A large living area had been cleared of civilians and surrounded by barbed wire. This was to be our prison camp. Those just arriving had a shock. The two-storey houses and the open places – in short the whole area surrounded by barbed wire – was packed with the dead bodies of those who had been taken captive in the Stalingrad South pocket and who had died here of disease. The number of dead was thought to be about 42,000 ...

After its victory at Stalingrad the Red Army threatened to roll up the entire German southern front. The situation was restored by a brilliant counterthrust masterminded by Field Marshal von Manstein, which by

March 1943 had stabilized the front. The result was a huge salient, 100 miles across and 70 miles deep, thrusting westwards into the German line between Orel and Kharkov. In July 1943 the Kursk salient was the scene of a colossal tank battle – the largest in history – as the German Army Group South attempted to eliminate the salient with concentric attacks launched on its northern and southern shoulders. The panzers were halted on the point of breakthrough by General Pavel Rotmistrov's Fifth Guards Tank Army, which had been held in the rear at the start of the battle by the overall Soviet commander, Marshal Georgi Zhukov. Rotmistrov, a vivid stylist, describes this crucial clash of armour.

At 0130 hours on 7 July, the Army began its strenuous journey in two echelons. The first was made up of two tank corps and the second of a motorised corps. The Army Headquarters advanced along with the main forces. This arrangement made it possible to control the Army on the move and to deploy our tank corps quickly to deliver a devastating strike on the march.

In July the nights are short and hardly anyone got a wink of sleep. At dawn I contacted the corps commanders by radio. Everything was all right. Their units were advancing smoothly and in order and our fighters were patrolling the skies overhead. Konev told me later that he himself had followed, from a plane, the advance of our columns.

It grew hot as early as 0800 hours and clouds of dust billowed up. By midday the dust rose in thick clouds, settling in a solid layer on roadside bushes, grain fields, tanks and trucks. The dark red disc of the sun was hardly visible through the grey shroud of dust. Tanks, self-propelled guns and tractors, which towed the artillery, armoured personnel carriers and trucks were advancing in an unending flow. The faces of soldiers were darkened with dust and exhaust fumes. It was intolerably hot.

Soldiers were tortured by thirst and their shirts, wet with sweat, stuck to their bodies. Drivers found the going particularly hard. The crew members tried in every way to make it easier for them by taking their place at the controls every now and then and letting them rest during brief halts. The hardships had to be endured as time was running short.

The tank crews did their best and by the morning of 8 July the main forces of the Army, after an exhausting and strenuous march, reached an area to the south-west of Stary Oskol. The rest of the day was spent bringing up rearguard troops and deploying units in their assigned concentration areas. Within 48 hours the Army had covered 230–280 kilometres [140–175 miles]. The number of tanks which had fallen behind because of mechanical failure was insignificant and they were promptly repaired and returned to their units.

This was the first instance of a tank army moving under its own power over such a vast distance in hot weather and on dusty roads. It was a rigorous test for the training standards of engineering and technical personnel, whose duty was to maintain the tanks while on the march. That day was also taken up by preparing for combat.

In the early hours of 9 July, we received our combat orders to reach the area of Prokhorovka by the end of that day in full combat readiness. Another march of over 100 kilometres was ahead, but the army coped effectively with that assignment too. Staff officers made all the necessary calculations. The troops passed the checkpoints on time and, defying the dust, heat and fatigue, reached their concentration areas before the deadline, ready for action.

On 10 July, the 5th Guards Tank Army was attached to the Voronezh Front. I was summoned urgently to the command post near Oboyan, of the Front Commander, General Vatutin. There I found Marshal Alexander Vasilevksy, representative of the Supreme Command GHQ, who coordinated the operations of the Voronezh and South-West Fronts,[1] and General Semyon Ivanov, the Front's Chief-of-Staff, who greeted me cordially and briefed me on the complex situation at the Voronezh Front.

The troops of the Front had been on duty for the sixth day in succession facing the fierce onslaught of a large concentration of Nazi troops, which included 8 panzer, 1 motorised and 5 infantry divisions of the Army Group South, which was commanded by Field Marshal Manstein, who was well known to us from Stalingrad. The 4th Panzer Army commanded by Colonel General Hoth, another 'old friend' of ours, launched an all-out attack at 0600 hours on 5 July from an area to the north of Belgorod, delivering the main strike towards Oboyan and Kursk.

Both commanders were favourites of Hitler, who seemed certain of their success, particularly as they commanded the flower of the German Panzer troops. These included the SS divisions *Adolph Hitler, Das Reich, Totenkopf* and the motorised division *Gross Deutschland*. The offensive of the German main strike was backed by a north-western thrust towards Korocha, carried out by the *Abt.Kempf* task force, which consisted of the 3rd Panzer corps reinforced by other troops.

In the fierce fighting, the enemy suffered heavy losses, but advanced 35 kilometres towards Oboyan and 10 kilometres towards Korocha.

---

[1] A Red Army Front was roughly equivalent to a German Army Group.

The Front Commander called me to the map and, pointing with his pencil to the area of Prokhorovka, said:

'Having failed to breakthrough to Kursk and Oboyan, the Nazis have apparently decided to shift the thrust to their main attack a little to the east, along the railroad to Prokhorovka. The 2nd SS Panzer Corps is being redeployed here and will attack Prokhorovka with the 48th Panzer Corps and the Panzer units of the *Abt.Kempf* group'. Vatutin cast a glance at Vasilevsky and, turning to me, he continued: 'So, Pavel Alexeyevich, we have decided to put up our Guards tanks against the SS Panzer divisions and to deliver a counter-strike with our 5th Guards Tank Army, reinforced with two tank corps. Incidentally, the Panzer divisions have new heavy Tiger tanks and Ferdinand self-propelled guns which inflicted heavy losses on Katukov's 1st Tank Army. Do you know anything about such a force, and how do you plan to fight it?', Vasilevsky asked.

'We know all about that, Marshal, as we have their specifications from Steppe Front headquarters and we also have drawn up plans on how to fight them'.

'That is good!'. Vatutin put in and nodded at me to continue.

'The Tigers and Ferdinands have powerful long-range 88-mm guns in addition to a thick front armour which gives them superiority over our tanks with their 76-mm guns. They can only be fought effectively in close combat, where the T-34 can use its greater manoeuvrability and direct its fire at the sides of the heavy German tanks'.

'Figuratively speaking, we should fight them in hand-to-hand combat and overwhelm them', the Front Commander summed up. He turned to talk back to the forthcoming counter-offensive, in which the 1st Tank Army and the 6th, 7th and 5th Guards Rifle Armies would also take part. Our Army, together with attached tank units, numbered about 850 tanks and self-propelled guns.

In the afternoon I returned to my command post with our combat orders. On the morning of 12 July, the Army together with the 1st Tank and 5th Guards Rifle Armies, was to launch a decisive attack to destroy the enemy to the south-west of Prokhorovka and to reach Krasnaya Dubrava and Yakovlevo by night.

Without wasting any time, I and the corps commanders, surveyed the theatre of operations and formulated their combat assignments. The deployment area for the main forces of the Army was chosen to the west-south-west of Prokhorovka, on a front stretching for up to 15 kilometres. Since we were to join battle with a strong enemy tank group which, according to our intelligence, had about 700 tanks, including over 100 Tigers and Ferdinands, and self-propelled guns, we decided to deploy all the four tank corps in the first echelon. The second echelon was made up of the 5th Guards Motorised Corps, and troops of the leading unit and an anti-tank artillery regiment were left in reserve under the command of my deputy, General K. Trufanov.

Marshal Vasilevsky arrived at my command post at about 1900 hours on 11 July. I reported how I had deployed the Army and my orders to the tank corps and artillery. He approved my decisions. He told me of a conversation he had had with the Supreme Commander-in-Chief, Stalin, who had ordered him to remain with the 5th Guards Tank Army and the 5th Guards Rifle Army in order to coordinate operations. Stalin had also told Front Commander Vatutin to remain at his command post in Oboyan while the Front's Commander-in-Chief, General

Ivanov, went on to Korocha. Then the Marshal asked to be shown the deployment areas assigned to the tank corps.

We went through Prokhorovka, our fast jeep bumping into potholes as we overtook ammunition trucks and fuel tanks crawling towards the frontline. Trucks carrying the wounded were advancing slowly in the other direction and we saw wrecked lorries and carts here and there by the roadside. The road meandered through vast yellow wheat fields and beyond them stretched a forest with a village at its edge.

'There, on the northern rim of the forest, the 29th Tank Corps has taken up positions and the 18th Tank Corps will attack to the right of it', I explained to Vasilevsky.

He peered ahead, listening to the mounting roar of battle. The frontline held by our infantry was marked by billows of smoke and blasts of air bombs and shells. Suddenly, Vasilevsky ordered the driver to stop. The car swerved to the kerb and came to a stop abruptly by dust-coated shrubs. We opened the doors and went out. The roar of tanks was heard distinctly and a moment later they came into sight.

'What is the matter, General?', Vasilevsky asked me with obvious displeasure. 'You were warned that the enemy must not know about the arrival of your tanks and yet here they are, rolling in plain view of the Nazis....'.

I raised my binoculars and, indeed, I saw dozens of tanks moving in combat order across a wheat field, firing as they went from their short guns.

'But Marshal, those are German tanks, not ours …'.

'So.... The enemy must have broken through at some spot; the Germans want to surprise us and seize Prokhorovka.'

'We must not allow this to happen', I told Vasilevsky and immediately radioed to General Kirkchenko to order the two tank brigades to advance to stop the German tanks.

On return to my command post, I learned that the Germans had been in action against most of our armies. The situation was thus heightened. The area chosen by us earlier for a counter-attack had now been captured by the Germans, so plans for the offensive, and in particular the choice of gun emplacements, had to be re done. It was vital to update orders, to organise cooperation between individual corps and units, to revise the schedule of artillery preparation and to ensure efficient troop control. The task was difficult because time was running out. However, all the staff officers reorganised the plans within a matter of hours and, in addition, the army combat order was updated.

Telephones kept ringing at the Army's field command post and liaison officers handled orders to and from the troops. General V. Baskakov, the Army's Chief-of-Staff, his face taut with fatigue and his eyes red from lack of sleep, reported to me periodically on the latest developments. I immediately analysed the reports, marked changes on my map, and issued new orders.

An operational report stating that the Army had taken positions for a counter-offensive and was ready to proceed was signed and despatched. However, at 0400 hours General Vatutin, the Front Commander, ordered me to send my reserves immediately to the operational area of the 69th Army as the enemy had committed the main forces of the 3rd Panzer corps of the *Abt. Kempf* operational group and had pushed back our two infantry divisions and captured three villages. If the enemy's mobile units continued to advance to the north, the left flank and rear of the 5th Guard Tank Army would be jeopardized and the entire left flank of the Voronezh Front could crumble. I contacted General Trufanov by radio and gave the order to despatch troops immediately to where the enemy had broken through in the section held by the 69th Army and with the 69th Army to stop the enemy tanks from advancing northwards.

At 0600 hours on July 12, I arrived with a group of officers at the command post of the 29th Tank Corps. It had been chosen as my observation post because the hill to the south-west of Prokhorovka afforded a good view of the terrain ahead. It proved a good choice for on this ground was fought an awesome tank battle. From a solid dug-out in an apple orchard with trees half-burnt and half cut-down, we surveyed a panorama of the undulating plain with small groves and ravines. The rich grain field, which seemed golden in the first rays of the rising sun, was edged by a large dark forest in which the enemy had taken positions.

General Kirichenko reported that the night had been relatively quiet. The Germans had conducted sparse shelling and had fired flares from time to time. Our scouts, however, had heard the roar of many engines in the darkness. To all appearances, the enemy had been redeploying their tanks and motorised troops to new positions. Meanwhile, everything was quiet except for the voices of telephone and radio operators lodged in trenches around the dugout and in a nearby ravine, where the motor cycles of the despatch riders and the armoured cars were camouflaged. There was an awareness, however, that the peaceful morning would be disrupted by the hellish roar of hundreds of guns and thousands of bombs. Enemy planes appeared in the sky at 0630 hours to warn off our fighters and to signal that an air raid was about to begin. At about 0700 hours we heard the monotonous drone of enemy bombers and dozens of Junkers appeared in the cloudless sky. Having chosen their targets, they banked heavily and, their windows glittering in the sun, they dived clumsily. They bombed villages and small woodlands. Plumes of smoke criss-crossed with red flames rose over the forest and villages and pockets of fire rose from a wheat field. Hardly had the enemy planes dropped their bombs than the Soviet fighters appeared overhead. Fierce dogfights erupted and planes, one after another, caught fire and plunged to earth leaving behind them thick billowing black smoke. Most of the Junkers, pursued by our fighters, turned tail, dropping their bombs haphazardly, or took their bomb load back to base.

Then our bombers appeared in the air. They flew in smooth formation to the south-west, wave after wave, escorted by fighters, making clear their determination to dominate the air. The counter-strike was supported by the 2nd Air Army, commanded by General Krasovsky, which had protected the 5th Guards Tank Army on the march so well that the Germans were unaware of its arrival at Prokhorovka. In addition, the Army's artillery opened fire and provided support for our tanks. Most of the fire was directed at the areas where we believed the enemy's tanks and artillery were emplaced. We had had no time to locate precisely where the enemy batteries and tank concentrations were and it seemed impossible to determine the effectiveness of their artillery fire.

Our own artillery was still firing when the regiments of Guards rocket launchers went into action. This was the signal for attack, which was repeated over my radio network. 'Steel, steel …', the radio station commander, Junior Lieutenant

Engineer Konstantinov, kept repeating and the commanding officers of the tank corps, brigades, battalions, companies and platoons took up the call immediately.

I raised my binoculars and saw our famous T-34 tanks leaving cover and rushing ahead, gathering speed. At the same time, I caught sight of a host of enemy tanks. Apparently, both we and the Germans had launched our offensives simultaneously. I was surprised to see how close to each other both the German and our tanks had been moving. The two huge tank armadas were set for a head-on collision. The rising sun blinded the German tank crews but clearly outlined the Nazi tanks for our gunners.

In a few minutes the first-echelon tanks of our 29th and 18th Corps were firing on the move, clashing into and breaking the formations of the German troops. The Germans seemed to be surprised to encounter such a large number of our tanks and to be attacked so resolutely. Control of the forward enemy troops had been disrupted and the enemy Tigers and Panthers, denied fire superiority in close combat, were attacked at close range by Soviet T-34 and even T-70 tanks. The battlefield was enveloped in smoke and dust and the earth was shaken by strong blasts. Tanks clashed, and locked together could no longer disengage. They fought until one caught fire or came to a standstill with a torn track. But even disabled tanks kept firing as long as they could.

Prokhorovka was the first major head-on tank battle of the war in which tanks were hurled against tanks. As combat formations became inter-mixed, all artillery fire ceased and neither air force bombed the battlefield although fierce dogfights continued in the air and the screams of disabled planes, plunging towards the earth, were added to the clamour.

Individual bursts of fire could not be distinguished but all the sounds were blended into a formidable roar.

The battle grew in intensity with devastating fierceness and it became more and more difficult to tell our tanks from those of the enemy because of fire, smoke, and dust. However, I plotted the progress of the battle from the situation reports of the corps commanders and from their radio dispatches. The intercepted radio orders, given in the open by both Soviet and German commanders also provided information on what was taking place.

'Forward!'; 'Orlov, take them from the flank!'; '*Schneller!*'; '*Tkackenko*, break through into their rear!'; '*Vorwarts!*'; 'Follow me!', and '*Schneller!*'. I also heard stronger words not to be found in either Russian or German dictionaries!

The tanks seemed to be caught in a giant whirlpool. Our T-34s, manoeuvring and running circles around the enemy, shot Tigers and Panthers at close range but then they themselves, caught in the direct line of the fire of heavy enemy tanks and self-propelled guns, would catch fire and perish. Shells, striking strong armour, whined off, tracks were torn to pieces, rollers were shot away by direct hits, and ammunition was detonating inside tanks blowing off their turrets.

General Kirichenko's 29th Tank Corps, which advanced along the railroad and the highway, was engaged in particularly heavy and fierce fighting. Against it were the main forces of the *Adolf Hitler* and SS Panzer divisions, which made one stubborn attempt after another to break through to Prokhorovka. However, the Corps stood its ground and did not yield one inch.

By midday, our success in the main sector of the battle became obvious. The first echelon of the 5th Guards Tank

Army was pushing back the enemy, inflicting on it heavy losses in manpower and machines. We did not gain much territory but we accomplished our main goal, which was to stop the enemy as he had advanced along the railroad towards Prokhorovka; the spearhead of enemy tanks, blunted near the Oboyan highway, had now been broken. However, the right flank of the Army faced a predicament. The enemy had failed to advance in the centre towards Prokhorovka, but had encircled our 18th Tank Corps with the 11th Panzer division of the 48th Panzer Corps and had attacked General Kozlov's 33rd Guards Infantry Corps of the 5th Guards Army. By 1300 hours enemy tanks had broken through the positions of two infantry divisions. It was therefore necessary to eliminate immediately the threat to the right flank and rear of the Army and to rescue the neighbouring 5th Guards Army which had no tanks and insufficient artillery. Moreover, General Zhadov's 5th Guards had joined battle virtually off the march, deploying while already in contact with the advancing enemy. Since my reserve had already been committed, I had to detach forces from the main group to help out General Zhadov.

I sent Colonel Karpov's 24th Guards Tank Brigade towards the Voroshilov state farm, where it was to join the right-flank forces of the 18th Tank Corps and the infantry of the 5th Guards Army in routing the enemy at Polezhayev. Simultaneously, Colonel Mikhailov's 10th Guards Mechanised Brigade was dispatched urgently nine kilometres to the north-east of Prokhorovka to block the enemy advance to the north-east. The swift march of those brigades to the assigned areas and their determined counter-attacks against the German tanks which had broken through stabilised the situation at the junction of the 5th Guards Tank Army and the 5th Guards

Army. The enemy, therefore, had to fall back and assume the defensive. The troops of 5th Guards Tank Army displayed amazing courage, unflinching staunchness, superb combat skills and mass heroism to the point of self-sacrifice during the enormous battle which broke out on 12 July.

A large group of German Tigers attacked the 2nd Battalion of the 181st Brigade of the 18th Tank Corps. The battalion commander, Captain Skripkin, boldly joined battle. He personally hit two enemy tanks and, having caught the third machine in his sights, pulled the trigger, but at that moment his tank was hit and caught fire. As the driver, Master-Sergeant Nikolayev, and wireless operator Zyryanov pulled the gravely wounded battalion commander out of the tank, they saw a Tiger rolling towards them. Zyryanov dragged the Captain to cover in a shell crater, while Nikolayev and loader Chernov jumped back into their burning tank and slammed it into the enemy tank. They perished, having fulfilled their duty to the end.

Every man, from every type of unit, whether tank crew, artillery, submachine gun or liaison office, displayed courage and valour in fighting the enemy on that day. All the fighting men at Prokhorovka were real heroes. The wounded refused to leave their positions, tank crews who had lost their tanks continued to fight on foot, and the gunners of anti-tank gun crews kept firing till none could stand on his feet.

By nightfall on 12 July, the enemy had committed their second echelons and reserves which stiffened resistance, particularly in the Prokhorovka direction. The corps commanders reported, one after another, of strong counter-attacks of fresh enemy tank groups. It was pointless to continue our offensive when the enemy had an obvious superiority in tanks. Having evaluated the situation I, with Vasilevsky's permission, ordered all the tank corps to hold their positions, to halt the progress of anti-tank artillery and to repulse enemy attacks with tank and artillery fire. The corps were to refuel their machines, to replenish ammunition, to feed the crews in the darkness and by dawn to be ready to resume the offensive. The wounded also had to be taken care of, the dead picked up and buried, and the incapacitated tanks towed into the rear echelon for repairs.

Night fell, threatening and oppressive. Fighting had ended on the entire front. I left my dug-out for a stroll to shake off fatigue. The air smelt of smoke and soot. The faraway stars were looking down upon earth and the moon cast a cold, dim light on to the battle ravaged fields. Fires cast a glow in the sky to the west and south-west: grain fields, forests and villages were in flames.

3

THE STRUGGLE FOR ITALY

The Allies invaded Italy. On 3 September Montgomery's Eighth Army crossed from Sicily to land virtually unopposed in the toe of Italy. A week later, they were followed by a remarkable reconnaissance group commanded by a Belgian lieutenant-colonel, Vladimir Peniakoff, universally known as 'Popski'. 'Popski's Private Army' (P.P.A.), as his unit was called, had a uniquely unconventional approach to the solution of ticklish military problems.

The occupation of the whole of Sicily concluded, Eighth Army crossed the Straits of Messina on September 3rd, unopposed (or nearly), and advanced into Calabria. Meanwhile negotiations with Badoglio came to a head, and the Italian Armistice was signed but not yet published.

Ignorant as yet of these developments, the Airborne Division was, on September 1st, put on a week's notice to embark at Bizerta. I was told that P.P.A. would provide five jeeps and their crews to land (wherever it was) with the first wave of troops – the remainder of the unit to follow later. The operation was to be seaborne, then landborne, and we put gliders out of our plans – as it turned out – once and for all.

We got ready. I recruited Sergeant Brooks, an L.R.D.G.[1] signaller, who had somehow got stranded in Msaken with his wireless truck. The arrangement was purely private, concluded in two minutes' talk (to be straightened out afterwards), but he stayed with us until the end of the war. He was a Londoner aged thirty-five, of extreme deliberation in his speech; a great reader of books with a thoughtful turn of mind and a gift of clothing common sense in expressions of crystalline originality. Conversing with him was a pleasure that I sought whenever I had an opportunity.

McGillavray, a young officer who had been seconded to us from the Derbyshire Yeomanry through the friendliness of its commander, Lieut.-Colonel (as he was then) Payne-Gallwey, rushed away to Alger to collect six new jeeps and came back having travelled over a thousand miles non-stop in his eagerness not to miss the embarkation. By the time he came back we were at twelve hours' notice: without troubling to get any sleep he prepared his jeep for action with his gunner, Gaskell, and drove away with us at sunset in a long, slow convoy which was carrying the first elements of the Airborne Division to Bizerta. When we arrived at the port at dawn he was not with us. We got on board the U.S. cruiser *Boise*, and watched our vehicles as they were swung on deck. McGillavray appeared on the quay, riding a motor-bicycle: the engine of his jeep had passed out half way between Msaken and Bizerta. In the middle of the night he had stolen a motor bicycle, found and woken up an American workshop and had so well succeeded in convincing them of his urgency that they were at this moment putting a new engine into his truck. He rode away

---

[1] Long Range Desert Group

to collect it, promising to embark on our cruiser, if he came back in time – if not, on one of the other ships of the convoy.

We sailed without him, but when we had been at sea a few hours, I got a signal from H.M.S. *Abdiel* saying that he and Gaskell were on board that minelayer with their jeep.

We sailed on September 7th. The next day the Italian Armistice was announced to us and our destination given: Taranto, the naval base under the 'heel' of Italy. According to the terms of the armistice our landing should be unopposed, but we were warned not to place too much reliance on this promise. On the afternoon of the 9th we caught sight of the Italian coast; then we saw the low shapes of naval vessels steaming out of port: the Italian fleet on its way to surrender at Malta. We entered the outer harbour and stopped. A launch flying Italian colours came alongside *Boise* – and the commander of the naval base, an Italian admiral, in white uniform, gold braid and medals, came up the gangway and stepped on deck; an Italian officer, yet neither an active enemy nor a prisoner-of-war, which seemed strange. Night had nearly fallen when we moored at a quayside: to starboard stood a row of gaunt, bombed houses, silent and dead; to port, under the glare of our ship's searchlights, a company of our red-bereted troops formed up on the quay and marched off to the harbour gates.

The winches lifted our five jeeps ashore, we got in, and, leading our small company, I drove out of the harbour, past the guard, through the deserted rubble-covered streets of Taranto into the sleeping countryside, alone with my nine men in the dark, hostile continent of Europe.

A landing at Taranto had been considered, with several others, at an early stage of the planning of the invasion of Italy, but the decision to carry it out had, as I believe, been taken at the last minute when it was realized that the main landing of our Fifth Army at Salerno would be opposed by powerful German forces. The object was to link up with the Italian forces in the Puglie, and having stiffened them by our presence and our example, create a diversion on the German left flank which would induce them to divert some of their troops from Salerno.

A.F.H.Q. were so doubtful about the fighting power of the Italians that all they had told us was that Badoglio had 'promised the co-operation of his troops'. Indeed the extent to which we counted on this co-operation of the Italian forces went no further than the hope that we should be able to lift from them transport and petrol, for we needed them badly as the cruisers which carried our division to Taranto had room on their crowded decks for no more than a few jeeps and motor bicycles.

About the situation ashore A.F.H.Q. had been unable to tell us anything either of the numbers or the location of our new allies, or of the strength of the German troops – if any – which might oppose us.

From the Italian admiral who came on board I had learnt that an admiral commanded at Brindisi, that there was an Italian infantry division with its headquarters at Francavilla, and that a Corps Headquarters was at Bari, which, he supposed, might have been informed of the terms of the armistice. The Germans, he said, had troops in various localities of the Puglie,[2] though some of them might have been withdrawn recently: more than that he wouldn't say. Being of a surly disposition, he

---

[2] This region covers the Adriatic watershed of the Apennines from the Gargano Peninsula in the north to the tip of the 'heel' in the south.

made it clear that it was no business of his to give us information. This was all the knowledge I had of the situation when I landed from U.S.S. *Boise* and drove out of Taranto in the night. My orders were:

To contact the general commanding the division in Francavilla and give him verbal orders from my general.

To contact the admiral commanding in Brindisi and give him his orders.

To inspect all the landing grounds dispersed in the flat country between Brindisi, Lecce and Taranto, and report on the facilities they could offer for prompt use by the R.A.F.

To get intelligence of the German forces in the area.

Though it was not later than nine o'clock, the whole population seemed to be already in bed. We saw no one in Taranto, then drove through San Giorgio Ionico and saw no one still. Half way to Grottaglie a flickering light zigzagged across the road: a cyclist, too drunk to understand my questions – my first contact with the Italian civilian population. Before entering Grottaglie we stopped a good while because of a convoy we heard driving somewhere beyond a railway embankment. When they had driven away along a side road, we pushed on without meeting a soul. In Francavilla I discovered, with difficulty, a military office: a sentry seated on the steps outside the door slept with his rifle between his knees. Woken up and disarmed, I put him next to me in the jeep, while Cameron in the back kept him covered, and under his guidance we drove to Divisional Headquarters. Bob Yunnie having placed the jeeps to cover the approaches, I drove up to the door of a villa where the general lived, and entered bravely the lion's den. I stated my business to a sleepy corporal, and ten minutes later a captain walked in and said in English:

'Good evening, Major. I *am* sorry I kept you waiting while I shaved but this *is* a pleasure *indeed*. Won't you sit down and have a drink? I have warned the general, who is now getting up and won't be a moment: he *is* looking forward to meeting you, I know.

'I do hope you had a pleasant trip. What kind of sea did you have for the crossing? The weather at this time of year is generally good, though perhaps a bit hot.'

There were no lions it seemed in the den, only lambs. The general's moment was a long one: in the meanwhile I pumped the young man. Despite his silly prattle he was no fool: I would find the army and the air force very eager to help us – the navy was different, snooty fellows, he said, but they would have to toe the line. With great satisfaction he rang up Naval Headquarters in Brindisi, and had the admiral brought out of bed to be told that a British representative would call on him at three that morning.

The Germans, he thought, had pulled out of the province by now, but I had better be careful on the way to Brindisi not to fall in with their rearguard. They had a large technical staff who had been working on the airdromes, but few fighting troops. Somewhere in the north was the German First Parachute Division, perhaps in Bari, with which town telephone communication had been interrupted earlier that day.

He was happy and excited. The war was over – the bitterness of defeat had been swallowed, and he saw opening up a delightful era of collaboration with English gentlemen: he was a bit of a snob.

We talked a long time of the campaigns in the desert. He was the intelligence officer I have mentioned before who gave me the Italian Staff's views of our raids on Tobruq, Benghazi and Barce. He knew much of our plans for these operations, and even pretended he remembered my name. I brought a bottle of whisky from my jeep and we shared it with his commanding officer when he at last turned up. The general, having been given his instructions by me, said he would call on General Hopkinson first thing in the morning, and would arrange straight away for his divisional transport, such as it was, to report at Taranto during the day. (As to bringing his troops to fight with us, his only answer was a hopeless gesture of the hands.) Walking out of Headquarters I was met by the sentry I had disarmed: with tears running and heavy sobs he begged me to return him his weapon or he would get into trouble.

Back with my men, I got Beautyman to put up his aerial and try to get in touch with Brooks at Divisional Headquarters. I enciphered a message giving my first scanty intelligence – then we had a meal. Beautyman was a long time tapping his key before he got a reply, so that, with one or another delay, when we finally reached the outskirts of Brindisi the time was, not three, but six o'clock in the morning. The few people about fled when they saw us, and we drove along the streets preceded by a clatter of shutters hastily pulled to. The experts had promised us a friendly welcome from the population, but it was through a hostile, surly and silent town that we drove to Naval Headquarters.

Grimy and unshaven I padded in my slovenly desert boots up a marble staircase into a vast and noble room: through six crimson curtained windows the rising sun shone from over the harbour on to a tubby figure standing alone in the middle of the floor in gimcrack finery. The admiral wore a sash, a sword and many medals; he stared peevishly out of a yellow, puffed face, for he had been standing there three hours, and his first words were a complaint about my delay.

I called to the orderly who had showed me in:

'Bring a seat for the admiral, immediately. Can't you see that His Excellency is falling with weariness?'

The poor admiral, his surrender scene utterly ruined, declined the chair, but led me into an office where he sulked, puffed and objected while I talked. His head ached, he said, and he would attend to business later in the day, but I was in no mood to humour him, and twenty minutes later we were driving out to view the harbour, the seaplane base and the airport. By nine we had finished, had dropped him at his headquarters and drove off through the town on our way to Lecce.

Brindisi had in the meanwhile undergone a peculiar transformation: Union Jacks, Italian flags, and carpets such as are used for religious processions, had been hung from the house windows, stalls in the market square sold small Union Jacks (some of them rather queer), and red, white and blue cockades; the streets were so packed that we could hardly drive. Waves and waves of cheers enveloped us: men climbed on to our jeeps, shook us by the hand and kissed us in ecstasies of enthusiasm. It seemed very odd: two days before we had been still at war with these people, and now they gave us a welcome that could not have been exceeded had we been their own victorious troops returning home after the utter defeat of the enemy. They longed desperately for a hated war to end, and they cared not if their country's military disasters were the price of the peace we brought. To their simple minds we were allies and friends, who had fought to deliver the suffering people from their wicked rulers and to put an end to nightmares of apprehension and terror: they loved us, their deliverers, hysterically. They were not, as some may think, trying to propitiate their new master, for their joy was uncalculating: obscurely, in their poor hearts, they felt that we had won the war for them.

I realized later that at our early arrival in Brindisi we had been mistaken for a party of Germans.

In every village that we passed that day events developed along a similar pattern: as we reached the first houses a wave of panic spread ahead of us, women gathered their children and bolted for their houses, slammed the doors and banged the shutters, carts backed up side streets, men on bicycles slipped furtively away, and the main square was empty when we arrived, except for two or three small boys who, curiosity having overcome fear, remained to watch us. As we drove by, their faces registered comically in succession surprise – incredulity – hesitation and then, suddenly, decision: off they darted, like mad, from house to house; bang, bang, bang, on each door, piping shrilly:

'Inglesi, Inglesi, Inglesi!'

As if they had been massed behind the closed doors waiting for the signal, crowds poured into the square and the streets: we were enveloped, submerged, cheered and kissed. If we stopped long enough, and often we had no other choice, locked as it were in the crowd, men of importance forced their way to my jeep and delivered speeches of welcome – offerings were brought: baskets of grapes, almonds and apples emptied over our knees, eggs, cheeses and loaves piled in the back of the trucks. Bottles of wine reached us, from hand to hand, over the heads of the people, glasses were produced and toasts proposed. In one village an old woman came forward with a pitcher of cool water and an egg, all she had, she said, for she was very poor. I took a long draught of water and, not knowing what to do with the egg, sucked it then and there. Everywhere the 'Americani', elderly men who, having worked in America for a term, had returned to their native village with a small hoard of dollars, came up, called ''Ello, Boy' and then stood mute, for they had forgotten the few words of English they had ever learnt.

The people who greeted us were all of the poorer kind, peasants and labourers, for in these parts the landed gentry and their satellites of the professions, doctors, lawyers and suchlike, don't mingle with the vulgar. The priests also kept aloof.

So much kindness might have overwhelmed us, but we managed to keep our heads, and during that day, our first in Italy, we visited all the landing grounds in Lower Puglie. From them all the aircraft had been removed and attempts had been made by the Germans to destroy the ground installations, but they had left in a great hurry without achieving much damage. The Italian Air Force officers in charge fell over one another in their eagerness to help us, each commander endeavouring eloquently to persuade me that *his* landing ground was more suitable than any other to be occupied immediately by the R.A.F., and they made a great show of starting repairs even before we had left them. The keenness of these fighting men was different in my eyes from the single-hearted enthusiasms of the poor people and left a bitter taste: they showed, to my liking, too much eagerness to fall on their former allies, the Germans, now that we had proved to possess the greater strength. They liked to think that their behaviour would commend itself to us, but I couldn't help feeling that their sudden change of face stank of treachery.

Towards evening, I reached an airfield, near San Pancrazio Salentino, with which my review of the landing grounds south of a line running from Taranto to Brindisi would be completed. Thinking of my job for the morrow, I asked the local commander for information about the installations further to the north, in particular about the airdrome at Gioia del Colle – the only one of importance, according to my knowledge, for the ground becomes rough and rocky as you proceed north from Taranto and is generally unsuitable for landing aircraft. He described the facilities at Gioia and said:

'As to the present state of the ground I am not informed, but if you don't mind waiting a moment I shall ring up my colleague at Gioia and find out from him.'

This very simple method had not occurred to me, as I had assumed, without giving the matter more thought, that all telephone lines to the north would be cut off. The colleague in Gioia said that German troops had occupied his airdrome early that morning, coming from Altamura, their headquarters. A little later we heard German voices and he rang off. Encouraged by this success we telephoned to various other places, talking either to the local Italian military commander, or simply to the postmaster. Many of the telephone exchanges were still functioning with their civilian staff, and so little were they adapted to the new situation resulting from the armistice and our landing, that no one questioned our business in asking for information: they had not realized yet that we had brought war to their peaceful backwater. I was enchanted by this easy method of getting inside the enemy camp. In less than two hours, just by sitting in an office and listening patiently on the phone over very faulty lines, I had been able to put the enemy on the map where before I had only a blank.

As a result of the talks, I had gathered that there were German troops to the north of Taranto and that they were concentrating in places of which I knew three: Gravina, Altamura and Gioia del Colle. Of their numbers, units and resources I was still completely ignorant.

By one in the morning on September 11th I was back in Taranto, twenty-nine hours after I had left it. Division Headquarters were now in a building in the town; such troops as had so far disembarked held a perimeter round the town and they had been in contact with enemy patrols on the main road to Gioia. I gave verbally the general information I had collected, dictated a report on the airdromes, told the general that I would try to reach Bari in the morning and thence go to the rear of the German positions on the Gravina-Gioia lines, and went to sleep for a couple of hours on the roof of Headquarters building.

My heart was heavy with sad news: early on the 19th H.M.S. *Abdiel* had foundered in a few minutes after striking a mine in the outer harbour; there were few survivors of the crew or of the troops on board, and neither McGillavray nor Gaskell was amongst them – our first death casualties in P.P.A.

I had placed great hopes in McGillavray: gifted with courage, imagination, singleness of purpose and tremendously active, he was, I think, the most promising young officer I ever recruited for P.P.A. I was fond of the man and it was the friend that I mourned, not the loss of a useful officer. In our tense little world affection developed quickly, went deep and lasted; unexpressed ties of friendship held us together, a band of brothers who shared a taste for strenuous action, and our allegiance was to each other, more than to a wider community; the inspiration of our enterprises was our common wish to perform well the difficult tasks which we set ourselves. As the general military situation became less acute the need to keep our country free from a foreign domination receded more and more into the background of our consciousness.

In our hazardous pursuits we suffered death and the loss of friends with an even mind, but it grieved me that this man should have been killed before he had given his measure, at the very moment when his toilsome preparations would have begun to bear fruit.

Early that morning our five jeeps were once more on the road, which climbed first to the top of the watershed and then looked down on to Locorotondo and the Adriatic. The houses here are made of stone; circular and domed like beehives, they are spread over the countryside under clumps of trees. The landscape of grey rock and red soil adorned, but not clothed, with wild vegetation and very ancient olive trees, is so beautiful that driving down towards the Adriatic I fell into a dream and saw the whole of Italy stretched out before me.

'Jock, four hundred miles up this coast lies Venice, an island town of canals and narrow streets, where no wheeled vehicle has ever been seen. One day we shall land our jeeps on the main square, which is called Piazza San Marco, and drive them round and round, a senseless gesture no doubt, an empty flourish – but it has never been done before and at that time we shall be able to afford showing off because the war will be nearly over.'

Cameron, who was watching the map, replied:

'No doubt indeed. The village we are coming to now is Fasano, on the main road. Hadn't we better slow down and inquire, or we may run into a German post? The war isn't over yet.'

Fasano turned out to be unoccupied, and nobody stopped us till we reached the outskirts of Bari, where an Italian guard on the road provided, at my request, a guide to Corps Headquarters. I left my men in the street and walked in to see the corps commander.

He was a fat, fussy little man in a state of considerable agitation. He said:

'I want immediate support from your troops. You have got a wireless, haven't you? Then signal your headquarters in Taranto to send up immediately five squadrons of armoured cars, ten batteries of field artillery and two battalions of infantry. We have had a battle with the Germans in the harbour yesterday' (a scuffle, as I found out, with some German engineers who wanted to blow up the port installations). 'We beat them off – but this very moment they are coming back along the main road from Trani.'

The poor man had in Bari three infantry divisions with their artillery and several squadrons of tanks, but he hadn't the faintest notion how to employ troops. He had not in his life held an active command, and was in fact no more than a depot commander, who had overnight, so to speak, found himself in command of front-line troops – he was in a panic and his headquarters, having none of the organization required for battle, couldn't help him at all. The whole staff was scared of the Germans. I refrained from mentioning that our forces in Taranto had no armour, no guns heavier than four-pounders and no transport, but I agreed to refer his request to my headquarters and infuriated him by declining to give him any information.

'You are worse than the Fascists,' he sneered. 'How can we collaborate if you mistrust me and tell me nothing?'

Mistrust him I did indeed – and he fared no better with those who came after me; he ended as a war criminal before a tribunal for ordering the execution of escaped British prisoners-of-war, and was eventually (years later) shot by a British platoon.

He had no intelligence organization whatever, but acted impulsively on market-place rumours. In his panic he had ordered his own telephone lines to be cut, so even this means of information was denied to us.

As a compromise I agreed to go out with his chief of staff, a weedy old man with the mind of a gendarme, to visit the outposts that had hastily been disposed outside the town, and advise him on defence. When we came back to Corps Headquarters a message came through that the German command in Foggia, eighty miles to the north, was on the telephone of the Water Company. A private company runs aqueducts all over the Puglie, and they have their own telephone lines which had been overlooked and had escaped destruction. We went round to the company's offices: the Germans, it seemed, in their ardour of destruction had blown up a conduit at Cerignola, intending to cut off Bari water supply, instead of which, by some mistake, they had cut themselves off at Foggia. They now wanted the Italian commander in Bari to order the aqueduct company to send their engineers to repair the damage. I took the receiver and gave my German colleague in Foggia the equivalent of a German raspberry – not before, however, I had got from him some information about their forces and their intentions. At the end of our talk I let out that I was the commander of the British armoured forces in Bari, which, I hoped, would spoil his night for him. In those early days after the armistice, the Germans were nearly as much upset as the Italians by the sudden change from peace-time to front-line activities, and in their agitation they had a tendency to speak freely on the telephone. Later that evening I rang up several places on the aqueduct line and got a sketchy picture of the position north of Bari – but nothing at all to the south, excepting that the Germans there were supplied from Foggia.

My task now was to find out the strength of the Germans in the Altamura area because our weak division in Taranto was condemned to remain on a fruitless defensive until they knew what enemy forces opposed them. The object of our landing in Taranto was to attract German forces away from Salerno on the other side of Italy, where our Fifth Army were finding themselves hard pressed: Airborne Division could achieve nothing by sitting on its perimeter round the town, and on the other hand, few in numbers as they were, with neither artillery nor air support and little transport, they couldn't risk annihilation in attacking blindly an enemy whom they suspected to be three or four times stronger than themselves. The matter was of some urgency because, if they waited till shipping became available to bring in reinforcements, the position in Salerno might, in the meanwhile, deteriorate a little more and Fifth Army might find themselves thrown back into the sea. To be sure, our small effort at Taranto was not the main diversion threatening the Germans: Eighth Army, having crossed the straits of Messina from Sicily, was moving northwards through Calabria, but they had still two hundred miles to go over difficult mountain roads, interrupted every few miles by the destruction of bridges and tunnels, and we couldn't guess how soon they would be able to make their power felt.

I had spent the remainder of September 11th, after we arrived at Bari, pumping courage into the Italian garrison and putting some order in their military dispositions, hoping they would find the heart to hold the place against an eventual German attempt to recapture it: it was of some importance for our future operations that we should find the harbour and the landing ground in good condition when we had built up enough strength in Taranto to move up and occupy Bari. There was also an appreciable amount of transport and large stocks of petrol which I didn't want to fall into Germans hands. I hoped that, as a result of my indiscretion on the telephone, the Germans, believing Bari to be now in British hands, would not attempt to re-occupy it before they had got together a fairly substantial armoured force, and we should be spared the mortification of seeing the place fall to a mere troop of armoured cars – for the Italians were so jittery that no reliance could be put on them.

Night had now fallen, and, urgent as it was that I should proceed with my reconnaissance, I found it necessary to give ourselves a night's rest: we had slept no more than two hours since the morning of September 9th, three days and two nights ago.

We had a fine meal at the Albergo Imperiale, all of us at one large table, rather upsetting an officer from Italian Headquarters who had come to see if we were comfortable, for he was not in favour of officers and men feeding together. Beautyman, as usual with our wireless operators, worked most of the night getting my messages across to Taranto, while we all slept.

Putting together the meagre information I had, and looking at the map, I worked out a provisional picture of the German dispositions: they had forces based on Gioia del Colle, Altamura and Gravina, holding the crests of the hills, with a good lateral road. This line possibly extended to Potenza in the west and on to Salerno. The forces with which I was immediately concerned were supplied from Foggia along the road running to Gravina. As Bari was in Italian hands and the first place held by the Germans on the coast, to my knowledge, was Trani, they had from Gioia del Colle to the coast an open left flank forty miles long, which I presumed they guarded in some manner, either with detached posts or with patrols.

I made a plan to slip through this guard with my small party the next morning, cross by night the Gravina-Foggia road, the main enemy lines of communication, and establish myself to the west of it, in what looked, on the map, a fairly remote hilly area. Being there well in the rear of the enemy and on the opposite side to his open flank, I thought it unlikely that we should be bothered by his patrols, and I hoped I should be able to investigate his positions in peace. I say in peace, for on this trip, I was out to obtain information, which might prove to be a slow business, requiring care and cunning, and I had no intention of giving myself away by indiscriminate shooting. We had larger issues at stake than the killing of Germans or the destruction of a few of their trucks. Consequently my orders were that once we had passed into enemy territory there would be no shooting except in self-defence and when flight was impossible.

We left the Italian lines at Modugno and proceeded along the main road to Bittetto, ten miles from Bari. We were greeted by the usual crowds and pinned down in the centre of the village. Picking out from amongst the frantic cheerers a man of more sober appearance, I asked him whether he had any knowledge of German troops.

'Of course,' he replied, 'there are two German armoured cars in the village now,' and laughed. What joke the yokel saw I don't know: we were caught in a compact mass of men, women and children, and if it came to a fight, God help us.

We discovered the two German armoured cars in the southern outskirts and chased them in the direction of Altamura. Where the road widened I spread out my jeeps to give a free field to each of our ten guns, and we let go with everything we had. One of the German cars stopped, but I let the other one go – it suited me well that the rumour should spread in the German camp that there were strong British forces in Bari.

I then retraced my way into Bittetto and left the village again to the west along a cart track. For two hours we wandered in a maze of tortuous lanes between high stone walls built to keep robbers out of olive groves. The map didn't help me much in this labyrinth but finally, unseen, we emerged where I wanted, in the foothills of the Murge, a barren plateau, forty miles by ten, stretching between the coastal plain and the valley in which runs the Gravina-Foggia road. Rising to fifteen hundred feet above the plain, its rocky, broken surface intersected by low stone walls, fit enough for sheep, would normally be considered inaccessible to any vehicles, but, as I expected, we found no great difficulty in driving our jeeps across it. When at last we could see the German road, we had not been detected and I felt that first the olive groves and then the rocks of the Murge were, between them, a discreet back entrance to enemy territory.

The road ran along a broadish valley, a thousand feet below the edge of the Murge plateau where I stood. On the far side rose the hills into which I wanted to go. Nearly opposite me was a hilltop village – Poggio Orsini, in which through my glasses I could see signs of military occupation. Between the foothills and the road there was a flat stretch of dark green vegetation, suspiciously swampy, which would have to be avoided. A mile down the road, towards Gravina, I spotted a small track leading off across the suspected bog into the hills: this track I decided to attempt after dark. The danger spots were: Poggio Orsini on its hilltop across the valley, Gravina ten miles down the road on our left, Spinazzola ten miles on our right, and of course the road itself with its German traffic. I called the men together, each one with his maps, explained the situation and told my plan. I then sent them in pairs to an observation post on the edge of the plateau to have a good look with their glasses at the country we were going to enter.

When darkness fell we eased our jeeps down a very rough gully into the valley, struck the road and turned into it, making for the side track. There was a little light from the stars and we crept along, hugging the verge, showing no lights whatsoever. Cameron, who was watching the speedometer, warned me when we had covered a mile: a moment later a high tension pylon loomed out of the dark, a landmark which I had seen from the top of the Murge, and I realized that I had overshot the mark: the turning into the track must lie a couple of hundred yards behind us. I stopped, warned the next jeep and started turning round: I was half across the narrow road when I saw the dark form of a truck bearing down on me from the direction of Gravina. I straightened out immediately and pursued slowly along the road in our original direction: there was no time to give a warning and I had an anxious moment wondering if the rest of my party would guess what I was doing and follow me quietly, or if they would carry on with the original purpose and get entangled with the German convoy while they were turning their vehicles round on the narrow road. A moment later Cameron reported the jeeps following on our tail and all was well. Twenty-eight ghostly German five-ton trucks crawled past our five jeeps, but their drivers, straining to keep on the dark road, took no notice, and our men had the sense not to open fire. A clash would probably have gone in our favour, but would have wrecked my chances of snooping into the German camp and discovering the information I required, for there would have been such a hue and cry the next morning that we should have had to leave the area.

When the convoy was past and out of hearing we turned round, undetected, found the side track and drove into it. I carried in the back of my jeep a man called Liles, a new recruit to P.P.A., whom I had taken with me on this operation for training, to give him experience of our ways. Now Liles fancied himself as an expert on all types of military vehicles, and after a while he said:

'I thought those trucks might be German five-tonners.'

'So they were, Liles, you are quite right.'

'What, all captured vehicles?'

'Not captured,' I said. 'That was a German convoy. I told you this road was German. We are now on the main German line of communication.'

Liles adjusted himself to a new situation with a sharp gasp. At the same time I learnt the lesson that infinite patience is required to make every man in a patrol listen to what he is told. We discovered that several of our new recruits were 'followers' who drifted along, trusting that when the time for action came they would be told what to do: the army had trained them too

128

well in unquestioning discipline, and we had to break them into a more lively awareness. Liles, by the way, was not a *congenital* 'follower'.

The side track took us to a deserted farmhouse, then petered out. A moment later we had two jeeps wallowing in a morass. While we were pulling them out, Sanders wandered off, and came back having found a firm route across the hidden stream: at the top of the rise we came upon a country lane, then upon a rural road which I identified on the map. We left Poggio Orsini on our right at a safe distance. I pushed on into the heart of the hills, along winding lanes, up and down, from crest to crest. At two a.m. I called a stop, after crossing a stream which I took to be the Basentello; according to the map we were now near the centre of a group of hills and well away from the main roads. There was nothing more we could do before daylight, and having found in the dark a gully just deep enough to conceal our jeeps, we drove into it, set two men on guard to be relieved every hour, and went to sleep.

At five a.m. I was called to take my turn of guard duty: I posted myself under a tree with my glasses and waited for dawn to break. I had succeeded in getting my patrol undetected into enemy territory: the coming day would be the test of my ability to put this achievement to a practical purpose. Between me and our division in Taranto stood an unknown force of German troops: my object was to discover how many there were, and to do so I should need help from the local civilians, because, though undoubtedly I could, by surprise, fight my way into the rear enemy formations, such an action would in no way give me the information I required. From my experience of the previous days I knew that the peasants were favourably disposed towards us, but unlike the Senussi Arabs they were not a warlike people. During the next few hours it would be my business to find out: firstly, if they had enough self-control not to spread the news of our presence so widely that the rumour would reach the Germans, secondly, whether I would find a single individual amongst them with enough guts to give me practical help, and lastly, if their untrained minds would grasp the nature of the military information which was useful to my purpose.

My assets were: an imperfect command of the Italian language (but none at all of the local dialect), a certain confidence in my powers of persuasion born of past successes with other people in another land, and a long, long patience. Intensely curious about the way events would develop, I was looking forward to a test of my wits.

The sky lighted and I began to see the landscape: our gully was slightly above the Basentello: further away from the stream bare fields rose to a crest on which I discerned a large group of buildings with a few big trees. Dim human shapes moved backwards and forwards from the buildings to a nearby field, but it was yet too dark to make out who they were or what they were doing: perhaps troops digging. The buildings, a large farmstead or a monastery, being on the skyline, seemed hardly suitable to be used as a strong point, but even Germans make mistakes, and I looked round to consider an eventual line of retreat for my party. There was time yet, however, and I waited for more daylight.

The troops digging turned out to be women, dozens and dozens of them, coming out of the farmstead for their morning squat. I could see them quite plainly now in my glasses, with their skirts up and gossiping, I guessed, actively. I made a note of this interesting local custom, and turned to other matters. I flicked pebbles at Bob Yunnie, who was sleeping below me in the gully, and asked him to rouse the men: I wanted them to wash leisurely and then to cook breakfast, without, however, showing themselves outside the gully. We still kept our desert habit of carrying our own water, so there was no need to go down to the river.

A small boy trotted past us, along a track that led from the farmstead to the road along the stream: I beckoned, he came over, I made sure he saw our company in the gully, gave him a piece of chocolate and finally dismissed him with a message for his father (whoever he might be) asking him to come and talk to me. The die was cast, I had made my first contact.

The boy's father drove down in a trap: he was the tenant of the farm, a middle-aged man of sober demeanour and good understanding, courteous but shy. I told him that we were an advance patrol of a large force of British tanks which would move down later from Bari to wipe out the Germans in Gravina. He saw our men stripped to the waist and washing – I hoped that the sight of our composure would banish the alarm he might have felt at our arrival.

I mentioned no more military matters for the time, but put him on to local gossip; he fell in readily with my lead and told me how, German troops having occupied Poggio Orsini the day before, the inhabitants had fled in fear: in his own farm up the hill he had at present over one hundred and forty refugees, mostly women and children. I told him not to worry, that we would clear the Germans out of the area in a few days – in the meanwhile how was he for food? He was all right, he said, the refugees having brought some food with them, and his farm was well stocked.

Would I not, he asked, move up to the farm with my men and accept a meal?

I declined the offer; it might give him too much trouble, and if ever the Germans came out and fought us, I didn't want any of his people mixed up in the clash.

'It is better,' I said, 'that the Germans shouldn't know yet that we are here. The crowd up at your place might gossip.'

He laughed. 'We know how to keep our tongues. This is Basilicata, not the Puglie. It is not such a long time ago that we had the bandits.'

I offered him a packet of cigarettes, but he only took one, which he lit.

'There is some information I should like to have,' I said. 'If you have got any friends who would like to talk to me, please ask them to come down.' He departed to reassure the crowd at the farm that we were not Germans.

The cat was out of the bag, there was no reason why we should hide any longer, so we moved out of our gully up the slope to a more open space among trees, where I thought we couldn't be surprised, and where we had room to manoeuvre, and an open field of fire if ever the Germans heard of our presence and became inquisitive.

The farmer's friends soon came down in droves. They were very excited and all thought they had vital information to give me. I interviewed them in turns and spent hours listening to fatuous gossip. I heard the story of the occupation of Poggio Orsini ten times over, and what the grandfather had said, and what the sister-in-law had seen. My difficulty was that these farmers didn't know their area. Apart from their own farms, and the towns of Gravina and Irsina where they went to market, they knew less than I did with my map. They couldn't tell me who lived over the next ridge but one, and none of them had ever been to Genzano, five miles away. I got the most fantastic accounts of the troops in Gravina: two hundred tanks, guns larger than a railway train, seven generals and so many soldiers that they couldn't be counted. 'Two thousand or thirty thousand, perhaps a hundred thousand!' Patiently I asked questions and listened: too often the talk digressed on to family matters and genealogies: these people were all related.

Still, a bit here and a bit there, I increased my knowledge – but by mid-afternoon I had a very poor showing for nine hours' work. I called to a little man who had been standing by for a long time waiting for his turn to speak, shy but less dim-witted than those other boobies. The first thing he said was:

'I know the quartermaster officer in Gravina, Major Schulz, the one who buys the supplies for the officers' mess. His office is in the piazza, the third house to the left of the trattoria, the one with the double brown door. My name is Alfonso.'

His words gave new life to my poor brain, dazed by so many hours of fruitless gossip.

'Alfonso,' I said, 'please tell those people who are still waiting that I shall talk to them tomorrow.' I took him by the arm and we sat down side by side on a stone. Alfonso had sold cheese, eggs and wine from his farm to Major Schulz, he had been in Gravina the day before and had noticed many things; he offered to go again and try and find out what I needed. Eventually we evolved another plan. First Bob Yunnie with four jeeps set off to watch the Potenza-Gravina road. He found a suitable hide-out on a height opposite the small mountain-top town of Irsina, close enough to the road to read the number plates of the passing vehicles. He organized the familiar routine of road-watching, and I pulled back three miles to a deserted railway station on the Potenza-Gravina line. From the station telephone I rang up Major Schulz: I had a long struggle to get through but eventually I got on to him. Speaking Italian mixed with a few words of German I told him, with a great show of secrecy, that I was the quartermaster sergeant of an Italian headquarters in a town which had recently been evacuated by the Germans; I had, I said, the disposal of eight cases of cognac which I would like to sell if he would offer me a good price. We haggled a good deal about the sum. When we had finally come to an agreement I said that for obvious reasons I didn't care to deliver the goods by daylight. If he would wait for me in his office that night at eleven o'clock I would drive up with the drink in a small captured American car. Would he give the word to the control post on the Spinazzola road to let me through without asking questions?

Major Schulz was a simple soul: he may have had scruples about buying stolen goods, but he wanted the cognac badly for the general's mess, and I had made free use of the name of his predecessor, Hauptmann Giessing, with whom, I said, I had in the past made several similar deals. (The relevant information came of course from Alfonso, a good schemer with an observant mind.) He agreed to my dubious request and promised to wait for me that night.

With Cameron we stripped our jeep and loaded in the back some compo-ration boxes, weighted with stones. At ten to eleven the guard on the road block lifted the barrier for us and waved us through, and at eleven exactly we pulled up on the piazza opposite Major Schulz's office. Cameron and I grabbed each end of one of our cases, went past the sentry, up the stairs into the office, where Major Schulz dozed at his desk. Woken up by the thump of the case on the floor, he opened bleary, drunken eyes and gazed at us uncertainly. Cameron didn't give him time to wonder at the nature of our uniforms, but hit him smartly on the head with a rubber truncheon – a gift to us from S.O.E. Schulz passed out and slumped in his chair. Cameron went down the stairs for another case – while I went through the papers in the room. By an amazing stroke of luck, open on the desk lay the ration strength of the units of the First Parachute Division and attached troops which were supplied by the distributing centre in Gravina, dated September 12th, 1943. While Cameron brought up the remaining cases I collected more documents out of the files. We placed a quarter-full bottle of whisky, uncorked, on Schulz's desk (the poor man deserved a reward), and walked out into the street. The German sentry was idly examining our jeep – moved by an impish gust of Scottish humour, Cameron, the sedate, shook him by the hand, pressed on him a packet of 'V' cigarettes, said:

'Good night, good German,' and we drove off.

Two hours later, from a fold in the hills, Beautyman tapped out:

POPSKI TO AIRBORNE STOP TOTAL STRENGTH ENEMY FORMATIONS OUTSIDE TARANTO 12 SEP ALL RANKS 3504 RPT THREE FIVE ZERO FOUR MESSAGE ENDS

On the 0900 call I received:

AIRBORNE TO POPSKI STOP PLEASE CONFIRM TOTAL STRENGTH ENEMY FORMATIONS TARANTO PERIMETER NOT MORE 3504

I knew that Intelligence had put the figure much higher. Slightly piqued, I fell to the temptation of showing off and, having by now sorted out the papers I had stolen from the unfortunate Schulz, I composed a lengthy signal which ran to four or five messages and took the rest of the day to encipher and to transmit. It went something like this:

POPSKI TO AIRBORNE STOP CONFIRM TOTAL STRENGTH ENEMY 12 SEPTEMBER ALL RANKS 3504 RPT THREE FIVE ZERO FOUR INCLUSIVE OFFICERS 441 STOP LOCATIONS FOLLOW GINOSA OFFICERS 61 ORS 500 MATERA OFF 72 ORS 570 ALTAMURA OFF 83 ORS 629 SANTERAMO OFF 58 ORS 469 GIOIA OFF 92 ORS 755 GRAVINA OFF 75 ORS 140 STOP ORDER OF BATTLE FOLLOWS ONE PARACHUTE DIV 19 RGT D COY O.C. LT. WEISS INITIAL W.G. GINOSA B COY LESS ONE PLATOON O.C. HAUPTMANN SCHWARTZ INITIAL ILLEGIBLE GINOSA....

and so on: Major Schulz had filed his strength returns with care.

With this flourish I considered that my first mission was completed, and I turned my mind to investigations much further afield.

A German propaganda leaflet urged the Allies to 'See Naples and die'. Climate, terrain and determined defenders combined to make life extremely tough for the British, Commonwealth and American troops slogging their way through Italy. As John Keegan has observed of Italy in the winter of 1943: 'The Allies enjoyed at best material parity in a battle with a resolute and skilful enemy who had nothing to lose and much to gain by standing his ground. The effort to make him loosen his grip on the crags and outcrops of the Apennines was to involve the British and Americans in the bitterest and bloodiest of their struggles with the Wehrmacht on any front of the Second World War.' The cartoonist Bill Mauldin, whose grizzled combat veterans swap sardonic comments in the rain-sodden ruins of Italy, has left a mordant description of how the 'poor bloody infantry' coped with the rigours of the campaign.

One thing is pretty certain if you are in the infantry – you aren't going to be very warm and dry while you sleep. If you haven't thrown away your blankets and shelter half during a march, maybe you can find another guy who has kept his shelter half and the two of you can pitch a pup tent. But pup tents aren't very common around the front. Neither is sleep, for that matter. You do most of your sleeping while you march. It's not a very healthy sleep; you might call it a sort of coma. You can't hear anybody telling you to move faster but you can hear a whispering whoosh when the enemy up ahead stops long enough to throw a shell at you.

You don't feel very good when you wake up, because there is a thick fuzz in your head and a horrible taste in your mouth and you wish you had taken your toothbrush out before you threw your pack away.

It's a little better when you can lie down, even in the mud. Rocks are better than mud because you can curl yourself around the big rocks, even if you wake up with sore bruises where the little rocks dug into you. When you wake up in the mud your cigarettes are all wet and you have an ache in your joints and a rattle in your chest.

You get back on your feet and bum a cigarette from somebody who had sense enough to keep a pack dry inside the webbing of his helmet liner. The smoke makes the roof of your mouth taste worse but it also makes you forget the big blister on your right heel. Your mind is still foggy as you finger the stubble on your face and wonder why there are no 'Burma Shave' signs along the road so you could have fun reading the limericks and maybe even imagine you're walking home after a day's work.

Then you pick up your rifle and your pack and the entrenching tool and the canteen and the bayonet and the first-aid kit and the grenade pouches. You hang the bandoleer around your neck and you take the grenades out of the pouches and hang them on your belt by the handles.

You look everything over and try to find something else you can throw away to make the load on the blister a little lighter. You chuckle as you remember the ad you saw in the tattered magazine showing the infantryman going into battle with a gas mask and full field pack.

Then you discover something and you wonder why the hell you didn't think of it long ago – the M-1 clip pouches on your cartridge belt are just the right size for a package of cigarettes. That will keep the rain off the smokes.

You start walking again but you are getting close now so you keep five yards between yourself and the next guy and you begin to feel your heart pounding a little faster. It isn't so bad when you get there – you don't have time to get scared. But it's bad going there and coming back. Going there you think of what might happen and coming back you remember what did happen and neither is pleasant to think about.

Of course, nothing's really going to get you. You've got too much to live for. But you might get hurt and that would be bad. You don't want to come back all banged up. Why the hell doesn't somebody come up and replace you before you get hurt? You've been lucky so far but it can't last forever.

You feel tighter inside. You're getting closer. Somebody said that fear is nature's protection for you and that when you get scared your glands make you more alert. The hell with nature. You'd rather be calm the way everybody else seems to be. But you know they're just as jumpy as you are.

Now they're pulling off the road. Maybe you don't have to go up there tonight. You don't. You start to dig a slit trench because the enemy might come to you if you don't go to him. But there's a big root halfway down. Mud and roots seem to follow you wherever you go. You dig around the root and then you try the hole for size. You look at the sky and it looks like rain.

A weapon carrier slithers up the trail and the driver tosses out the packs you all threw away a couple of miles back. Maybe the army is getting sensible. Hell, you got the wrong pack and somebody else got yours. The blankets are damp but they would have been soaked anyway even if you had carried them.

You throw some brush in the bottom of the trench. You squeeze in. You don't like it. You get out and sleep beside the hole. You wake up two hours later and you're glad you didn't get in the hole because it's raining and the hole is half full of water. Your head still feels fuzzy and your heart is still pounding but its better because you have been lying down. A pool of water has collected right in the center of the shelter half you threw over yourself and the water is dribbling right through to your skin. You brush the water out and pull the canvas tight around you. The rain continues, the weather is getting colder, and you try to go to sleep quick so you won't feel it.

Sometimes when the doggies are on the march they find a gutted house with part of the roof still hanging out from the

139

top of the wall. This makes very fine shelter indeed and it's a happy time when they go into bivouac near such a house. But when the guys are really lucky they find a barn, and every doggie knows that barns are far better than houses. He knows that vermin are awful things to have and, since he never gets a chance to take a bath, he avoids houses and questionable mattresses if he can find a luxurious barn full of hay. A farmer who has reason to be suspicious of soldiers prefers to have the guys sleep in his barns because even if the doggies swipe some hay they can't carry off his favorite rocking chair and daughter.

When you are in a barn you don't have to bother about being nice to the hostess because she is probably a cow. You can put one blanket under you and one over you and lots of hay on top of that and you will be very, very warm.

The only bad thing about a barn is that you find a lot of rats there. You don't mind it so much when they just scurry over you if they leave your face alone and don't get curious about your anatomy. A barn rat likes nothing better than to bed down with his guest and carry on a conversation in Braille all night.

The best nights I've spent in the field have been in barns. And the best night I ever spent in a barn was when I woke up and found a cow standing over me. She had a calf but I shouldered the little creature aside and milked the mother in my best New Mexico style. The farmer came in when I was almost finished and I pointed to a small lump in the cow's udder. That showed he hadn't stripped her well and I showed him how to do a nice job of stripping with thumb and forefinger. He was well content when I left and so was I because that was the first fresh milk I had drunk since I left the States.

The dogfaces love to find haystacks and an infantry company will tear down a stack in five minutes. They line their holes with the stuff and, if they've got bedsacks, they'll fill them too. If they don't have bedsacks they find some stack that hasn't been torn down and dozens of guys will crawl into this one stack and disappear. It's wonderfully soft and wonderfully warm but if it's old hay a lot of people who suffer from hay fever have to pass it up. But even if you don't have hay fever there's another bad thing about haystacks: the enemy has used them and he figures you are going to use them too, so he often mines them and, if he is within shooting range, every now and then throws a shell into them. Bombers and artillerymen blow up haystacks and barns just on general principle sometimes.

Caves are nice and you find them sometimes in the mountains. Nice thing about a cave is that you can throw up a little dirt around the entrance and you're safe from almost anything. Air bursts and butterfly bombs make open holes uncomfortable sometimes.

Barns are still about the best, though.

Abandoned towns are wonderful places for guys who have time to make homes in them. Many doggies prefer wrecked houses to undamaged houses because as long as there are walls to break the wind and a roof to stop the weather the men can fix the places up without any qualms about scrounging.

There is a difference between scrounging and looting. Looting is the stealing of valuables, but most evacuees take their valuables with them. Scrounging is the borrowing of things which will make life in the field a little more bearable. Since the infantryman carries everything on his back, he can scrounge only temporarily, borrowing a chair from this house and bedsprings from that one.

The headquarters units which follow the infantry have a little motor transport and they can carry many things with them. Go into almost any field CP and you'll find a pale-pink upholstered chair which looks pretty silly sitting there in the mud.

In combat, infantry officers usually share the same conditions as the dogfaces. But when the doggies get back to a temporary rest area they have to be careful about fixing up a wrecked house too well because the officers may suddenly remember that they are officers and take over the premises. Noncoms can be just as bad about it, too.

It's strange how memories of peacetime life influence these makeshift homes. If a soldier has fixed himself a dugout or an abandoned house, and has cleaned it up and made it look presentable, his visitors instinctively feel that this is a man's house, and he is its head. They use his C-ration can ash trays and they don't spit on the floor. But no matter how much time or effort a guy is able to spend making his dugout livable, and no matter how many of his friends may come to shoot the breeze with him, there are only a few subjects of conversation: wives and girls and families, just plain women, or home.

Many dugouts in Anzio were fixed up surprisingly well. Some guys sat there for five months without moving, and they had to do something to relieve their boredom. They scrounged a little lumber here, a set of bedsprings there, and some of the boys even found mirrors.

The farther behind the front line the dugouts were made the more elaborate they became. Some blossomed out with reading lamps made from salvaged jeep headlights and batteries, and a few huts had wooden floors and real rugs and charcoal stoves made from German gas cans and the flexible tubing that had been used to waterproof vehicles for the landing. Old brass from shells made good stove parts, and the thick cardboard shell cases were used to line walls and to make 'sidewalks' through the mud.

All the dugouts were sunk deep in the sandy, damp ground, and had thick roofs made of layers of logs and planks and dirt. That made them almost invulnerable to shells. Guys who were able to find enough planks to line their walls combined insulation and decoration by covering them with cardboard wallpaper from ration boxes. But these more elaborate jobs weren't to be found very often right up at the front, because the guys up there couldn't move around freely enough to do any scrounging.

The Germans must be given credit for rigging up some very fine dwelling places. They had the advantage of time. Their dugouts at Cassino were fantastic. One was so deep that its roof, almost flush with the surface of the ground, consisted of a four-foot layer of dirt and rocks on top, then a section of railroad ties, a thinner layer of stones, a layer of crisscrossed steel rails, and beneath that a ceiling of more thick wooden ties. Its roof indicated that many of our shells and bombs registered direct hits on it, yet I doubt if the explosions even disturbed the sleep of the occupants. The walls were lined with real plywood, nicely fitted, and there were springed bunks which folded into the wall. There was a radio, too, and a number of German magazines. It was easy to see how the krauts were able to snooze blissfully through our worst bombings and shellings, and then come out and fight off our infantry when the big stuff stopped.

The dugout's only weakness was its one entrance – a screen door to protect the delicate krauts from predatory mosquitoes. Cassino was entered by the foot infantry who knocked down the dugout doors with their grenades and bayoneted the occupants.

Then our guys occupied the luxurious dugouts for a while.

4

WAR IN THE PACIFIC

To secure their vast Pacific perimeter, the Japanese sought to lure into battle and destroy the US Pacific Fleet. In two crucial naval encounters, Coral Sea (4–8 May 1942) and Midway (4 June), they were first halted and then decisively defeated. The previously all-conquering Japanese were now forced to defend an ocean empire which might be attacked at any point by the gathering might of the American war machine. The point the Americans chose was the Solomons chain. On 7 August 1942, US Marines stormed ashore at Guadalcanal, the first move in an epic battle which marked the beginning of the Allied reconquest of the Pacific.

On 2 November, during fighting near the Matanikau River, First Lieutenant John Doyle of the 5th Regiment, 1st Marine Division, rescued three wounded men while under heavy machine-gun and mortar fire, for which he was awarded the Silver Star. Not long afterwards he wrote to his father.

Guadalcanal
British Solomon Islands
11 Nov., 1942

Dear Dad:

It's relatively quiet now. Perhaps I can, without fear of violating naval censorship regulations, bring you some idea of these three months' active combat.

Green troops, and we were green although excellently trained, have a quantum of fearlessness almost approaching foolhardiness, and, well led, will accomplish their mission against veterans. This battalion of Marines (the one I was in) saw the first combat and rode roughshod over the Nips. We attached tremendous importance to our every step, and, emerging victors, thought ourselves world conquerors. Then we began to look around, at the casualties, at the defeated enemy, and finally at ourselves. We were under control only because of training. We lost many more than was necessary. We had wasted all our energy in a few hours. Nerves and excitement kept us intact from there on. There were no instances of cowardice; many of cool bravery and courage.

The 2nd, 3rd and 4th contacts were of a different color. The second is the toughest for all leaders. You cannot doubt or mistrust yourself. Every command and order must be put so boldly that even you are almost convinced of your personal infallibility. Sometimes you must resort to cruelty. Never let a man falter. One lapse and the whole command falls through, and you're left with just a few to fight for all. In these fights men begin to show their souls.

Our 5th fight was and still is the pride of the Division. This one battalion was called upon to join in an attack when all knew that we had more than done our share, and that better than any others. Of course, there was the bitching and belly-aching from more than a few. But all went out and fought a regiment's worth. They battled their own way; then helped those to the right and to the left. It was real Marine stuff. The accomplishment was astonishing....

What has it done to me? What does it mean to me? I know that I have not become cruel or callous. I am sure that I am hardened. If a man cannot produce, I'll push him into the most degrading, menial task I can find. A man that shrinks from duty is worse than a man lost. He should be thrown out of the entire outfit. He's not fit to live with the men with whom he is not willing to die. Death is easy. It happens often.

The toughest part is going on, existing as an animal. Wet, cold and hungry many times, a man can look forward only to the next day when the sun, flies and mosquitoes descend to devour him.

Few men fear bullets. They are swift, silent and certain. Shelling and bombing are more often the cursed bugaboos. But because we retain some mechanics of reasoning, we can predict something of the artillery shell's course. We listen to the sound of the gun, for its location and calibre. We await the whisk of the shell as it splits the air. We know that it can hit in only one place and can generally isolate that spot. Mortar shells are terrifying. Their high angle of fire hides their coming until too late. The gun only coughs. I'm a mortar man and know their worth. I've had to call for my own to fire close by when I'm observing. Because my crews are the best in the Corps, the rifle troops trust my presence, and that's a wonderful compliment.

Bombing is something different. You cannot hope to silence the offender by counter-barrage or seizure. You just wait. We all can distinguish plane motors miles away. The 'thrum-thrum' of the Mitsubishi 97 was the first our minds recorded. If they are directly overhead and still you can hear no bombs falling, you are safe. You crawl just a little outside of your foxhole and watch the show. The Marine fighters and AA crews are marvelous. No wonder this is fast becoming known to the Nips as 'Suicide Island.' All the time you hear the bombs shrieking their way down, and you pity the poor souls in that area. The

147

next time it may be your turn. The heavens are burst by the falling bombs. Prayers and curses run intermingled off your lips and the earth retches and writhes. The close ones all but bash your head in. You pray that yours won't be a near miss but will take you in one blast. At first, I was innocent and never quivered. Then a few close by shook me inside out. A few weeks more and I reached the veteran stage. Indifferent but watchful!

Our stomachs have been ravaged with the food we've eaten and the way in which we eat. We've fought the Japs for water and cigarettes. Often we have shot and ripped off a Jap's pack and canteen before he has a chance to fall. I've buried both Japs and Marines. That is probably the most odious task of all. Decomposition begins within four hours in this climate. Some of the sights I've had to see would sicken a good intern. But I have to go back and eat lunch. There may not be another for a while.

But all is quiet again. I'm sitting by. Long ago I wished to go into aviation. I'm convinced now that it is the only way for me to finish out this war. Today, my request for a flight physical goes to the regiment. I pray that I pass. My superiors have commended me on my action to date, and were glad to recommend me in my preference of duty. Have all keep their fingers crossed, and I may make it. It will take time, though. But time to me ended yesterday.

Love,
Jack

The Allied strategy to recapture the Pacific islands consisted of isolating the important Japanese base at Rabaul and then driving on to the Philippines. The final attacks on the Japanese home islands were to be launched from the Philippines through Okinawa, from the Marianas through Iwo Jima, and from the Aleutians. The strategy was dubbed 'island hopping' as, one by one, the island stepping stones were bypassed, isolated and left to 'wither on the vine'.

As they approached the Japanese home islands, the Allies encountered fanatical resistance. Much of this gruelling 'gut fighting' was undertaken by the US Marine Corps. On 21 July 1944, US 3rd Marine Division landed on Guam in the Marianas. With them was Alvin M. Josephy, a Marine combat correspondent. First and foremost Marines, combat correspondents went through boot camp and learned to shoot a rifle and use a bayonet; they were enlisted men who lived, worked and fought with their units.

Reveille was at two-thirty in the morning. It came through the loud-speaker in the hold, like a hammer hitting us on the head.

'Reveille, Reveille! All up! All up!'

Most of the sailors were already up, standing general quarters at their gun watches out on the black, silent decks. The 'head' was crowded with Marines, many of whom had been there all night, smoking and talking about the landing. The little red lights around the toilets had been the only illumination in our hold, and the 'head' was the natural gathering place. The room was filled with smoke and the heavy odor of sweat.

One man came back from the mess hall. 'Beans and joe for breakfast,' he announced.

We were disappointed. We had expected our last meal to be an unforgettable one – steak and fresh eggs perhaps.

'A swabbie said the skipper of this ship always serves beans and coffee as the last meal before a landing,' the Marine who had been in the mess hall continued. 'A tradition with him.'

'That's all right,' a man answered bitterly. 'If they didn't say it was a tradition, they'd probably hand you the line that beans are filling. They stick to your ribs.'

The pharmacist with the big handlebar moustache came into the head excitedly. 'You want to see something?' he said. 'Go up on deck.'

We went up the ladder into the cold blowing night air.

Off on the horizon we saw it – a great fireworks display of red, yellow, and white lights zipping through the air, crashing out in the blackness, hovering in the sky like flares. When we listened we could hear it – a dull steady rumble like distant thunder.

A sailor at the rail nodded solemnly. 'There's the Fleet,' he said. 'Been at it sixteen days. They're putting on the finishing touches.'

We stared into the darkness at the far-away coloured streaks. Suddenly we saw a great burst of red flame.

'See that?' said the sailor. 'That's Guam.'

This was my first combat. I had never been under fire before and had a vague dread of what it would be like and how I would stand up to it. For weeks I had given my imagination full play, trying to visualize the scene on D-day as we landed on a Jap-held island and moved inland against the enemy. I tried to imagine myself wading across a reef with enemy fire coming at me. I tried to realize what it would be like when I saw my first dead American. I wanted to be prepared. I didn't want to be shocked. I thought that by such mental preparation I might take the actual event easier, and I think it did help. As the real thing approached, it seemed as if I were seeing a scene already familiar and undergoing things for which I had thoroughly rehearsed. The sounds of shells and bullets would not be strange. I had reconstructed what they would sound like from many elements in my past experience – newsreel sounds, maneuvers, etc. – and on D-day morning that was just the way they were. It was as if I had been through shellings many times, and there was nothing strange or unusual about what was going to unfold.

Back on Guadalcanal I had been in a tent with five veterans of Bougainville, men who had been overseas for sixteen to twenty-five months and who had already experienced the terrors of combat. We used to lie awake nights under our mosquito netting, listening to the pounding of the rain on our tent, and I would ask them what it had been like on Bougainville. Mostly they remembered the landing and Jap planes. Some of the waves had had to land in the face of Jap fire and had been strafed by low-flying enemy planes along the beach.

'Getting onto the beach is the worst part,' one of them said. 'It's a nightmare. After you're on the beach, you can try to find cover. But on the way there, you're wide open.'

They also remembered the jungle and the mud and the long nights in watery foxholes, and one of the boys recalled a Jap bomb – a 500-pound aerial – that had fallen in the middle of his camp around midnight.

'It was terrible,' he said. 'Nobody knew what happened. You couldn't see. There was somebody moaning in the darkness to please shoot him and end his pain. Most of us were too scared to get out of our foxholes and crawl around. There were Jap snipers among the trees. But finally somebody couldn't stand it any longer, and he crawled out and got the wounded man to aid. But he died before it was light.'

Such stories as this, also, had helped to prepare me mentally for my first combat. They were in my mind when, at 0600 on D-day morning, I followed John Wheaton into the halftrack in our hold and began describing into our recording machine what was happening.

Ours was the first vehicle to be lifted from the hold. While Seabees put braces beneath the halftrack and attached them to lines from the winches, Wheaton and I knelt in the vehicle and prepared to be hoisted topside. Marines huddled about the hold, smoking cigarettes and watching us.

The halftrack was filled with gear: packs, blanket rolls, ammunition boxes, machine guns, water cans, camouflage netting, and weapons and paraphernalia that would be needed on the beach. Our recording equipment was lashed in among the gear, and Wheaton squatted on a pile of packs to operate the machine. He was going to stay in the vehicle all the way in. When we reached the reef, I would have to get out and wade along with the other men in the outfit. That was because the halftrack, lumbering across the 450-yard-wide reef, would be too big a target for the Japs. Besides Wheaton, only the driver and radioman-machine-gunner would be allowed to ride in the vehicle. The rest of us would have to stay as far away from the halftrack as possible.

With a clatter and banging, we were slowly lifted out of the hold and swung over the side of the transport, down into a waiting LCM – a small tank lighter. As soon as we were secured in the tiny bobbing craft, a cargo net was dropped down to us, and we heard a roar through the transport's loud-speaker: 'First trip of boats! Man your debarkation nets.'

The next instant Marines poured down the net into the boat. Thirty-two men, including the crew of the halftrack and members of the Weapons Company headquarters, were assigned to the LCM. They half-fell from the lower rungs of the net into the boat and scrambled to assigned positions around the LCM's bulkheads. A trailer filled with flame-throwers and communications gear, and a rubber boat, were also lowered to us. The trailer was attached to the halftrack to be towed across the reef. The rubber boat was for any casualties we might have. Two of our men were assigned to pull it, once we left the LCM and began to wade.

When all our men were down the net, we pulled away from the side of the transport and joined a group of small LCVPs[1] – Higgins boats – that were circling near by in a rendezvous area. We could see sailors and Seabees waving goodbye to us from the deck of the transport. Some of them were standing watch in gun tubs, ready for a possible Jap air raid. One man hallooed across the water at us: 'Get some Japs for me!'

H-hour was to be at eight-thirty. Our first waves would come from the LSTs[2] which were standing close off shore. While they were landing we would gradually move toward the beach, passing from one line of control to another. These control lines were spaced several thousand yards apart. Small craft were at each line, organizing and directing the boats of each wave, so that they moved on schedule and in an orderly fashion toward the section of the beach on which they would land their men.

The transports were about seven miles off the beachhead. As we moved away from the big ships, we could see Marines of the next wave flowing down the cargo nets like brown waterfalls into more landing boats.

---

[1] Landing-Craft, Vehicles, Personnel.
[2] Landing Ships, Tank.

From our first rendezvous area, Guam was just a purple smudge on the horizon. Between us and the island were our warships, still shelling the Jap positions. We could see orange flashes shooting out from the big guns. As we moved nearer the island, we could smell the powder and make out the fog of smoke that hung over the water off the beachhead.

We passed all kinds of ships, anchored like an armada off the Jap beach. There were big, green-painted landing ships, repair vessels, communications boats. They flew colored pennants, each of which signified something to our coxswains trying to guide our boats in toward the correct beach.

One man said the scene reminded him of a boat race back home. 'It's as if we were coming up to the starting line,' he said.

Just after eight-thirty the radioman in our boat leaned over his walkie-talkie and pressed his headphones tighter against his ears.

'First wave ashore,' he yelled.

We gathered around him, as he listened to the radio conversations between units on the beach and the command ship. After a moment, he looked up and smiled.

'Casualties light.'

No one said anything. The men looked at each other and nodded.

We passed a battleship, then two destroyers, shelling the island. The noise around us was thunderous.

One man shouted into the ear of the Marine beside him: 'You think anything's left on the island?'

The other man yelled back: 'Tell you when I get there!'

Major Gammon moved from one man to the next, shouting final directions: 'Soon as we hit the beach, get around the halftrack as security!'

We had been thoroughly briefed before and knew that our first job was to get to a prearranged location, set up a command post, and await orders from the regimental commander.

About ten minutes after the first wave landed, our group of boats reached the line of transfer. We waited while infantrymen in Higgins boats around us transferred into amphibious tractors that would take them across the reef. Because a tractor couldn't carry our halftrack, we would have to get out of our LCM at the lip of the reef and wade in the open, while the infantrymen in tractors clanked over the coral beside us.

We could see Guam clearly. The beachhead, which lay between two points, smoked from end to end. The points, jutting out toward the reef, seemed to be on fire. The more prominent one, Adelup Point, on our left, was topped by a concrete building that looked like a Spanish-type hacienda; the Japs had converted it into a fort.

When the infantrymen in our wave had completed their transfer, a control boat raced up beside us and gave our coxswain an order to follow him. The coxswain for the first time during the morning put on his helmet. Another Navy man in the boat pulled a canvas hood from a machine gun and took his position behind a steel shield. The coxswain gunned the motor of our LCM, and we shot forward. On each side of us, the amphibious tractors churned even with us, their radio aerials bent backward like long fishing rods. We could see placards held up in each boat, showing the wave and the boat number. The tractors were low in the water. We could scarcely see the Marines huddling in them. Only their big pot helmets stuck up above the bulkheads.

Ahead, we suddenly saw explosions in the water. Big shells were landing near the reef. For the first time, we began to hear the chatter of machine guns. We got down low in our boat and looked up at the clear, blue sky.

'Lots of noise!' a corporal shouted.

'And it ain't a maneuver,' another man answered.

'It's like Scollay Square on a Saturday night,' a man from Boston yelled.

Some of the men laughed. We felt our stomach muscles tighten and relax in spasms.

Our LCM paused suddenly, and we realized we were at the line of departure – the last line. The control boat signaled to us, then turned back for the next wave.

'We're going in,' the coxswain yelled. 'Get ready to hit the reef.'

The men crouched and pulled back the bolts of their rifles and carbines. A clicking ran through the boat as the weapons were cocked. We roared forward. Somebody called, 'Good luck!'

The next instant we hit the reef. A shudder ran through the boat. The ramp crashed down on the coral and the coxswain yelled to get going. One by one, the Marines stepped out into the water. The driver of the halftrack pressed his accelerator, and the vehicle ground down the ramp and dipped with a splash onto the reef. The rest of us followed, jumping into the warm water.

It was difficult wading across the reef. The coral was sharp and slippery, and the water in some places was ankle-deep, in others almost hip-deep. One man fell and picked himself up quickly, looking around and laughing nervously. The air was full of a loud, composite noise, a roar made up of the sounds of shelling, small-arms fire, the halftrack's motor, and the rattle of amphibious tractors over the coral near us. The beach was wrapped in smoke. In places we saw shattered palm trees, looking like burnt telephone poles. Explosions came from our left. One man shouted and pointed: through the smoke obscuring Adelup Point we could see orange flashes – Jap guns firing straight at us, sweeping in flanking fire across the reef. The Point still hadn't been knocked out, despite our naval bombardment. We looked up. American planes were diving over the Point and the looming hills back of the beach. The hills rose above the smoke. They seemed to go straight up – directly behind the beach.

On the sand we saw a man get up and run; the smoke swallowed him. In the water to our right an amphibious tractor was burning. Jap mortar shells threw up fountains of water near it. Ahead of us were more fountains. We would have to go through them. We felt lonely.

'Hey!' I shouted, trying to laugh. 'Don't leave me alone.'

A man near by turned and grinned. I saw small splashes in the water almost next to him. I gripped the small hand microphone I was carrying and tried to concentrate on what I was saying.

'Machine-gun fire!' somebody yelled. And another called: 'Spread out!'

The word passed from man to man. Instinctively, the men moved farther apart. We were spread over an area almost one hundred yards wide. Some of the men, a hundred yards ahead of me, went down to their necks in the water, trying to hide under the surface. They held their rifles above their heads; then they got up again and pushed through the water.

A fountain of spray shot up near me. We could hear the high crack of rifles. The halftrack paused suddenly. I looked at the wire connecting my microphone with the recording machine in the vehicle. I felt like dropping the microphone and getting farther away from halftrack; if it was going to get stuck, I didn't want to be near it. A man who had been swimming in front of the vehicle, looking for boulders and potholes, stood up and waved the driver in a circle around him. The halftrack lurched ahead again.

The trailer suddenly turned over and dragged through the water. Someone yelled to the halftrack driver to stop, but he couldn't hear. Communications gear fell into the water and floated around us. A man was hit – our first one. Two men pulled him to the rubber boat and laid him across it. Two others on the opposite side grabbed the injured man's arms and helped lay him down evenly. Another man was hit, and sank in the water. Major Gammon yelled to get him. 'Don't let him drown!' he shouted.

A third man, and a fourth, went down. Bullets were whistling around us. A splash of water hid two men from view. When the spray fell, one of the men spun around backward, his neck bleeding. The other man caught him. By now the rubber boat was full of wounded, and a Marine walking beside it was trying to give one of the men a sulfa pill. Another injured man was hanging onto the trailer with both arms, dragging through the water. He had dropped his weapon, and his face was drawn with pain as he tried to hang on.

We were almost on the beach. We could see Marines lying on the sand. Other men were moving cautiously among the debris. At the edge of the beach a man lay on his back, his feet in the water, his eyes open. Blood was pouring out of him.

Three halftracks were piled on the sand near us. Marines were crouched behind them. An amphibious tractor backed out past us. Its placard hung crazily over the side where the members of a preceding wave had dropped it.

Our halftrack came to an abrupt stop. It was half on the beach and half in the water. There was no place to go. The preceding waves were still in the tangled rubbish of the shattered coconut trees at the top of the beach. We saw Major Gammon scramble up the sand and fall flat behind an uprooted coconut tree. The rest of us crouched around the halftrack. Behind us, we could see another wave coming in. Marines were wading across the coral, trying to keep as low in the water as possible without wetting their weapons. They were spread out around another halftrack. Jap bullets cut through the water. One man was carrying an injured Marine over his shoulder.

We heard heavy explosions near us, and a spray of coral drummed on the halftrack. Major Gammon began to shout: 'Get the hell away from the halftracks. They'll be hit. They'll blow up!'

We had to end our recording.

Wheaton snapped off the machine and jumped out of the vehicle; we huddled behind it, the water lapping our feet. All around us, men knelt and lay, most of them bleeding. One, who was hysterical, was being held by a corpsman, while with his free hand the corpsman tried to press a battle dressing against the forehead of a man who lay mostly under the halftrack. Two other Marines with bloody dungarees watched him, their eyes wide and staring. Another man ran into our group, stumbled over one of the wounded Marines, and shouted at no one in particular: 'Jug's killed! Jug's killed!' He looked at us wildly. 'The Major says to get out of here. The halftrack's drawing mortars. Get up to the coconuts!' Then he turned and bolted back up the sand.

We helped the corpsman for a moment. Then he dropped the compress on the man half lying under the halftrack. 'He's dead,' he said calmly.

One of the Marines took the hysterical man and guided him away. They walked around the halftrack, moving as nonchalantly as if they were on a Sunday stroll, and disappeared from sight.

One by one we dashed up the beach. From the hills, from their hundreds of observation and firing positions, the Japs looked down on us and let us have it. They had recovered from the initial shock of the prelanding bombardment and had made up their minds that this was to be our main invasion. Our first waves, which had landed without much opposition, had got halfway up the hills overlooking the beach. But the rest of us were in trouble. The Jap fire was increasing in intensity each minute. Enemy artillery and mortars were being brought from other parts of the island. They were being registered in. Machine guns, Nambus, and rifles were cracking at us from all the hills. We could hear the crashing of mortar shells closer and closer. We could see the black fountains going up on the beach, in the water, and among the coconut trees, and could hear the whistle of bullets flying past our heads. We didn't want to leave what seemed to be the shelter of the halftrack's steel body for the dash across the open. But the big vehicles were targets; one might be hit any moment.

Stumbling and sliding through the sand, we ran across the open, a distance of about fifteen yards. It seemed like a hundred. We fell scared and out of breath behind a sand dune and lay on our stomachs panting. Why were we still alive? – No time to think about it. The only thing was to stay alive. Save yourself. Don't raise up. Don't move. It was like Tarawa. Men crowded on the sand. When would it end? How would we get out of it?

We wondered suddenly whether this was any different from what men had undergone during every other amphibious landing in this war. We had sat at home comfortably and read about them – stories under a one-column head, impersonal stuff written at a rear base about our side: landing somewhere, moderate opposition, light casualties, progress made ...

There was a terrific crash. Then another, like a house falling down. Sand and coral rained through the air like ashes. A moaning started, high, like a baby whimpering. The odour of blood and cordite filled our nostrils.

A man slid past us, almost crying. His foot was a pulpy mass. 'Where's a corpsman?' he sobbed. 'Where's a goddamned corpsman?'

Somebody motioned back to the water. 'Down there, Joe.'

The man with the injured foot paused and wiped his nose, then dragged on. 'Gotta get a corpsman,' he cried. 'Gotta get a corpsman. There's boys dying back there.'

We knew that at home somebody would soon be getting the news and saying to somebody else: 'I see we landed on another little island.'

The fighting in the jungle of Bougainville, in the Solomons chain, which had lasted from November 1943 to March 1944, was every bit as grim as the tales Alvin Josephy had been told on Guadalcanal. Captain John Monks served with the 3rd Marines at Bougainville.

The officer shouted the Division Code name into the 'phone.

But the Division lines were all busy. Very busy. A Japanese landing force had been reported and countermeasures were burning up the wires.

'Bright and early on the morning of November 7th I noticed shell splashes off the point of land to my right, west of the Koromokina River,' reports Major Dick Moss, who was in his Regimental Weapons Observation Post on the beach. 'Finding out it was friendly artillery, I decided to help, and rolled the two halftracks out on the beach to engage the target. We put about twenty-five high-explosive shells per gun on the point. It was direct fire at about 1400 yards, and we really bounced them in there.'

But by the time the first report of the landing had been checked and fire orders had been given to the artillery and beach defense units, the Jap barges had already hit the beach.

How many barges? Where had they landed? Some had been seen coming in beyond the left flank near and beyond the mouth of the Koromokina River. But how many more had landed west of this area, up near the Laruma, out of sight beyond the point of land west of the left flank of the beachhead? A sixty-man outpost from K Company of the Ninth Marines and a forward observation team from the artillery battalion were down near the mouth of the Laruma River. They had been out of communication all night. What had happened? Had their radio gone dead? What had happened to this outpost? Another platoon from K Company of the Ninth was out on patrol along the Laruma River. Where was this patrol now? What had happened to it? The Third Battalion of the Ninth was holding this left flank of the beachhead. K Company of this battalion anchored the flank to the beach. Their line would be stretched dangerously thin. How large a force had landed? Had some landed during the night? How far inland had the enemy advanced?

These were some of the pertinent questions that must be cleared up immediately. And at the same time countermeasures had to be taken. If that flank was breached and a hard-hitting, fast-moving Jap force poured through the gap, we would be in serious trouble. Action! Immediate action! But where? What was the enemy trying to do? What could we do without weakening any portion of the perimeter? Perhaps this might only be a diversion. The main attack might be made at another section of the perimeter. Messages shot along the jungle lines. Division to the Third Regiment … Regiment to the C.P.[1] of the Third Battalion Ninth … back to Regiment … back to Division … then to the First Battalion Third, the battalion in reserve.

The First Battalion had had a bad night. There had been three long bombing raids. The Japs had concentrated on this section of the beachhead. The day before a battery of 90-mm. anti-aircraft guns had moved in right next to their bivouac area. During most of the night the ground shook as the guns blasted the air. Right on schedule the rain had arrived at 3:30 in the afternoon, and it kept up all night. Only a limited supply of rations had been brought up. The company commanders had made their complaints. The men had enough to eat that night, and sufficient rations were on hand for one meal in the morning; but they didn't like it. 'Always have an extra two-day supply of rations on hand for an emergency.' They were straining to carry out their orders. Company executive officers had tried to get additional rations from the Third Battalion, but

---

[1] Command Post.

the Third didn't have any extras either. The quartermasters were doing the impossible to fill immediate demands. There were just so many amphibian tractors; all were being used. Complaints passed through the chain of command. Regiment bore down on the quartermasters. No excuses. Get those emergency rations up to the lines and the reserve battalion. Supply men worked faster and harder. Tractors bogged down with their heavy, precious loads. Men put cases of rations on their shoulders and plodded through the waist-deep mud. The ugly, gluey, flooded jungle swamp laughed at them.

The men of the First Battalion climbed out of their foxholes that morning, cleaned their rifles, and talked about the night bombing raid. Word had drifted in. One bomb had dropped in the Division Headquarters area. A newspaper correspondent who had been sleeping in a jungle hammock had been killed.

Up to this time a jungle hammock issued to the Army had been a coveted piece of equipment. Some of the men had 'borrowed' a few from the Army on Guadalcanal, but all the equipment of the front-line troops (save combat packs) had been left on the beach. A man who had a hammock in his blanket roll down on the beach never expected to see it again. This morning none of the owners cared. Anyone who wanted it could have it for a present. And if any of the men wanted to go over to Division they could get any number of them free. That particular bomb had missed the First Battalion's bivouac area by a few hundred yards. Even with every man below the surface of the ground, they had been lucky.

Before they had finished their breakfast ration the morning's news exploded in amongst them:

'Five hundred Japs have landed on the left flank and have broken through the perimeter.'

In a matter of minutes after Major McMath, 'The Traveler,' had reached Major Chuck Bailey, executive officer of the First Battalion, by 'phone, the First Battalion had gone into action. Chuck Bailey and Major Steve Brody, the Battalion Commander, had issued their orders and were tearing down the tractor road to join The Traveler on the beach. Captain Gordon Warner had assembled his company, had issued his terse orders, and was moving out at the head of B Company. Captain Shorty Vogel and C Company were right on their heels. Here was the emergency. No rations. No extra water. No extra ammunition. Every weapon, all combat packs, and all fighting equipment had been snatched up. No one thought about what wasn't there – men grabbed what there was. Action! Immediate action! Time, man's most precious gift, was running out. The enemy had landed. They had broken through the beachhead perimeter. No one had to define that situation – it was only too clear. This was a time of lightning estimation on the part of the leaders, brief explicit rapid orders, speedy, thorough, immediate execution on the part of the men. Think fast, talk fast and clear, anticipate, act with speed and accuracy. Do something, and do it right now, and do it well – but, by God, *do something!* Two companies of the battle-tested First Battalion smelled urgency. Under perfect control, alert to orders, straining through the mud, determined, keen, vicious, mad, with blood in their eyes, they double-timed toward the beach. The battle of the Koromokina had already begun.

The two company columns halted on the trail running parallel and just off the beach about a thousand yards west of the tractor road. Here, amongst a small clump of coconut trees on the edge of the jungle, the First Battalion had set up its C.P. Here The Traveler was analyzing the situation, with Steve

Brody and Chuck Bailey passing on every bit of information that had arrived at regimental headquarters from the Third Battalion, Ninth. K Company of the Ninth had been hit hard by the Japs who, landing over a broad area, had been faced with the choice of taking the time to assemble their forces and organize a full-scale attack, or of attacking immediately hoping to find the line weak enough to effect a break-through and then pour the rest of their forces through the gap as they arrived. They decided on the latter action.

How many of the Japs had already infiltrated through K Company, the remainder of which had advanced and was tied down by Jap fire about two hundred yards in front of its original perimeter line, no one knew. There was no time for preliminary reconnaissance. The plan of action had already been decided on by the time the troops arrived. Steve led the troops into position as Chuck and The Traveler, remaining at the C.P., quickly reviewed the situation and plan to Big Mac, who had just arrived. Captain Tom Jolly, a battery commander who was acting as liaison officer for the supporting artillery battalion, arrived at the same time, together with a forward observation team which was immediately assigned to B Company. But it was a bad situation. An artillery concentration which would harass the Jap forces moving up in support of their troops attacking K Company could not be laid down, for out in front, somewhere between the Laruma River and our front lines, were over a hundred of our own troops: the sixty-man patrol which might have been wiped out or was working its way back toward our lines, and the platoon patrol scouting out the area along the Laruma River. Until reports from these friendly troops could be received, artillery – so precious now – could not be used.

Steve issued his order to his company commanders, Warner and Vogel, and led them into position. Less than fifty yards ahead of the Battalion C.P. a narrow trail led north along the original perimeter line of the Third Battalion Ninth. C and B Companies of the First Battalion, Third Marines, moved up this trail for about 600 yards. They formed quickly into their attack formation. The brief and simple attack order had given the company commanders little to work on. No enemy information. A part of K Company had pushed west, about 200 yards to their front, and was tied down by Jap mortar and machine-gun fire. That was all. The terrain was totally unknown. How much swamp? How much open space? How much thick jungle? All a mystery.

The two companies abreast, covering a front of 600 yards, would attack in a line of skirmishers, each company with two platoons abreast forward and one in reserve. B Company would anchor its left flank platoon to the beach. Both companies would advance immediately on a compass azimuth of 280° until their forward elements struck K Company. They would then halt and await further orders from the battalion C.P.

For two companies attacking, with two platoons abreast, 600 yards means 150 yards of frontage per platoon. In the thickness of the jungle this is a very wide front, and each man in that forward moving line is required to keep contact with the men on his right and left. But 600 yards of front had to be covered. By figuring time and what had already happened, the Japs could be that far inland and ready to attack anywhere along that line.

Warner with the left flank company decided to move forward with his left platoon. He had a new lieutenant in command, and Warner knew that the Japs could move more rapidly near the beach. He anticipated that this platoon would make the first contact with the enemy. His right flank platoon was under the command of First Sergeant Le Guin. His executive officer, Lieutenant Joe Nolan, would follow with the company command group of about twelve men, directly behind the narrow gap separating the first and the second platoons. His reserve platoon, under Lieutenant Jackson, together with the 60-mm. mortar section from the weapons platoon would follow the command group at an interval of fifty yards. Vogel's company on the right flank was dispersed in much the same way.

Both companies were in position when a lieutenant from K Company came dashing back with the urgent request: 'For God's sake, get up there fast. We need help' – punctuated by the sound of firing up ahead. In possession of no information on the whereabouts of the enemy, knowing nothing about the terrain in front of them, Warner and Vogel gave the order to advance. Both companies, moving entirely by compass azimuth, started off through the thick jungle growth.

Joe Nolan and the command group moved cautiously forward in a column of file. Their azimuth led them over dry, dense ground right along the edge of a deep swamp on their right. They had gone about fifty yards through this thick underbush and were approaching a small clearing when Gunnery Sergeant Duncan, a tall, slow-drawling, seasoned Marine old-timer from Tennessee, signalled to Joe Nolan up ahead. Joe halted the column and everyone took cover. Gunny Duncan pointed out a tall banyan tree overlooking the group about 150 yards to their left front.

'What's the matter, Gunny?' Joe asked him.

Gunny had his head cocked to one side and was squinting toward the top of the tree.

'That's a likely place for a sniper,' he drawled. 'Yes, I do believe there is one there.'

Slow and easy, Gunny dropped to a comfortable position on his right knee, never taking his eyes off the target. Then he tucked his carbine into his right shoulder and sighted in. As if he were firing for record on a rifle range and straining for a possible, he lowered his carbine slowly and adjusted his position. That felt better. Once again he raised his carbine to his shoulder and took a bead on the target. Ten seconds built up into half a man's life-span as this slow, methodical, accurate squirrel-hunting expert held that pose and squeezed the trigger a thousandth of an inch at a time. A lone bullet cracked through the air. Still holding his position, Gunny watched the form of a Japanese jungle sniper emerge slowly from the upper foliage of the large tree … slowly at first, then – as gravity picked it up from there – plunge through the air and crash into the heavy brush sixty feet below. With the same premeditated slowness, Gunny lowered his carbine and drawled to Joe: 'You know … I deliberately killed that man.'

The sound of the fire fight to their left front grew louder. Joe gave the signal to move forward. The group circled the small open spot, keeping in the shadowed underbrush, and proceeded on their azimuth.

Joe Jackson and Gunner McAlexander with the reserve followed fifty yards behind. Then a new twist occurred. A runner suddenly dashed up to Jackson: 'Warner needs your platoon and the 60's over on the left flank. He says, "Make it fast!" '

'Pass the word up to Joe that Warner has sent for us to reinforce the second platoon,' yelled Jackson. Then he pulled out and rushed the urgently needed reserve over to Warner. But the word never got up to Joe Nolan. The group continued to move forward.

As anticipated, the Japs had made their farthest progress toward the perimeter on the left flank nearest the beach. The left flank platoon was hit almost immediately by a Jap force strongly equipped with 50-caliber and rapid-firing Nambu machine-guns. They had immediate fire superiority. Warner had two light machine-guns and a platoon of riflemen. He needed fire power badly, and he needed it in a hurry. Fifty yards to his rear was the regimental and battalion command group sweating over map and field 'phones. A few yards farther back was the field dressing station. Warner knew well what it would mean if the Japs broke through here. He had a fight on his hands.

In the meantime Shorty Vogel's company, presumably moving abreast on the right flank of this new line, advanced ten yards and struck a waist-deep swamp. His orders were to cover 300 yards of front and move on a particular compass direction. He and his men started through the swamp. It was hard, slow going.

The jungle grew thicker. Joe Nolan's command group continued to move forward. The front had been spread much too thin for an advance through thick jungle underbrush. The units on his left were not only tied down by fire but were desperately fighting to prevent a break-through. Vogel's company on the right was bogged down by the swamp. The reserve was no longer following behind them. Nolan with his group of twelve men continued to move forward. He didn't know it, but they were really out on the limb. And they were walking into a situation that would soon separate the men from the boys.

Lieutenant Herron, who had been attached to company headquarters, suddenly appeared from the brush in front of the advancing group and signaled to Nolan. The group halted. Herron rushed over to Joe and whispered, 'Japs – up ahead!' He pointed to the front.

Knowing that Herron had started off with Warner, Joe figured that the two forward platoons on his left were keeping up with his rate of advance.

Again they started forward. Three ground snipers opened up. Everyone hit the deck. Three men worked their way off to the left. Selkuski, a B.A.R. man up in front, kept the snipers tied down. Other men moved off to the left. The rest of the group waited patiently under good cover. When the snipers were eliminated, the group again moved forward. The ground started to rise. It was still very thick.

Twenty yards farther, Allicon and O'Keefe, the forward scouts, broke through some heavy underbrush that was screening a recently cleared area on somewhat higher ground. Thirty Japs frantically digging foxholes looked up from their work and into the faces of the two rugged jungle-fighting Marines. The men in the command group would have plenty to tell their grandchildren – they had walked into a Japanese strong point in the process of construction.

Allicon fired. O'Keefe's Tommy-gun jammed and failed to fire. Joe ran forward and shot a Jap in the forwardmost foxhole. The rest of the Japs started yelling, threw down their tools, and sprang for their weapons. Allicon and Selkuski got two of the scramblers before they reached their rifles. O'Keefe threw his Tommy-gun into the bush, screaming, 'For Christ's sake, somebody give me a weapon that'll shoot!'

'Six others already in the rear holes opened up,' Joe later related. 'My first instinct was to charge. But Herron, who had made his way back past them, told me there were more a short distance up ahead. We could hear them cutting trees and jabbering. He knew we had to get possession of these foxholes. Then we could hold them off until Jackson's platoon caught up to us. Thinking Warner was on my left, I knew they couldn't outflank us on that side. I had lost contact with Le Guin's platoon from Shorty's company on my right, but I could protect my own right flank until that platoon came abreast with us. They couldn't be too far behind. I didn't know how wide the swamp was or how far it extended.

'Herron saved our lives. He said if I would hold them down by fire to the front he would outflank them. Herron and four men started off to the left. I tried to roll two hand grenades into the rear holes. But the Japs were on higher ground and had us pinned down. The grenades hit the brush. I couldn't get one in there. We got every weapon on them and covered for each other. Gradually I was able to work the men one at a time into the forward holes. I dashed ahead and reached a hole in the center. Herron had moved off to the left. That was the last time I saw him alive. One of my men yelled that Herron had been hit. I sent another man over to the left to give him a hand. But he couldn't help him. Herron had been shot through the heart.

'Then the Japs charged. I yelled for the men to fire faster. The Japs kept coming with fixed bayonets. I fired as fast as my carbine would work. I don't know how many rounds were left in the clips I kept changing, but I wasn't going to get caught with an empty. One mean-looking bastard charged practically on top of me. I dropped him not more than three feet from the foxhole. A bullet struck the front of Selkuski's foxhole and kicked dirt in his eyes. The bullets tore through the trees as the muzzle of the B.A.R. went skyward. Selkuski slumped in his hole as if he had been hit. I yelled, "Black John, for God's sake take over that B.A.R." But Selkuski discovered he wasn't hit and got the B.A.R. back in action. Selkuski told me later that he had thought, as he heard me call to Black John, "That friggin' Nolan don't care if I was dead or alive as long as the B.A.R. kept firing!" We stopped the charge. Some of the Japs ran to the rear, and some into the swamp to the right.

'Then the Lieutenant from the K Company platoon dashed over. He told me his men were over to our left, badly shot up. He asked me for some help to knock out a machine-gun up ahead of them. I told him that we had just stopped one Jap charge but there were more of them reorganizing behind the cover to our front. I knew they'd be back. I told him to hold tight, that a platoon in his rear was moving up and would soon be there. I asked him to support us with fire while we took the rest of the foxholes. He went back to his platoon, and I signaled to the men to work themselves forward.

'Then I remembered the Japs who had run off into the swamp. I pulled back and worked my way around to the right. I dashed toward Duncan, who was over too far on the right to hear me. As I got off the deck the second time on the way over, I felt as if somebody had hit me in the shoulder with a large hammer. I kept going until I fell on my face alongside of him. "Watch the right flank, Gunny," I yelled.

' "All right, Lieutenant, take it easy," Gunny kept repeating. "Now take it easy … take it easy."

'The blood started to soak through my dungaree jacket. It didn't hurt, but I kept thinking about going into shock. I wasn't worried about the blood, but I knew I had to get some morphine into my arm. Klinger crawled over to me, opened my first-aid pouch, and tried to get the morphine in my arm. He was fired at. He picked up his rifle and fired back. Then he got the morphine into me and bandaged my arm.

' "Withdraw! They're going to lay down mortar fire." The word started from over on the left and passed across the line. "No one will withdraw!" I screamed back. "God damn it, *I'm* giving the friggin' orders." Gunny never moved a muscle. He kept watching a foxhole out ahead. I sent Haberson and O'Keefe back to find Warner and see if any order to withdraw had been given.

'Then the Japs charged again. Gunny changed his position where he could take over. He kept every man firing just as fast as they could. I was still lying on the ground. Gunny and the men stopped the charge.

'I looked down at my arm and tried to move it. It wouldn't work, so I pulled it up and stuck my wrist through the rawhide compass cord I was wearing around my neck.

'We had been fighting for the foxholes about two hours. Things were quiet now for a while. I started to worry about the mortar fire. If that order was correct, we were in a bad spot. Where in the hell was the reserve platoon? I couldn't understand why they hadn't gotten to us.

'I went over to Gunny Duncan and told him to take over. Then I worked my way over to where the platoon from K Company had been catching hell. There was no one there. On my way back I ran into Sergeant's Dougherty's squad from C Company. Either they had gotten separated or else Shorty had heard the fire fight and had sent them over to help us out. O'Keefe came running up and told me the order to withdraw was straight dope and that we were about 150 yards ahead of the front line. I sent Dougherty and his squad over to Gunny to help him fight a withdrawing action and pull the rest of the men out.

The mopping-up operations on Bougainville were conducted by Australian troops. Peter Medcalf, a young infantryman with the 15th Battalion, 29th Brigade, describes the character of the jungle. It was a savage war, with few prisoners taken, and the jungle itself could be either friend or foe. The Australians stalked the enemy for days in an eerie silence which was suddenly shattered by close-range gun battles; all this amid the rotting stench of the jungle, where the dead were shovelled into shallow graves.

B Company were glad to be relieved, and we quickly took over the shallow holes they had scratched in the dank earth. Behind us the bottle-neck was a waste of smashed and splintered trees and odd bits of abandoned Japanese equipment. Nugget lay propped against his pack, waiting for the order to retire. His hands shook with delayed shock.

'You know', he said, 'they were tied up in the trees, firing down at us. The 25-pounders finally shifted them'. He gave a weak grin. 'I tell you, Slim, this was no place for me mother's little boy!'

We took over and dug in, and the rain started. Heavy, fat drops slapped the leaves, slowly increasing to a driving downpour. Dusk deepened to night, and the rain kept on, roaring through the undergrowth, hour after hour. Pickets were blind and deaf in the deluge, holes were quickly filled. We squatted through the long night under groundsheets and felt the water rise slowly ankle-deep through the perimeter. The Japanese could have walked through our positions if they had returned. Gritty-eyed, we squatted without sleep, and waited for morning.

Dawn brought fitful light, and a waste of water, trees and bushes standing in a black sea. All signs of dry land had disappeared. The rain eased to a fine drizzle, and on all sides creeks rushed and riffled through the tangled underbrush. Listening posts were thrown out and we tried to make the perimeter liveable. The rain stopped and the sun finally shone, bright golden shafts breaking through gaps in the dense canopy overhead, reflecting rainbows in the steam already rising from the surface of the water.

A patrol splashed up the track, and returned by mid-afternoon – no contact.

The weather stayed fine. Slowly we improved our new home in the bottle-neck, and patrols daily confirmed that the enemy had pulled back towards the dry country to the south. The water receded, the cooks provided hot meals of a sort, and mail caught up with us. It grew hotter, and we gradually became aware of a peculiar smell about the place. After a few days the sickening stench pervaded the whole clearing.

Early one morning, filing out on patrol towards the river, we found the answer. B Company had obligingly left a dead Japanese just outside the perimeter. As the water drained away and the hot sun went to work he was making his presence felt. Finally the stench became too much to bear. We had to face the unpleasant task of burying the swollen, rotting remains. The job was made bearable by the varied jokes and comments from several humorists as the burial party sweated with shovels alongside the offending corpse. Finally the work was done, and the detail walked back to the perimeter before heaving sighs of relief.

But the smell persisted. It became stronger. Day by day it was in our water, our food, our clothes, in every breath we took. Only on patrol could we escape it.

One morning I sat on my bunk, and looked at the ground between my boots. A large white maggot wriggled out of the dry ground – and another, and another. We had pitched our shelters on top of the shallow graves the Japanese had dug for their own dead during the battle the week before.

As Sad Sack observed, 'You got to admit, the place has atmosphere!'.

Thick clouds gathered, and thunder muttered in the foothills; short, sharp storms swept the swamps, and rain gradually set in. The water level in the surrounding marshes rose and slowly invaded our home. We improved our tattered shelters with large banana fronds and jacked our bush bunks higher out of the mud. Food was short again, and several men were sent back suffering from skin diseases and unknown fevers. A patrol tried to find a short cut to the coast, and became lost for two days in the swampy wastes of the Tavera estuary.

An urgent radio message: Japanese reported in Sisiruai, a village about six miles inland; so Perce decided to take our platoon and find the place, and clean it out.

Early morning, overcast, and the scouts led us through the wire; ten yards into the heavy growth the water was knee-deep. Slowly the line splashed ahead. We sank to the waist in clammy brown slush as the ground fell away. Bert backed up suddenly and prodded a lump of floating bark with his rifle. A foot-long centipede, bright orange in the dim light, rode on the debris, its wide head waving gently as it bobbed by.

We were heavily loaded with spare ammunition; the weight around our necks dragged us off balance as we tripped and stumbled on tangled snags below the surface. I clambered over a half-submerged log and a grenade slipped from my belt to be lost in the mire. An hour passed and we halted for a smoke. Sad Sack floundered up and took the Bren from Bomber; and word filtered back, a big creek, too deep to cross. The lead section changed and turned inland to see if the creek narrowed or grew shallow. It showed as a twenty-yard gap in the undergrowth, with the water moving sluggishly coastwards.

Hours passed, and we found a tall tree fallen across the stream. Gingerly we inched over, straddling the slippery trunk until we could swing down into the shallows on the far bank. Midday, but too cloudy and dim to see the sun. We leant against tree trunks, up to our knees in the black mire, and munched dry biscuits and bully from the tin. Joey from 6 Section was shivering and running a temperature; he could not eat, but would not let us carry his pack. We swigged dank chlorinated water from our bottles and moved on.

Ahead thunder rumbled, light faded, and lightning flickered through the trees. No sign of dry land, black tree boles anchored in a black, liquid desolation. We floundered on in increasing darkness. Lightning flared closer; sharp thunderclaps, and a dull roaring through the undergrowth. Rain started, sharp, stinging drops, intensifying, bitterly cold. An ear-splitting crack and a blue-white glare, the air sharp with ozone, and the rain lanced down. The line stopped. We turned our backs to the deluge; it hammered down upon us, harder, harder, deafening. The surface of the swamp was smashed upwards in flying spray – we were blind, disoriented, staggering in the flailing dark chaos. A faint, thin shout, lost in the din. I staggered, bumped into a sapling and clung frantically; someone clutched my belt, and hung on.

Slowly the uproar died away. The downpour slackened and we lifted our heads, mouths gaping, gasping for breath. Men stood waist-deep, shivering as if beaten. The light dull, glaucous, thick with moisture – leaves and branches littered the surface of the swamp.

'Jesus!' a shaky voice said, 'wonder what it's like when the bloody drought breaks!'.

We slowly re-formed, and the line moved ahead. My equipment weighed me down, boots sinking in the soft viscous slime, my body forcing a slow, turbid wave before me as I lurched forward. The day dragged to a close, the light died, and the patrol weaved to a halt in a tangle of trees looped with trailing vines.

Slow drops of moisture formed silent rings on the dark surface of the water. I felt totally done, standing legs apart, hip-deep, drooping, completely and absolutely miserable. I looked at the rest of the section – they seemed no better.

Perce floundered by. 'Eat something, and make yourselves comfortable for the night. We won't need pickets in this place.'

We looked at him in thorough disgust; he had a large, fat leech clinging to the back of his neck. He deserved it!

Slowly we gathered ourselves and looked for somewhere to sleep. The ground was impossible – if there was any, it was under three feet of dark, muddy water. Fergie climbed a tree, hung his equipment on a branch, and draped his long frame along a thick limb. Others followed suit, wedging themselves in tree forks or making rough nests of branches and vines.

It grew dark, and I was too tired to look for a decent tree. An inch-thick vine looped from the tree-tops; I cut a long length, threw it over a branch and passed it under my armpits. I relaxed, hanging in the loop, leaning back against the tree trunk.

A firefly drifted by – blink, blink – his cold green light softly reflected on the black water. Quiet rustlings, a cough, a muttered curse, as the platoon tried to settle. The water round my hips slowly grew chill. Rotting tree limbs and vegetation shone around us in a soft, eery phosphorescent glow.

Half asleep, I heard a scrabbling noise, and a loud splash. Someone had fallen out of bed.

The night grew pitch-black, mosquitoes whined and stung. Too tired to care, I hung in the vine. The long night dragged on.

I woke gasping, choking – I was almost under water. The bloody vine had broken! Stagger up, clutch the tree trunk, stand shivering, hugging it in the darkness. Incredibly, somebody snored.

Slowly the night passed. Dim morning light: we choked down a few mouthfuls of cold rations, slung our loads and pushed on following a compass bearing, looking for Sisiruai.

We never found it. For two nights and three days we struggled through a waste of rotting swamp. At dusk one night we heard dogs barking, but we could not find Sisiruai. We saw no living thing, other than an army of leeches and mosquitoes. Always the mosquitoes! They even stung through our shirts; our faces swelled, and the backs of our hands and our faces became lumpy and stiff.

On the third day we staggered back to the perimeter. Some were sick, all completely beaten down; we resembled pale, yellow-skinned corpses as we splashed out of the swamp and lurched tiredly to our shelters.

After a time I sat up and awkwardly unlaced my boots and gaiters. I slowly peeled off my rotting socks.

The soles of my feet came off with my socks.

Ambushes were the staple of this kind of war. Medcalf describes one, and its consequences.

We could barely see. The road was a pale break in the timber above, dawn still minutes away. At least the rain had stopped.

Stealthily we checked a hundred yards of the dimly seen track. It was ten feet wide, dark pools of water gleaming oilily in the dim light, with the scrub on each side a black, tangled wall. Jeff finally picked a spot where the trail curved; we stationed ourselves along the outside of the bend, moving as quietly as possible and hiding behind a thin screen of brush a few feet off the open roadway. Sad Sack and the Bren were on our right flank, where his fire could pass across the curve. Fergie and I were on the extreme left. They would come from that direction, and we had the short-range firepower.

A twig snapped, a tiny rustle of leaves. Silence. Slowly the light grew. I was looking past Fergie down the dim trail through a sparse screen of fern fronds. 'Gawd!' I thought, 'Sad Sack's fire will pass about three feet in front of us'. I hoped the idiot wouldn't get careless!

A bird twittered, and sunlight brightened the upper air. As if by magic the thin ground mist formed above the surface of the road, gently swirling as the growing warmth sucked the moisture from the sodden ground. I checked again that the gun was on full automatic. Maybe they won't turn up.

A shiny, iridescent beetle slowly climbed the frond in front of my face. As I crouched one leg was becoming cramped. My clothes were drenched, the half-empty pack on my back sodden and heavy. Fergie stiffened suddenly and hissed a soft warning. He turned and snapped his fingers towards the others, hidden in the tangle on our right. Then clearly I heard the jabber of voices, coming closer. My breathing stopped – I froze. The beetle flicked his wings and buzzed away and my stomach jumped. Movement, and a shape appeared dimly – then another!

Two scouts out ahead, coming closer, behind them a large shifting group, talking loudly now as the light grew. I stared fixedly at the first scout and tried to shrink further into the leaf mould below me. Jesus! He had to see us! He had a rifle and a dirty white tunic – marines! Fat moon face beneath a cloth cap. He was looking at his feet, hidden in the thick ground mist. He passed six feet from us. The second one was busy scratching his backside – tall for a Japanese – dull, rusty steel helmet, his face in shadow. He turned and called to the group behind him. They laughed loudly and one said '*Hai! Hai!*'. He passed by.

My hands wanted to shake; thin, sick stomach pains. There were at least twenty, more behind. They were getting closer. For Christ's sake, now!

Two rifle-shots, almost blending! The concussion slapped my ears and I jumped a foot. Then the pounding hammer of the Bren. Heave up on my knees, swing the gun on the bunched group fifteen paces away, fire! fire! Muzzle smoke flares from the oily barrel, swing the burst across the milling targets, fire smashing a few feet past me, six or eight down in a threshing pile. In my mind a warning voice – the magazine, must be nearly empty. Short bursts, short bursts! The gun suddenly runs dry, snatch a new mag, change; a stumbling figure tries to break away into the bushes. Knock him down! The pile in the middle of the road was still. Suddenly, unbelievably, three shapes charged screaming towards us up the track! The Bren swept them away – they were smashed backwards, falling into the swirling ground mist.

Fergie, beside me, was coolly firing short bursts; I saw bodies fall, sudden silence, then Bunny's call, 'Grenades! Grenades!'. Snatch one from my belt, pin out, arm swings up in time with Fergie's and throw. Lunge to the ground, waiting for the explosions. They thundered through the smoke-filled scene, blasting leaves, branches and swirls of mist aside. Again!

Then Jeff calling, 'Pull out! Pull out!'.

Suddenly I was exultant! Turn with Fergie and scramble away, rise after a few yards and run, run into the thick timber beyond. I was ten feet tall! I bounded over logs and bushes, choking with excitement. I turned to Fergie, running beside me. 'Did you see 'em go over! Jesus!' I panted. 'We must have got at least fifteen or twenty! You little beauty!'

Dimly behind us I half heard an echoing bang. 'What was that?'

'Mortar!' said Fergie. 'Shut up and run!'

I hurdled a low bush, and plunged towards a thick sheltering wall of scrub ahead. Above us a thin buzzing, growing quickly louder. I half stopped – a cracking explosion almost over our heads. Too late I sprawled on my face while smoke swirled and hot metal fragments zipped and sizzled past. Another explosion, but thirty yards away to one side. I staggered up and turned towards the thick cover for a few paces, then looked back …

Fergie was lying on his face, very still. While I watched, a tremor shook his long frame; he was shuddering. Oh Jesus! I knelt beside him. 'You all right, mate? Get up, come on, get up!'

The shuddering grew smaller. I put a hand on his shoulder. There was a large black hole in the middle of his sodden shirt, high up in his back. Oh Jesus!

I knelt beside him, shaking him gently. In the distance another heavy explosion. Someone crashed through the bushes, and Jeff was beside me. He knelt by Fergie, and gently we turned the still form over. Jeff was panting. He swallowed, and said in a strange voice, 'He's done, he's had it!'. There was a mess of blood slowly welling from the front of Fergie's shirt.

I did not believe it. 'We can carry him, he'll be OK. Give us a hand!'

'For Christ's sake! He's gone, he's had it!' Jeff snarled at me. 'Get his gear, move! We've got to get out of here!'

Dumbly I looked down at Fergie. His face was slack; he seemed to be shrinking; the bright blood slowly welled. Jeff reached for the meat tickets around his neck and sawed one off with his knife. Thudding feet, and Sad Sack and Bert arrived panting. Sack was cradling his Bren. He looked down at Fergie and said, 'Ah shit! No!'.

Jeff snapped at me, 'Come on! Get his gun and magazines!'. I slipped the magazines into the front of my shirt and took up the Owen from Fergie's right hand. I eased the sling away. This gun had killed for him twenty-four times – more after today.

Suddenly Sad Sack called urgently, 'Hurry it up! Here they come!' He swung the Bren, firing from the hip, the bursts swaying his heavy frame backwards. Dumbly I watched the empties pour smoking from the bottom of the gun, and looked down at Fergie.

Jeff punched me hard on the shoulder. 'Move! Move!' I heaved to my feet and turned stumbling towards the heavy jungle behind us. Fergie's magazines clattered and thumped inside my shirt. The thick bushes closed around us as we ran. I felt empty inside, my feet were leaden. We ran, and ran, and ran …

Every hundred yards we turned and slashed fire at the dimly seen shapes behind us – turn and run again. Slowly we lost them in the wastes towards the Wapiai.

Finally, panting and shaking like blown horses, we stopped and re-formed, sullenly glaring at our back-trail. I sank to my knees beside Bert, and rubbed a shaky hand across my face. He slipped another clip into his rifle; mouth open, he was gulping the thick, dank air. 'We lost the bastards!' he said.

Sad Sack was heaving like a bellows, sweat running in streams from his face and chin. 'Ah Jesus!' he panted, 'Ah Jesus!'. He snapped the Bren's bipod legs down and rolled behind it, resting his face on the butt. Slowly we settled down.

Jeff pored over his map. 'In a minute, that way.' He waved to the north.

I did not care. I looked down at Fergie's gun, but Fergie was dead. And we had had to leave him …

For Australian troops there were few more hellish fighting environments than that of New Guinea, which was not completely cleared of Japanese until May 1945. The climate and conditions on the Kokoda Trail, a track leading across the Owen Stanley mountains to Buna, were probably the worst in which any troops fought during the war. The Australian war correspondent George H. Johnston paints an evocative picture of the Buna front in the winter of 1943.

Sunday, 29 November
The harsh white light of mid-afternoon has softened and there is a misleading hint of coolness in the light breeze that ruffles the wide waters of the Gerua river. This is the beginning of zero hour on the Buna front. Up here 'zero hour' isn't used in its

last-war sense. It is the period of the day towards evening when the American fighter cover generally disappears and the Japanese Zeros can be expected to show their snub noses again, and perhaps enliven the ending day with strafing and dive-bombing. Sometimes the Zeros don't come, of course, but air spotters are vigilant, and every man looks upward expectantly as the drone of a plane is heard over the trees.

They settle back again to their little tasks of stoking the campfires, filling the billies and dixies, getting the night's supply of cool river-water into water bottles, writing letters home while there is still sufficient light to see. The plane is only an army co-operation aircraft heading toward Sanananda Point to spot and register targets for the night's artillery shoot. The last transport plane for the day wheels overhead, its enormous wings almost brushing the tree-tops, and heads toward the cloud-capped Owen Stanleys.

The setting sun is daubing colour into the previously dried-out whiteness of the glaring tropic day. The smoke-clouds over Buna and Gona and Sanananda are tinted now with orange. There is a warmth of tone in the tree-trunks, and the Hydrographers Range, which rears its craggy peaks behind us, is deep purple in the shadows and rich gold on the high-lights. Naked me, white and black, are swimming in the shallow stream. The scene is no more martial than a Boy Scouts' Christmas camp. From the front, a couple of miles ahead, there has been no sound now for two hours.

A sergeant, wearing only shorts, and with his three chevrons drawn on his bare arm with indelible pencil, calls his men in the voice of a Stentor – 'Don Company. Here's your soap issue and cigarettes. One cake of soap and one razor blade, 40 cigarettes per man. And don't any of you mugs try and come the double!'

The men assemble quickly. Another voice cries: 'C Company Tucker.' And there is the noise of many bare legs swishing through the undergrowth and the clatter of mess-tins and pannikins. From the bushes comes a mocking voice that feigns girlish delight – 'Oh, goody, goody. Isn't this a thrill? Bully beef and biscuits. Oh, what a lovely surprise!'

Chuckles ripple through the bustling bivouac area. The sky is purpling and the shadows in the trees are mysterious black caves and chasms.

The sun drops swiftly, and there is an air of tenseness and expectancy that comes suddenly and without reason. For the first time for hours one can imagine crouching figures in the jungle, men flattening to earth and fingering triggers of automatic weapons, slant-eyed Japanese peering from loopholes in their tree-trunk weapon-pits, men looking at the dense wilderness all round them with the faint, uncontrollable feeling of fear that comes each evening in the jungle when the trees seem to be hiding watching eyes, when every sound is magnified by the awful hush that precedes the nightly cacophony of the insect world.

The hush is broken by the sudden frightening roar of 25-pounders just ahead of us – the curious double bang followed by the strange, rushing whistle of the shell and the distant 'fruump, frump, frump, fruuump' of the explosions. It is the regular overture to another night of battle.

Mortars start to cough, and on the Gona track and north of Soputa there is a wild rattle of machine-gun fire. The Japanese are nervous. They have been hammered solidly for many nights now, and they are jittery at what this new night has in store for them. Their fire ripples unevenly along the wall of jungle.

Occasionally, I can see the flash of a rifle, once the orange splash of a bursting grenade.

Over the east bank of the river, where Australian and American guns are supporting the infantry attacks on Buna mission and the airfield and the Cape Endaiadere pill-boxes, the guns begin with a full-throated roar that echoes crashingly from the dense walls of the jungle. The earth shakes and the air is filled with sound and movements. The rushing roar of the shells is like an express train plunging through a culvert. The air throbs and is still.

A sun-tanned Digger, spooning bully beef into his mouth grins across at me. 'Here they go again,' he says. 'Pity help the Buna boys on a night like this. No sleep again to-night, I suppose.' He laughs out loud.

'I was speaking to an artillery bloke to-day, and he said that the guns had been in action at night to make sure the Japs didn't get any sleep. Trouble is we aren't getting any ourselves.'

There was no bitterness in his remark. The troops know how wonderful it is to have that ring of guns supporting them. When the 25-pounders were first brought up by transport planes and towed into action by jeeps, the track was lined with cheering Australians, and the shouts of 'You bloody beauts' must have been heard by the Japs.

It is almost dark. Crickets and strange insects are filling the night with sound. Strange birds with narrow-gutted bodies and great wings – the troops call them flying lead pencils – are rocking in the green branches and cawing like crows. Overhead is the nightly procession of giant black fruit-bats, countless hundreds of them, all flying on exactly the same course from the seashore toward the jungle hills behind. The fireflies are flitting everywhere. One soldier has caught two in his hair, flickering like brilliant diamonds.

A signals sergeant whose tobacco has filled my pipe looks up to the silently flitting bats. 'A man must be going troppo,' he remarks quietly. 'About three nights ago I was looking up at those bats heading inland from Buna, and I jokingly said to a cobber. "There go the black souls of Japs killed at Buna, heading back to that big cemetery we found at Kokoda." Do you know that now, every time I see those blasted bats, I can't get that thought out of my mind. Those bats are evil-looking things, and I guess if the Japs have souls, that's what they look like.'

The brief twilight has ended and the thick tropic night has begun, a night filled with many small sounds – the murmur of voices, the crackle of cooking-fires, the sharp slap of a hand on bare flesh, and the soft cursing as a man carries out a brief blitz against the mosquitoes, the distant sound of a concertina and of a man playing 'Colonel Bogey' on a battered tin whistle.

Pretty soon the real battle of the darkness will begin; but all the preparations for it are hidden in the jungle. Thirty yards from a Japanese forward post an artillery officer whispers instructions into a tiny field telephone. Less than a mile behind him another man picks up his message and relays it back to the battery control post, so well camouflaged that you could never see it if you walked past it only a yard away. An operator screws his eyes as he listens at the headphones and turns to a sun-tanned captain: 'Blank's owe pip reporting, sir'. A pencil scratches on a pad and the gun-crews receive their instructions.

Up forward, weary Australian infantry are slumped among the tangled vines and tree-roots snatching sleep for an hour or two while they can. Sentries peer into the black, firefly-spangled jungle towards where the Japs are chopping down trees and driving stakes into the ground. That probably means another post to be taken when this one falls. A twig cracks in the night. There is a rattle of machine-gun fire from the Japs. The Australian sentry moves away from his position, blasts off a few rounds at the point where he saw the stabs of flame from the enemy guns, and then whips back to his old position. Another spatter of fire and a couple of bullets whack the tree he has just fired from. The sentry grins.

A patrol squirms silently through a black, evil-smelling swamp on a flanking job to try to get behind the enemy positions before dawn. Almost in a whisper, a private curses the leeches clinging to his legs and arms.

The artillery has started now in its full measure. Sleep is no longer possible in the unbroken crash of sound that runs from one end of the front to another. The noise is travelling queerly tonight, and it often sounds as if the Japanese are shelling us. A soldier nearby asks his mate: 'They reckon there are a couple of destroyers off Buna to-night. Sounds as if they're shelling our guns, doesn't it?'

'Dunno,' the reply comes out of the darkness. 'It's hard to tell tonight. But one thing's certain: somebody's at the receiving end of an awful heap of metal, and I'm glad it isn't me.'

Hour after hour the firing continues. There are destroyers somewhere off Buna, and the guns have the job of preventing any barge or small-boat activity between ships and beaches. The right is an almost uninterrupted medley of noise – the double cracking bark of the 25-pounders, the deeper roar of heavy Australian mountain howitzers every now and then, the thunderous bark of big American 105-mm. howitzers. There is little break in the rushing hiss of torn air between each gunshot, and over on the northern beaches the 'frump, fruuump' of falling shells marks a regular and grim anthem of destruction.

Gun-flashes flicker yellowly round the entire sky-line. Once a great searing flash of white light splits the darkness over Buna. 'Must have got a dump,' suggests a man nearby. 'Looks like it,' I reply.

There is a great roaring drone overhead. 'Bombers,' somebody yells, and we all listen for the engine note. 'Ours, I think,' somebody says, and we accept his opinion with only slight reservations. They are ours, however, and in a few minutes the north sky is weirdly lighted by falling parachute flares, two white and one red. It's five minutes before the bombs fall with the great rolling thunder sound that seems to reach us at the same time as the shaking of the earth.

The same thing goes on hour after hour. Men sleep fitfully, if they sleep at all, tossing restlessly and muttering unintelligibly.

A half-moon rises hugely over Buna, and soon afterward we hear a Zero overhead, droning round and round above the tree-tops. 'Put that bloody light out,' comes a roar as a man strikes a match to light a cigarette. The light goes out. But the Zero isn't looking for us. He's trying to spot the artillery positions by the gun-flashes. The artillery-men don't fall for that. One battery over which the Zero is circling stays silent, but three or four miles away another battery opens up with a terrific salvo. The Zero drones across to investigate, and as soon as he's gone the other battery blasts out its shells, while the one that has been firing remains silent.

The cat-and-mouse game goes on for more than an hour. The Zero drops a red parachute flare, but apparently can't see anything, and drones away in disgust after having dropped one bomb irritably in the scrub.

A Japanese 75-mm. gun, firing at random, plonks a few shells down our way, but they fall harmlessly in the tangled trees. There is a heavy clash somewhere on the front at first light, and we can hear mortars and machine-guns kicking up a terrific din. It dies away after half an hour, and firing is light and scattered all along the front.

The sun pops suddenly above the range. Aircraft drone in the pure, dew-drenched light of dawn – our fighter cover over the top to begin the daylight business. An A.I.F. private looks up at the Airacobras speeding beneath the clouds, and yells out: 'Good on yer, Yank'.

Another night on the Buna battlefield is over.

Conditions were equally grim on Peleliu, an island only two miles wide and six miles long, where William Manchester fought as a sergeant in the US Marine Corps. The clearing of these specks in the ocean was a dirty and dangerous business. Peleliu was garrisoned by 10,000 Japanese dug into a honeycombe web of connecting caves and bunkers. It took the Americans seven weeks to secure Peleliu and its surrounding islands. The Japanese, who had brought in 4,000 reinforcements during the fighting, lost 13,600. The Americans suffered 7,900 casualties, including 1,750 dead, the highest casualty rate of any amphibious assault in history.

Now the slow, horrible slugging of attrition began. Hummocks of shattered coral changed hands again and again. Cave entrances were sealed with TNT; the Japs within escaped through tunnels. Corsair fighters dove at pillboxes; their bombs exploded harmlessly. Tongues of wicked fire licked at Nip strongpoints from flamethrowers mounted on Shermans; Japs appeared in ravines and knocked the Shermans out with grenades. Using the airfield was impossible; cave entrances overlooked it. Slowly, moving upward in searing heat – the thermometer seemed stuck at 115 degrees in the shade – Marines rooted out enemy troops or sealed them off, hole by hole. The island was declared secure on September 30, but eight weeks of desperate fighting lay ahead. By the end of October, when GIs arrived in force, the defenders had been reduced to about seven hundred men. The Japanese commander burned his flag and committed hara-kiri. Yet two months later Japs were still killing GIs poking around for souvenirs. The last of the Japs did not surface until eleven years later.

We used to say that the Japanese fought for their emperor, the British for glory, and the Americans for souvenirs. One wonders how many attics in the United States are cluttered with samurai swords and Rising Sun flags, keepsakes that once seemed so valuable and are worthless today. I collected them like everyone else, but I shall never understand men whose jobs kept them away from the front, who could safely wait out the war – 'sweat it out,' as we said then – yet who deliberately courted death in those Golcondas of mementos, the combat zones. You heard stories about 'Remington Raiders,' 'chairborne' men ready to risk everything for something, *anything*, that would impress families and girls at home. I didn't believe any of them until I saw one. Even then I wondered what he was looking for. I suppose he was partly moved by a need to prove something to himself. He succeeded.

Our war, unlike our fathers', was largely mobile. It was just as bloody and, because of such technological achievements as napalm and flamethrowers, at least as ugly, but we didn't live troglodytic lives in trenches facing no-man's-land, where the same stumps, splintered to matchwood, stood in silhouette against the sky day after desolate day, and great victories were measured by gains of a few hundred yards of sour ground. Nevertheless, there were battles – Bloody Nose Ridge[1] was one – where we were trapped in static warfare, neither side able to move, both ravaged around the clock by massed enemy fire. I saw similar deadlocks, most memorably at Takargshi. It wasn't worse than war of movement, but it was different. Under such circumstances the instinct of self-preservation turns the skilled infantryman into a mole, a ferret, or a cheetah, depending on the clear and present danger of the moment. He will do anything to avoid drawing enemy fire, or, having drawn it, to reach defilade as swiftly as possible. A scout, which is essentially what I was, learned to know the landscape down to the last hollow and stone as thoroughly as a child knows his backyard or a pet a small park. In such a situation, certain topographical features, insignificant under any other circumstances, become obsessions. At Takargshi they were known as Dead Man's Corner, Krank's Chancre, the Hanging Tree, the Double Asshole, and the End Zone. It was in the End Zone that I met the souvenir hunter. We were introduced by a Japanese 6.5-millimeter light machine gun, a gas-operated, hopper-fed weapon with a muzzle velocity of 2,440 feet per second which fired 150 rounds a minute in 5-round bursts. Its effective range was 1,640 yards. We were both well within that.

At Takargshi, as so often elsewhere, I was carrying a message to the battalion operations officer. All morning I had been hanging around Dog Company CP, content to lie back on the

---

[1] The highest point on Pelelin, officially named Urumbrugol Mountain, but given a more expressive name by the troops.

oars after a patrol, but the company commander wanted heavy mortar support and he couldn't get through to battalion. The Japs had jammed the radio; all you heard was martial music. So I was drafted as a runner. If there had been any way to shirk it I would have. There was only one approach from here to battalion. I had come up it this morning, at dawn. The risk then had been acceptable. The light was faint and the rifles of the section covered me on the first leg, the one dangerous place. Now, however, the daylight was broad, and since I wasn't expected back until dusk, I couldn't count on covering fire from anybody. Still, I had no choice, so I went. I remember the moment I took off from the Dog CP. The stench of cordite was heavy. I was hot and thirsty. And I felt that premonition of danger which is ludicrous to everyone except those who have experienced it and lived to tell of it. All my senses were exceptionally alert. A bristling, tingling feeling raced up my back. Each decision to move was made with great deliberation and then executed as rapidly as a Jesse Owens sprint. I had that sensation you have when you think someone is looking at you, and you turn around, and you are right. So I made the ninety-degree turn at Dead Man's Corner, stealthily, dodged past Krank's Chancre, burrowed through the exposed roots of the Hanging Tree, bounded over the Double Asshole – two shell holes – and lay in defilade, gasping and sweating, trying not to panic at the thought of what came next. What came next was the End Zone, a broad ledge about thirty yards long, all of it naked to enemy gunners. Even with covering fire three men had been killed and five wounded trying to cross the Zone. But many more had made it safely, and I kept reminding myself of that as I counted to ten and then leapt out like a whippet, my legs pumping, picking up momentum, flying toward the sheltering rock beyond.

On the third pump I heard the machine gun, humming close like a swarm of enveloping bees. Then several things happened at once. Coming from the opposite direction, a uniformed figure with a bare GI steel helmet emerged hesitantly from the rock toward which I was rushing. Simultaneously, I hit the deck, rolled twice, advanced four pumps, dropped and rolled again, felt a sharp blow just above my right kneecap, dropped and rolled twice more, passing the shifting figure, and slid home, head first, reaching the haven of the rock. My chest was pounding and my right knee was bloody and my mouth had a bitter taste. On my second gulp of air I heard a thud behind me and a thin wail: 'Medic!' My hand flew to my weapon. Infantrymen are professional paranoiacs. Wounded Marines call for corpsmen, not medics. As far as I knew, and it was my job to know such things, there wasn't supposed to be a GI within a mile of here. But as I rose I saw, crawling toward me, a wailing, badly hit soldier of the U.S. Army. His blouse around his stomach was bellying with blood. And he wasn't safe yet. Just before he reached the sanctuary of the rock, a 6.5-millimeter burst ripped away the left half of his jaw. I reached out, grabbed his wrist, and yanked him out of the Zone. Then I turned him on his back. Blood was seeping through his abdomen and streaming from his mangled chin. First aid would have been pointless. I wasn't a corpsman; I had no morphine; I couldn't think what to do. I noticed the Jap colours sticking from one of those huge side pockets on his GI pants. It wasn't much of a flag: just a thin synthetic rectangle with a red blob on a white field; no streaming rays, no *kanji* inscriptions. We'd kept these thin, unmarked little banners earlier in the war and thrown them away when we found that the Japs had thousands of them, whole cases of them, in their supply dumps.

The GI looked up at me with spaniel eyes. One cheek was smudged with coral dust. The other was dead white. I asked him who he was, what he was doing here. Setting down his exact words is impossible. There is no way to reproduce the gargling sound, the wet sucking around his smashed jaw. Yet he did get out a few intelligible phrases. He was a Seventy-seventh Division quartermaster clerk, and he had been roaming around the line searching for 'loot' to send his family. I felt revulsion, pity, and disgust. If this hadn't happened in battle – if, say, he had been injured at home in an automobile accident – I would have consoled him. But a foot soldier retains his sanity only by hardening himself. Though I could still cry, and did, I saved my tears for the men I knew. This GI was a stranger. His behaviour had been suicidal and cheap. Everything I had learned about wounds told me his were mortal. I couldn't just leave him here, but I was raging inside, not just at him but he was part of it, too.

The battalion aid station was a ten-minute walk away. This trip took longer. I had slung him over my shoulders in a fireman's carry, and he was much heavier than I was. My own slight wound, which had started to clot, began bleeding again. Once I had him up on my back and started trudging, he stopped trying to talk. I talked, though; I was swearing and ranting to myself. His blood was streaming down my back, warm at first and then sticky. I felt glued to him. I wondered whether they would have to cut us apart, whether I'd have to turn in my salty blouse for a new one, making me look like a replacement. I was wallowing in self-pity; all my thoughts were selfish; I knew he was suffering, but his agony found no echo in my heart now. I wanted to get rid of him. My eyes were damp, not from sorrow but because sweat was streaming from my brow. Apart from unfocused wrath, my strongest feeling was a heave of relief in my chest when I spotted the canvas tenting of the aid station on the reverse slope of a small bluff.

Two corpsmen ran out to help me. He and I *were* stuck to each other, or at least our uniforms were; there was a smacking sound as they swung him off me and laid him out. I turned and looked. His eyes had that blurry cast. There we were, the three of us, just staring down. Then one of the corpsmen turned to me. 'A dogface,' he said. 'How come?' I didn't know what to say. The truth was so preposterous that it would sound like a desecration. Fleetingly I wondered who would write his family, and how they would put it. How *could* you put it? 'Dear folks: Your son was killed in action while stupidly heading for the Double Asshole in search of loot'? Even if you invented a story about heroism in combat, you wouldn't convince them. They must have known he was supposed to be back in QM. I avoided the corpsman's eyes and shrugged. It wasn't my problem. I gave a runner my message to the battalion CP. My wound had been salted with sulfa powder and dressed before I realized that I hadn't looked at the corpse's dog tags. I didn't even know who he had been.

5

A FOOTHOLD IN EUROPE

The 'Second Front' in Europe was finally opened on 6 June 1944 when, in the greatest amphibious operation in history, the Allies landed in Normandy. After a month-long air offensive and an Allied deception plan that convinced Hitler that the main attack would come in the Pas de Calais, Operation Overlord got underway. By midnight on 6 June more than 150,000 British, US and Canadian troops had been landed on the Normandy beachheads. However, it was not plain sailing for every one. Norman Smith went down with his Cromwell tank off the British 'Gold' beach at Arromanches.

The LCT[1] was lifting and banging down on the water about four or five feet each time with the huge waves, but we had to undo all the chains holding the tanks to the hull of the craft. The tanks began to slide about with the loosening of the restraining chains and it was clearly instant death to be between two tanks or between a tank and the hull of the LCT when they clanged together. Our training had taught us respect for the weight mass of tanks and we did not loiter when our feet still had to be on the deck of the craft getting the chains out of the way.

As quickly as possible, we got to our battle stations, loaded the main gun and machine guns and got ready for the dive into

---

[1] Landing Craft Tank.

the 'drink'. This was no rehearsal and we were keyed-up and ready to go. In my experience it was like sitting on the corner-stool in a boxing match waiting for the bell to go to release you at your opponent. But a hell of a sight more so.

We knew we might hit one of the mines which Rommel[2] had ordered to be installed completely under the water at three-quarter high tide and we did not expect to go down the landing ramp too daintily in any case, so everyone took a good grip on the solid features of the tank nearest to them in their battle stations; in my case, I hung on to the turret rim of my open turret flaps. A hard knock around your chest, back or shoulders would not be too bad (and would not stop you functioning properly as a member of the crew) but a bash in the face might break your nose and split your eyes open and then you could be part of the problem and not part of the solution.

The landing ramp was lowered and the Royal Navy skipper put a rod quickly into the water and said,

'Right, off you go!'

We had the engine running already and drove off and down into the drink: far too deep, far too deep. The first wave tore through all the ropes holding our bedding on the back of the tank as easily as cotton tied on a rolled up handkerchief; the second wave swamped the specially built up air-intake shute on the back of the tank. We were drowned. The engine stopped and we had water over the whole of the hull and lashing around the turret.

'Knocker' Knight, our tank commander, a short, fair, square-shaped man from the north of England, leaped down into the water, opened up the flaps and pulled 'Ianto' Evans, our driver,

---

[2] Rommel was now commander of Army Group B.

and Billy Bilton, the co-driver, out. It must have been one of those moments when the body provides extra strength because those flaps are very heavy: with the weight of water on top of them as well … But he was down in the water and had them out and up on the turret with the rest of us before we realised what he was doing. (Sgt Major 'Knocker' Knight, MM was killed in action near the end of the big tank battles at Caen and the world became a little diminished by his going).

We could hear our colonel up on the craft shouting at the LCT commander that he was craven-hearted, had lost us a tank and that he, the colonel, would personally have him court martialled. Perhaps fortunately for the navy man, Col Holliman was killed some weeks later, very much in the thick of things with his men. The colonel ordered the commander to back the LCT off and make another approach to the side of our tank; this time to run his craft in – never mind the mines – until he touched bottom. Meanwhile we were hanging on to the turret of our tank as the mountainous seas lashed over us. We had a small barrage balloon (the idea was to inhibit dive-bombers) tied to the turret; that was something extra to hang on to. There were five of us in the crew and two Middle European 'pioneers' with mine clearing implements on the back of the tank also. One of them shouted above the general noise that he had been an Olympic swimmer and he was going to survive. The beach was 60 yards away at most. He pulled off his boots and dived in. We saw his head go under the great waves and watched for his surfacing but he never came up at all. Then, miraculously it seemed, a little armoured navy launch came alongside. We jumped in, the craft bounced its way to the beach and we scrambled ashore. A few yards away a vehicle hit a mine and men and debris were blown high in the air. Shells were still coming over, some landing in the water and some on the beach but there was no sign of the enemy immediately ahead of us. In the other direction, the Navy big ships were continuing their bombardment and their shells were whistling over our heads.

There were many marine commandos lying dead on the beach and we could see by the denseness of the mines sticking out of the water how lucky we had been to get ashore without hitting any of them. Billy Bilton, another solid-shaped north countryman and, like Knocker Knight, an old Desert Rat, was our co-driver; he bent down and dextrously peeled a pair of socks off one of the bodies. Billy saw my face and said, 'He hasn't got any more use for them, Smudger – I might have.' (Trooper Bilton was killed too, much later, up on the Maas in Holland).

Knocker said,

'We'll look for some cover beyond the beach.'

So we made our way forward hoping not to step on any mines. Immediately we saw some little signs at the side of the path we were taking which said, '*Achtung Minen*'. We were suspicious as it seemed an odd thing to leave warning signs for the convenience and preservation of the invader but they must have been for the benefit of the German troops manning the coastal defences. Presumably they had not had time to remove the notices when our invasion began.

We moved along in single file minimising the risk from anti-personnel mines. I thought, '*This* is hardly the way we planned to come ashore'. There were no civilians about and the area immediately beyond the beach, among the knocked out concrete pillboxes, was a ravaged place: there were no trees left standing and the handiwork of man was here in the slaughtered bodies like discarded toys around us.

As we reached the road which served the houses immediately on the little ridge above the beach, we saw our first German prisoners being brought in; some looked dazed and some were wounded. I thought, 'These are men who were trying to kill us a very little while ago.'

Knocker decided that we would settle in a deep German slit trench until the morning, when we would try and rejoin 'B' Squadron, wherever they were. We had no food or water, of course, as it had all been lost with our other little possessions on our drowned tank. Our bedding was gone for ever, probably now on the sea bed somewhere. We huddled in the slit trench with only what we stood up in. It was, for me, the first introduction, in that slit trench, to the prevailing sickly smell of the German soldiery which we found everywhere, probably due to some disinfectant soap combined with the smell of stale sweat on ersatz garments.

The night came on and we tried to sleep. We were too cold, so we watched the flashes of gun fire and listened to the scream of shells overhead, going both ways. As we stopped talking among ourselves my mind went back to the beginning of it all....

The fiercest fighting on D-day was for Omaha beach, the target of US V Corps, which was defended by the experienced and well dug-in German 352nd Infantry Division. At one point the commander of US First Army, General Omar Bradley, considered a withdrawal from the beach, but the Americans won through with a combination of willpower, inspired leadership and many acts of personal bravery. Private Warner 'Buster' Hamlett describes the ordeal of 116th Infantry Division on 'Bloody Omaha'.

It was critical that we hit the beach at low tide, because thousands of obstacles with mines attached lined the beach. At high tide, many of these were concealed. Many assault craft stopped far short of the beach, in fear of hitting mines. As the men jumped into the water, it was often over their heads. Heavy equipment caused them to be pulled down into the rough water. The two coxswains, two young sailors on our boat, saw what was happening to other boats and they drove our craft into the sand as far as possible. We were in only four feet of water as we cleared the ramp. Constant 88 artillery shells, machine-gun fire and rifle fire criss-crossed the beach, mowing down helpless soldiers who couldn't find cover or fire their sand-clogged rifles.

I was to take my squad to the left of the boat. However, machine-gun fire was ripping the water and hit several of our men, so I turned to the right with my squad. After we were in the water it was every man for himself. I waded parallel to the beach with my squad because the heavy fire was directed towards the boats. As I was going towards the beach I saw Lieutenant Hillshure go down on his knees as a shell exploded. He fell into the hole caused by the explosion and died there on the beach.

When I finally reached the edge of the water, I started to run towards the sea wall under a deafening row of explosions and bullets. I saw a hole about seventy-five feet away, so I ran and jumped in, landing on top of O.T. Grimes. As soon as I caught my breath, I dashed forward again, but had to stop between the obstacles in order to rest. The weight of wet clothes, sand and equipment made it difficult to run.

One of the South Boston soldiers, Mervin L. Matze, had run straight to the sea wall and was motioning for us to come on.

At the same time he was yelling, 'Get off the beach!' Our only chance was to get off the beach as quick as possible because we were sitting ducks. While resting behind the obstacles, Private Gillingham, a young soldier, fell in beside me, white with fear. He seemed to be begging for help with his eyes. His look was that of a child asking what to do. I said, 'Gillingham, let's stay separated as much as we can 'cause the Germans will fire at two quicker than one.' He remained silent as I jumped up and ran forward again.

I heard a shell coming and dove into the sand, face down. Shrapnel rose over my head and hit all around me, blowing me three or four feet. My rifle was ripped from my hand and my helmet went twenty-five or thirty feet in front of me. When I started to jump up and run, a sharp pain hit my spine from my neck to my lower back. I pulled myself by my elbows to my rifle, then retrieved my helmet and dragged myself into the hole the shell had made. As soon as I felt stronger, I got out of the hole and ran forward as machine-gun bullets kicked up sand to the right of me. As the bullets came closer I dropped to the sand and waited to be hit. I looked up to see the bullets hitting on my left side. Again, I jumped up and ran, falling down each time machine-gun fire came close. I continued doing this until I reached the sea wall.

The shell that injured me took Gillingham's chin off, including the bone, except for a small piece of flesh. He tried to hold his chin in place as he ran towards the sea wall. He made it to the sea wall where Bill Hawkes and I gave him his morphine shot. We stayed with him for approximately thirty minutes until he died. The entire time, he remained conscious and aware that he was dying. He groaned in pain but was unable to speak.

We were forced to wait at the sea wall until wire cutters could cut the tremendous web of wire that the Germans had placed on top of it. During this time, Lieutenant Ernest Wise of F Company was directing his team behind the sea wall when a bullet hit him in the forehead. He continued to instruct his men until he sat down and held his head with the palm of his hand before falling over dead.

Germans began firing mortars, trying to knock out those few of us who had made it across the beach and were waiting behind the sea wall. They also shot out a type of fire bomb that contained a yellowish powdery substance that would ignite everything it touched. One of these bombs exploded so close to me that the yellow powder got on my clothes, but fortunately there was not enough to ignite. The Germans took advantage of the men that jumped up to avoid the powder and heavy mortar fire caused shrapnel to rivet the air, injuring one of my squad, Pfc Tway from Wisconsin. He was hit in the back and leg. I looked around to see who had survived and most were injured in some way.

We waited at the sea wall until the time to cross over the path cleared by the wire cutters. As I crossed the wall, I thought I saw my brother, Lee, lying face down dead. His clothes had been blown from his body. The back of his head looked just like Lee, but I chose not to know for sure. (It was weeks before I learned that Lee, who was in the 16th Regiment, had also survived the first wave.)

As we crossed the sea wall, Germans in pillboxes fired on each man as he dashed forward. After crossing the sea wall, the ground provided more protection, with small bushes and gullies. As I examined my injuries, I realized a large hole was torn from the jacket and shirt on my shoulder. My skin was not touched.

We took time to reorganize and planned to knock out the pillboxes. First we tried direct attack using TNT on the end of long poles, but this was impossible because the Germans could shoot the men down as soon as they saw them coming through the barbed wire strung in front of the pillboxes. It was then decided to run between the pillboxes and enter the trenches that connected the boxes. These trenches gave the Germans mobility and a means of escape. We entered the trenches, slipped behind the pillboxes and threw grenades into them. After the explosion we ran into the boxes and killed any that survived the grenade. Rows of pillboxes stood between us and the top of the cliff. Slowly, one by one, we advanced. The bravery of the soldiers was beyond belief. They were determined to do their job, whatever the cost. During this time, other boat waves of soldiers were joining us to push the Germans beyond the cliffs.

When we got near the top of the cliff, I talked to Sergeant England, who had also been injured. He told me I was pale and I showed him my leg, which was now swelling and turning different colours. My spine was sending jabbing pains through my body.

Sergeant England told me to go back to the beach and get a medic to tag me so that I could be transported back to a ship. The two of us returned to the beach. As I painfully walked back to the beach, thousands of bodies were lying there. You could walk on the bodies, as far as you could see along the beach, without touching the ground. Parts of bodies – heads, legs and arms – floated in the sea. Medics were walking up and down, tagging the wounded. As I stepped gently between my

American comrades, I realized what being in the first wave was all about.

6

THE ROAD TO VICTORY

At the beginning of August, the Allies broke out of the Normandy bridgehead. There have been few better descriptions of the fierce tank fighting that followed than the British tankman Ken Tout's searing, impressionistic account of forty hours of battle in the Normandy bocage.

Tout was a gunner in C Squadron, 1st Northamptonshire Yeomanry, during Operation Totalise, in which 2nd Canadian Corps, with 51st Highland Division and 33rd Armoured Brigade, advanced through strongly held German positions south of Caen.

8 AUGUST 1944:

12.35 hours: Full noon. August heat. Smoke and dust. A static skyline. Crowded with green shadows. Empty of people. One distant, menacing roof. Hidden fires. Ourselves watching. Intense. Silent. Sweat-soaked. Poised between tiredness and fear. Crackle of static. Voices of distant battles. Crash and shatter of shells. Ours. Theirs. Brilliant blue skies. Torrid sun. I wipe my eyes with sweat-soiled cotton waste. Wipe the periscope rubber. Wipe telescope. Eye to periscope again. Empty oblong world. Smoke bursts. Crash and shatter of shells. Mainly theirs. Birds sing in sudden silence.

'Hullo, Oboe 3 Charlie. Hullo, Oboe 3 Charlie. View Hallo! Three Tigers, moving north, line ahead on road. Twelve hundred yards at one o'clock. Oboe 3 Charlie, over.'

'Hullo Oboe Able to 3 Charlie. Hold your fire if you can till I join you.' (That's Tom Boardman.) 'Able to 3 Charlie, over.'

'3 Charlie, holding fire. Off.'

Harvey: 'God, man! Tigers!'

Now the moment of true fear has come. Tigers! They say each Tiger will take out three Shermans before it succumbs, if then. They say one Tiger took out twenty of our tanks way back. Now the huge steel hand of fear clutches and squeezes my lungs, heart, throat. Like molten metal pouring down the throat and behind the eyes.

Keith: 'Driver, start up. Loader, check loaded with AP. Gunner, traverse right. See what you can see. Co-driver, keep watch ahead.'

Oboe Able is making his way to the right flank to take direct control of the shoot-out with the Tigers. The German 56-ton tanks (almost twice as big as the Sherman) are heading down the Falaise road towards Caen, oblivious to our presence. I swing my gun onto the short stretch of road which I can see across the distant cornfield. No Tigers there. Yet. In any case at this range my 75 mm would be like a pea-shooter against a concrete wall.

'Hullo, Oboe Able to 3 Charlie. I see them now. Keep under cover and hold fire until about eight hundred yards. Then fire at the last one while I pepper the others. Over.'

'3 Charlie. Will do. Off.'

(Stan: 'If Oboe Able is going to take on the first two Tigers with his 75, he needs to be ready to duck.' Harvey: 'Or jump. Or say his prayers.')

'Oboe Able to 3 Charlie. Near enough. Fire! Over.'

'Charlie, OK. Gunner, fire!' (In his excitement Charlie has forgotten to switch back to I/C, but his gunner can hear A set clearly.) 'Gunner, on! Fire! … Got him, you golden boy. Got him. Charlie, got him. Over.'

'Able to Charlie. Get the middle one. I'm hitting the first in line to keep his head down. And use your I/C. Off.' I see a thick sprouting of smoke over trees beyond my range. 'Oboe Able to 3 Sunray. Charlie's Sunray hit. Get over there and keep Charlie shooting. 3 Over.'

'3. On my way. Off.'

I traverse gently back and forward but can see no more of the road. The growing cloud of smoke shows where one of the Tigers is blazing.

SLAM-CRASH of an 88 mm! Almost simultaneous crashes. Flat trajectory. Tremendous muzzle velocity. An anti-aircraft gun used point-blank against tanks. Firing and impact explosions coming almost together. No smoke in A Squadron positions. SLAM-CRAASH! Another Tiger fires unseen. A Squadron's 3 Troop Leader will be dodging through the orchard trees. Lifting the commander from the turret. Giving orders. Bearing on the middle Tiger. One Tiger blazing and the other two swinging round to look for shelter and still not sure where the pesky Shermans are. We see it clearly in our mind's eye.

BLAM-CRASH – slightly different sound, equally imperious, of the seventeen-pounder.

'Oboe Able to Oboe. Second Tiger brewing. Am keeping third busy while Charlie brings to bear. Over.'

'Oboe, bloody good show. Off.'

Black gush of smoke over trees hiding road. Another Tiger burning. SLAM-CRASH of 88 almost together with BLAM-CRASH of seventeen-pounder. One … two … three crashes nearby. An answering roar of sound. New spouts of flame beyond the distant trees. I shout, 'They've got him! They've hit Tiger three!'

'Hullo 3 Sunray in 3 Charlie. Got the second Tiger first shot. Hit the third with three shots. Charlie Sunray hit by falling flap, result of near miss. Send van for Charlie Sunray. Charlie otherwise OK. Over.'

'Oboe to Able and 3. Good shooting. Off to you. Able to Oboe. Can see first two Tigers smoking and abandoned. Third Tiger blew up. Beautiful fireworks. Over.'

'Oboe to Able and 3. You earn a Tiger's tail each. Off.'

(Stan: 'Hear that? Three bloody Tigers gone up in smoke for none of ours!')

I chew a boiled sweet and fold the paper. The chewing of the sweet is incidental. The folding of the paper is critical. The brief, unseen but uncomfortably close clash with the Tigers has been exciting, stimulating but also terrifying. A split second's delay or a yard's error of judgement by Oboe 3 Charlie and the Tigers could have been in among us by now, smelting some of us into writhing ash. The brief delays and errors of judgement were on the enemy's side and he paid the price. But where the three Tigers led, others must follow – Panthers, SPs, Mark IVs. The hedgerows ahead may be thick with enemy tanks, gingerly pressing their guns through hedges, ranging on us already, ready to fire. Smash us in the turret, driving compartment, gunshield, engine. Tear us limb from limb. Seal us within our own crematorium tomb. Spark the conflagration that nothing can douse.

So I suck a boiled sweet and fold the paper. And the folding of the paper is therapeutic. My crying need is for an occupation for the surplus part of my mind which is not concentrating on the periscope view and the earphone chatter. Now I apply the rest of my mind to the ritual of folding a sweet paper. The first fold, apparently simple, is in fact crucial because the slightest error in alignment affects later folds. The second fold is indeed fairly simple. The third fold finds the paper already wanting to slip out of the exact square pattern. On folding the paper for the fourth time I find considerable complications because of the thickness of the little wad related to its surface area. Invariably I try a fifth fold and inevitably all my efforts to fold, straighten and compress the paper end in utter failure. Sometimes during the calm which lies at the centre of the tornado-like battle raging about us, I sit for ages struggling with the problem of folding a sweet paper for the fifth time, compressing my own fears and anxieties into the stubborn paper as I work towards the unattainable and my eyes continue to scan the empty world outside.

When Stan first saw me concentrating on folding a sweet paper, he thought it a tremendous joke and accused me of tottering on the verge of lunacy. Now he sits at the other side of the gun intent on the same scientific experiment with a used toffee paper. And that corner of the mind which is still free to roam asks whether perhaps we have seen the last of the Germans for today? Or are there more Tigers in that jungle?

12.55 hours: 'Hullo Roger 1. I can see our little strange telegraph friends on the left. Dozens of them. In a cavalry charge across country. Roger 1, over.'

'Roger 1. Good to know they've arrived. Keep our left secure. Leave them to get on with it. Over.'

'Roger 1. OK. Off.'

Harvey: 'What the hell is Roger 1 talking about? Telegraph friends?'

Keith: 'Poles, of course. Telegraph poles!'

Harvey: 'Then why can't he say Poles? Surely Jerry can see them by now.'

Keith: 'Jerry isn't supposed to know that there is a Polish Armour …'

'Hullo Oboe 3. Number of nasty hornets straight ahead. Crossing from right to left. Some turning towards us. Ten … twelve … fifteen or twenty I can see. Over.'

'Oboe 3, OK. All Stations Oboe. Did you hear? Fifteen to twenty hornets ahead. Oboe 1, 2 and 4 over.'

Keith: 'All crew watch half right. Nasties should be moving behind hedgerows either side of gully.'

Bookie: 'Christ! Twenty of the buggers!'

And now SLAM-CRASH, again and again, unseen but near. Ours and theirs intermingling whilst we watch and wait and shudder.

'Roger 2 Charlie. Have brewed one Mark IV. Two more in sight, right of me, three o'clock. 2 Charlie, Over.'

'2 Charlie, good shooting. Off.'

(Harvey: 'Hey, that's little Sonny Bellamy. Bloody good shooting, Sonny. That's paying them one back for Corporal Astley.')

'Roger 2 Charlie. Tally Ho! Number two brewing. Watch for it. Here goes number three. Third Mark IV flaming. That's all we can see. 2 Charlie over.'

(Bookie: 'Good old Sonny boy. Bash 'em for the Colonel. Bash 'em for Astley. Bash 'em for the V bombs.' Keith: 'Cool it then. Watch out. That's only three gone.')

'2 Charlie! Behind you! Behind you, I say! 2 Able, traverse right! Charlie! Charlie! Oh my God, 2 Charlie is brewing. 2 Able, can't you traverse, right? Right! Traverse … Oh my God … bale out … bale!'

Fire shoots skywards across the gully, not where the Germans should be. Where 2 Troop should be. The slam-crash double explosions overlay each other, and the day degenerates into chaos, noise, flame, smoke, grilling sunshine, sweat, fear; and our tank shuddering and juddering even as it stands still on the exposed, oh so exposed ridge crest.

Stan: 'That was a Sherman.'

A second fire blasts even higher a few yards to the right of the first. Not where the Germans should be. Where 2 Troop should be. Two towers of flame gushing into the sky, spilling out foul black smoke.

'2 Able. Both Sunray and Charlie gone … Hullo, Roger 2 Able. May I do … God, I'm hit … baling …'

(Me: 'Sonny's had it then.' Bookie: 'You never know. There's always a chance …')

'Hullo Roger 3.' (Hank calling Hughie.) 'Move up to cover Roger 2's front. 3, over.' 'Roger 3, OK. Off to you. All Stations Roger 3 move up in line with me. Off.'

Keith: 'Driver, advance slowly. Gunner, I think all 2 Troop tanks have brewed. Any vehicle you see moving will be enemy. Shoot first. Ask after. Co-driver, do not, repeat, not fire on walking men. They may be 2 Troop survivors. Have you got that?'

I work my gun along the known hedgerows and woods. From this new angle I can see more of the woods across the gully. Trees. Undergrowth. Branches. Intricate, twisting tracery of branches, twigs and leaves. Those twisted variegated shapes are safe. I count them. Assess them. Trees and branches. Twigs and leaves. A box shape. A box ... BOX! Jab gun elevator, twist grip, crosswires ON! STAMP! (Keith: 'Hornet! Hornet! Front!')

Suddenly everything seems to slow to a thousandth of normal speed, like a film running down. A single second is packed with so many thoughts, so many sensations, so many occurrences, each one fully comprehended and savoured to the full. The bulbous gush of fire from our own gun muzzle, dazzling the telescopic sight. The huge recoil of the 75 gun by my left cheek. The clang of the breech block springing open and belching out heat and sulphurous fumes into the turret. The entire tank lurching back in the agony of the firing act as the great gun gives birth to the heavy shot jammed tight within it. The agonizing drive of the shot up the rifled gun barrel, the curving grooves grasping the shot as it gathers speed, acceleration fighting against deceleration, the shot twisting into a spin which hurls it from the gun at tremendous velocity. The spark of tracer racing across space.

Whilst the tracer is still in mid-air, a brilliant flash lashing from the box shape in the hedgerow, identifying it as a gun turret. A shot fired at us or ours. Then our tracer dipping in slightly towards the enemy tank and, in the last moment of its flight, another twin tracer speeding in from another angle, merging with it so that both tracers hit almost in the same instant and within inches of each other.

There is a tiny puff of smoke from the box shape. It jerks back into the wood out of my sight. Even as it does, thick black smoke spouts around it, black smoke tinged with crimson. Stan slaps my leg and I stamp again, holding the gun on the base of the ascending smoke pillar. Slap. Stamp. Fire again.

'Hullo 3 Able. Have brewed a Mark IV in the area of Roger 2. Roger 3 Able, over.'

'Roger 3 Able, well done! Keep your eyes open, Off.'

Stan: 'What the Hell! Ken got that one. The two shots landed together. But ours hit first. What is 3 Able talking about, just because he is a Sergeant and we are only a Corporal?'

Keith: 'What does it matter, as long as it burns?'

Bookie: 'Go on, burn, you buggers, burn!'

By the beginning of September 1944 the Allies were driving north in pursuit of the retreating Germans. Brussels was liberated on 3 September. Now arguments broke out in the Allied camp over the best way to bring a speedy end to the war. General Eisenhower, the Allied supreme commander, became embroiled in a dispute between his subordinates, the British Montgomery and the American Patton, respectively commanding the left and right flanks of the Allied advance across Europe. Both were straining at the leash to mount a strong thrust into Germany on a narrow front to clinch victory before Christmas. Eisenhower favoured a 'broad-front' approach, but he yielded sufficiently to allow Montgomery to mount Operation Market Garden, an unsuccessful attempt by British 1st Airborne Division to seize and secure a crossing of the Rhine at Arnhem (17–25 September). In the memorable phrase used by Lieutenant-General Sir Brian Horrocks, the operation was a 'bridge too far'. Major John Waddy of the 156th Parachute Battalion recalls his part in the fighting at Arnhem.

On our return to the UK from Italy at the end of 1943, we trained hard for the coming invasion of Europe, and it was, therefore, a blow to all of us in 1st Airborne Division that we did not take part in the D-Day landings, but merely stood to on the airfields as an immediate reserve in case there was trouble in the bridgehead. During those long summer months we became increasingly frustrated as we waited for action. We planned and prepared for a number of likely operations which were cancelled. One near Caen was highly dangerous, with the DZs[1] littered with panzers, and there were other targets – Brest, Le Havre, the forests south-west of Paris, canal bridges on the Belgian border; and in early September, Operation Comet, the later Market Garden task but to be carried out by the 1st Division only and the Polish Brigade.

On the morning of 17 September we were all thrilled to see large formations of Dakotas wheeling over our base at Melton Mowbray: it was the first lift of the operation flying in, and we knew the operation was, at last, on. Even then during the night there was a postponement in time of take-off. It was strange early next morning as we drove to Saltby airfield seeing the townspeople of Melton Mowbray going to work as we went to war. Even then at the airfield there was further delay to low mist. Our American aircrew finally came out, and I checked the aircraft with the pilot, who was dressed immaculately in service dress and cap, but wasn't sure if he had to fly in north-to-south or south-to-north! I told him to sort it out, but he said, 'Shit, I'll just follow the rest.' At last we were off, flying in huge circles to get into the formations of nine aircraft in Vs – what the Americans call 'nine-ship elements'. We crossed the Dutch

---

[1] Drop Zones

coast when there was a little flak, and flew on over the fields flooded by the Germans, waving back at the Dutch families huddled on the roofs of their farmhouses. The aircraft formations tightened up as we flew about 50 miles inland, bearing north-east over S'Hertogenbosch on to the final heading for our DZs, 30 miles away. Here the fighter escort, 1200 aircraft in all, closed up expecting attack from the Luftwaffe; we started to fly through light flak and small arms fire; puffs of black smoke could be seen bursting among the aircraft ahead and there were a few near us, but we were hit only once with no damage. Flying as low as 700 feet, I could see the white upturned faces of the German flak gunners. An aircraft just to starboard received a direct hit and, on fire from nose to tail, passed just under my aircraft and crashed in a huge ball of white and red flame below, just missing two terrified carthorses. RAF Typhoons were also diving below our aircraft and strafing the German guns.

Finally we crossed the last river, the Rhine, hooked up and ready. I had a RAF flight sergeant from Ringway in my aircraft to help (several had come with the 4th Brigade as a result of a private arrangement between our brigadier, Shan Hackett, and the PTS. They were ordered by the RAF not to 'fall out' of the aircraft). This sergeant was great, and he might have been dispatching over Tatton Park, dressed in a shapeless RAF battledress and scuffed shoes. At last, with a huge shout of 'GO' from the whole stick, I jumped, to be followed down the slipstream by a call from our RAF friend, 'Give 'em hell from Ringway.'

I did my usual untidy landing, getting entangled in my Schmeisser carried in the harness. I had landed just north of the new autobahn under construction, and so had a good half-mile walk to our battalion RV on the north-west corner of Ginkel Heide in the woods. I trotted slowly towards it, collecting some of my soldiers: I passed my company 2 i/c strolling up a track, saying, 'Hurry up, Monty, there's a war.' He replied, 'So I see.' The aircraft formations continued to roar overhead and the air seemed to be full of parachutes – over 2,000 men were dropped in a little over ten minutes. The American aircrews were superb and, despite the flak and now the small arms fire, they flew on in perfect formation but I could see at the end of the DZ, where there was a considerable belt of fire (and where the 10th Battalion had to fight for their RV) that as each 'V' of nine aircraft completed their drop, they poured on extra power to climb out of danger and into a more dispersed formation.

At the battalion RV the well ordered drill of rallying the battalion was working well. My company had to push out patrols to the north to protect the RV from enemy reported in the nearby Ede barracks. One was captured but when interrogated in German, answered in perfect English; he was a Pole. After about an hour the battalion was ready to move, less about 90 men missing, either from aircraft shot down, or killed, wounded by enemy fire or injured from the drop: one of my platoon commanders was missing, later found shot on the DZ. Just short of the Wolfneze crossing and as dusk was falling we joined up with the glider lift of the battalion: HQ and support company jeeps and carriers and anti-tank guns, which had landed on a LZ south of the railway. Soon after we were strafed by some German ME 109s. We continued to move forward slowly in the dark and the first fatigue was starting to set in, despite our fitness; it had been a long day with an exciting flight and drop, and a march forwards with everyone carrying heavy loads of 80–120 pounds.

Our leading C Company met strong opposition as it approached the railway cutting at Oosterbeek and the night was full of orange and mauve tracers, and soon burning houses lit the sky. Our battalion was ordered to halt and to move again at first light: fresh orders were issued. C Company were to push on again to take the high point (high for Holland!) in a wood just north of the railway, and I was to give fire support from the houses by the railway station. It was a slow job moving through the hedges and fenced suburban gardens of the neat houses, where surprisingly we met some Dutch families calmly sitting down to breakfast. Soon a fire-fight ensued, including tank fire against our houses, but our supporting fire role had been completed and we had to withdraw all the way back again along and over the railway and into the Johanna Hoeve woods.

I reported to my CO on the edge of the wood to be briefed. He had just been visited by Brigadier Shan Hackett, who had left with him saying, 'There are a lot of English faces down at the bridge eagerly awaiting us …' which in his words meant that we had to get a move on. I was told of C Company's position and that A company had attacked past their left onto the road running south to Oosterbeek, and I was ordered to pass through and move on to the Lichtenbeek feature in the woods 300–400 yards beyond the road. I was told that there were only a few snipers.

Later, I found out that A Company had been held up by heavy fire from the road, and that John Pott (who had won an MC in 1943 leading his company in Italy in a gallant attack against a strong position of German parachutists), had made a left flanking attack to reach the road to fight a desperate battle among the houses beyond the German armour and infantry. He with a group of his men then got on to the Lichtenbeek feature, and held it for several hours under repeated attack, until finally he and most of his men were either wounded or killed, and finally overrun.

I advanced with two platoons forward either side of a main ride in the woods, and only after a short while we encountered very heavy Spandau fire and bullets were ricocheting off the trees in all directions. I came to a clearing of felled timber, and by a pile of logs there was a Platoon HQ of A Company, all dead. Ahead a quick-firing gun was slamming HE shells into the scrub where my left-hand platoon was trying to edge forward, and they were taking heavy casualties. I then saw the gun at the end of the ride about 150 yards ahead on the road – it appeared to be a twin-barrelled 20-mm flak gun on a half-track chassis. As it was opposite my line of advance I decided to move forward myself to try to knock it out, with some of my soldiers and with Tom Wainwright, OC Support Company (what was he doing up there?).

Hearing the noise of fighter aircraft Tom suggested a dash across the clearing while the enemy's heads were down but the aircraft, as they passed very low overhead, had that prominent black cross on their sides – they were ME 109s and not Spitfires or Typhoons. God knows we could have done with the latter there! Nevertheless we pushed on through the scrub until we were within about 15 yards of the gun; the Germans were all shouting at one another and I could hear the empty shell cases rattling down on the deck; one could now sense that there were a lot of other armoured vehicles on that road.

Just then the soldier on my right was hit smack in the forehead by a bullet, and I saw that there was a sniper in the tree above the gun. I had only my .45 Colt and no Schmeisser and so I fired five rounds at him and he, or someone else, shot me in the lower stomach. When I came to, and started to crawl away he fired another shot, hitting the ground near my hand. I collapsed and lay doggo, until I heard a crashing through the bushes and a large Rhodesian private, Ben Diedricks (we had about 20 Rhodesians serving in our battalion since our stay in the Middle East), picked me up in his arms and carried me back some 200 yards to Company HQ. At the battalion RAP our doctor, John Buck, must have thought that I had had it for all he did was to chuck me his silver whisky flask! At the Field Ambulance casualty post half a mile back I was given a plasma transfusion, which was better than the whisky, and then, wrapped in a billowing parachute, I was taken on a stretcher jeep to Oosterbeek to the Tafelberg Hotel where 181 Airlanding Brigade Field Ambulance had set up a main dressing station. The billiard room was used as the operating theatre, and after I was operated on, I was moved out into the dining room. After about a day, as more wounded came flooding in even faster, I was moved out to a nearby house.

As no resupply had been received, the initial quantities of food and medical stores were fast running out. The Germans shelled and mortared the perimeter throughout the day and of course the dressing stations, being in the front line, were being repeatedly hit and the wounded were being wounded again or killed. The nights were cold and it had started to rain, a dismal drizzle: there were very few blankets and most of us were lying half-naked on the floor (having had our clothes cut off by the medics) or sharing mattresses from the hotel. Smells are usually held to be one's most evocative memory, and I can still smell today that mixture of wet earth, burnt cordite, brick and plaster dust, and pus that permeated those days. Towards the end of the battle there must have been over 3,000 casualties in this situation on the perimeter. A large proportion were evacuated to German hospitals towards the end during a short cease-fire organized by the ADMS, our head doctor, Colonel Graeme Warrack and a German medical officer. Graeme Warrack was truly a tower of strength and a source of encouragement to all of us lying helplessly in these battered houses. He was one of the greatest unsung heroes of the battle, as were his medical orderlies, who carried on without rest for over a week in their task of caring for the wounded, despite the fact that the dressing stations were under fire from snipers and from mortar and tank fire. On one day the room in which I was in received a direct hit, killing about six men and wounding others including myself, and this was followed by a rush of steel-helmeted Germans through the house. A counter-attack was launched and the Airborne troops drove them out, and this was repeated several times until finally we were in German hands. Two Germans came in and set up a fire position in the wrecked bay windows, but soon one of them was hit by an airborne sniper firing from a house across the road. A huge German feldwebel came in and lectured us on the evils of our soldiers firing at a house flying the Red Cross flag, and then he proceeded to shout at the wounded German, who was moaning pitifully. The next day in the morning the whole area around us was subjected to an even heavier concentration of fire, but this time it came from our own medium artillery (5.5 inch), which had been providing superb close fire support around the perimeter over the last few days: this was a very unfortunate lapse. Our room again got a direct hit and particularly the wounded German. I woke up, wounded again, under a pile of rubble but most of the others were killed except for a glider pilot-officer, who had had both legs smashed when his glider had crash-landed, lying screaming underneath a large piano across his shattered legs. Our house soon caught fire and the medical orderlies carried us out. I found myself on a house verandah behind, and close to, a gruesome sight of some 30 bodies stacked in a pile; they must have been those who had died of wounds or had been killed by mortar or shell fire in the dressing station.

A jeep suddenly drove up and out jumped a Sergeant Chivers, not only from our own 156 Battalion, but also from my original regiment, the Somerset Light Infantry. He said, 'Good God Major Waddy, what are you doing here?' and I said, 'Just get me out of here.' I was, with some other casualties, loaded onto his jeep and driven down a road strewn with wrecked vehicles and fallen tree branches. I thought that we had been relieved by Second Army, but too soon the jeep turned a corner, and drove into a space behind what I now know to be a fire station, and there in a huge semicircle were some 100 SS soldiers with machine-guns mounted on tripods. The wounded and the stragglers were being rounded up by the Germans, in company with Airborne medical staff and the padres, all of whom had stayed behind to carry on their care for the wounded. If battle honours could be awarded to the RAMC, then Arnhem/Oosterbeek should be one of its finest feats.

All the wounded, and there must have been over 4,000, were taken to a large empty barracks of the pre-war Dutch Army at Apeldoorn where the division's medical staff were establishing a British hospital nearby. I was taken to a German hospital full of their wounded, mainly from the SS Panzer divisions that we had been fighting, but one might have thought that they were on our side by the way they helped our soldiers as they came in and were put into their wards. A lightly wounded SS corporal helped me onto a bed, took off what was left of my blood-soaked and dusty clothes and, seeing that I was hit in the jaw, then carefully peeled and cut up an apple to feed me. I asked him to find out what had happened to a young soldier of the 1st Battalion with a badly smashed face who had been with me; next day the SS man came and sadly told me that 'der Junge' had died.

The German doctors and staff were very correct and attentive throughout my six weeks' stay in that hospital, although their medical resources were limited, consisting mainly of paper bandages and lashings of acriflavine; anaesthetics especially were in short supply for anything other than major surgery. Colonel Graeme Warrack visited us twice on his rounds of other hospitals and he said that the German Army were ten years behind in battlefield surgery. One day two German surgeons at the end of my bed discussed whether they would amputate my foot (amputations were apparently an all-to-common remedy in the German Army and an elderly German orderly gave me an example of heavy German humour – 'never report sick with a headache'). The two doctors abruptly broke off their discussion when one said, 'The major speaks German'; anyway the matter was solved by a large, blonde, German nursing sister who later pulled out a two-inch-long mortar splinter in one excruciating moment, complete with some sock knitted by Ann, my fiancée and now my wife.

There were one or two dramas: once after a RAF Spitfire had put a burst of cannon fire through the operating theatre, killing a German nurse and a British soldier, I got a bollocking from the hospital matron about the British disregard for the Red

Cross on the roof: she was a formidable lady like so many of our military matrons. On another occasion, a soldier from our own battalion, Private Greer, the battalion humorist, climbed out of his bed one day, walked across the ward and turned a picture of Hitler face to the wall, saying, 'I can't stand looking at that bastard any longer.' At first, the Germans laughed. 'He's mad', they said, meaning Hitler of course, but the arrival of a German nursing sister changed the situation and we all got another rollicking. Eventually, sometime in November the last of the Airborne wounded were shipped or rather railed out of Holland into Germany – the inevitable 'das Transport' had come. Colonel Warrack's hospital in Apeldoorn had been emptied, and he himself with a number of his doctors had at the end slipped away into the efficient and caring hands of the Dutch underground, and most would finally make their way home to safety.

We left Apeldoorn station in a German hospital train, the centre two coaches of which contained British wounded. The journey through the shattered railway system of Germany down into Graz in Austria to offload the Germans ('nichts fur Tommy', we were told) and back up to a Stalag hospital took over six days. The painful tedium of the journey was relieved by the usual irrepressible humour of the British soldier. The panels on the outside of the coaches were soon chalked with huge Victory 'V's which caused consternation as the train pulled into platforms crowded with German military and civilians. At one station, some of our soldiers had blown up condoms and drawn on the end Hitler's well-known features, and when these were displayed to the waiting throng on the platform, at first they evoked some merriment until the arrival of an officious Nazi official.

Stalag VIIIA, Moosburg, was a mixed camp for Russians, French, Polish and British soldiers, but it had a hospital (or what passed for one), and here I spent another three months before being passed fit enough to go out into the compound, where some 120 officers were held, mainly airborne and from special forces taken in south-east Europe. Food was almost non-existent in the whole camp but much more so in the Russian compounds which were at starvation level, and this enabled the Germans to recruit Russians into their army as late as April 1945.

As the spring of that year blossomed, the sounds and sights of the approaching fronts became more evident. We had a superb grandstand view, almost daily, of the massed daylight bombing raids by the US Air Force on targets all around us; and for several hours each night we could hear and feel the RAF heavies doing their stuff. After the war, the Allied bombing offensive has been denigrated as having achieved little in the strategic field, but certainly from what we saw and heard from the Germans in our camp, it had a significant effect on their morale.

Finally, in early May, artillery fire was heard during the night a few miles off and in the morning tanks could be seen several miles from the camp; before long they swept past and through the thick pinewoods in a headlong advance to Munich and beyond. It was George Patton's army on the move, and highly efficient it looked. About noon a huge Stars and Stripes flag was seen high on the church tower of the hill-top village of Moosburg: in front of me was the figure of a broad-based American Air Force officer, who remarked, 'Well, kiss my naked ass, it's the flag.' We were liberated. A few days later, we were flown out to Rheims, courtesy of the USAAF, and from there back to England, after a day's delay, by RAF Bomber Command, after they had recovered from their VE-Day celebrations. At an airfield in Buckinghamshire we were met by the charming ladies of the WVS with a cup of tea and a packet of ten Gold Flake cigarettes: we were home, almost.

Eisenhower's emphasis on the 'broad front' strategy led him to dismiss the possibility of an advance through the Ardennes by either the Allies or the Germans. On 16 December 1944 he was obliged to revise this assessment when the Germans attacked in the Ardennes along a 70-mile front, achieving tactical and strategic surprise. The salient the Germans drove into the Allied line was not eliminated until 16 January 1945. Both sides had suffered heavy losses. The Allies made good theirs in two weeks, but the German losses were irreplaceable. On 5 January 1945, First Lieutenant Robert Dean Bass, serving with 324th Engineer Battalion, US 99th Infantry Division, fighting on the northern shoulder of the salient, wrote home to his parents.

Dearest Mother and Dad:
This is the second letter that I've written in almost a month now. I've really tried to write but just haven't been in a place where I could, except when I spent the night in a Belgian home a few days ago. I did write you from there.

Dad. I received a letter from you today written December 24, the day before Christmas. I was in a fox hole, when you wrote that letter, as I had been for ten days previous and four days afterward.

I imagine that you all have been reading the newspapers about the big German counter-offensive. If I were a novelist, I could write a magnificent tale about a bunch of soda jerks and grocery clerks. After all, that's what all these American soldiers are. They're not professional military men but just a bunch of guys over here doing a job, and a darn good one, and proving themselves much the superior soldier to the German, who has spent the better part of his life pursuing military training.

I'm going to tell you a little of what my battalion has done in the last three weeks. Not just my outfit, but every outfit on the Belgian front did the same thing.

As I've told you, my division moved up to the line in early November. We were in a quiet sector though and not much was happening. My battalion moved into a little village and took the place over. We quartered all our men in houses and things went pretty smoothly. We went out every day and built roads, bridges and performed other engineering tasks in our division sector. But at night we had a house to come home to. We even had a couple of picture shows a week shown in our mess hall, the old Belgian beer garden. Remember, I've told you all that in my letters before.

During the second week in December, we were called out to build a supply road and several bridges to one of our front line infantry battalions. It was just a three or four day job, and then we were to return to our little village and go on as before.

While we were building this supply road, the big German counter-offensive began, but we didn't know it. We could hear small arms and artillery fire on both sides of us but just imagined it was the normal thing, since the infantry battalion we were supporting was making an attack.

Finally, we got an order for our whole battalion to retire to a little town in the rear and re-organize as an infantry battalion. We moved back, dropped all of our engineer tools and equipment, left our trucks, put our machine guns and rifles on our backs and after dark marched up into the line as infantry. We were supposed to have tied in on our right and left flanks with the infantry units of our own division. But we never saw another American unit. For two days and two nights we sat on the side of a hill waiting for a German attack. We could hear fighting on both sides of us and in our rear, and we couldn't figure out what was going on. We still didn't know the Germans had opened a counter-offensive. Finally, since we had no communication with anyone nor had we for two days, and since we never could find our own infantry units which we were supposed to tie into, our battalion commander (whom you know) led us out of this hole down through a valley and on to the rear. The Germans never knew that we were on the side of that hill. They had us practically surrounded, and if they had known we were there, it wouldn't have taken much to fix us. We hadn't had one bit of food in over two days and had just enough ammunition to fill our guns. We had to march up there and therefore couldn't carry much with us other than our weapons. We were supposed to have been supplied, but no one knew where we were.

The division had given our battalion up as lost, and, as we came marching through a small American-held town, a Chaplain rushed out and asked what unit we were. When my company commander said 'The 324th Engineers,' the Chaplain said, 'Thank God.'

We marched on for a day and finally reached the little village where we had been staying. There for the first time, we found out about the enemy offensive. We ate our first meal in three days, received a new complement of ammunition, and were sent right back up on the line. This time, however, we tied right in with an infantry unit on our right and one on our left. We were told to dig in defensive positions and get ready for an enemy armored attack.

Sure enough, we had only been in these positions a day and then came the German tanks followed by their infantry. Their main thrust was in our own sector. Our own small arms fire stopped the infantry, but those tanks kept coming. There was an artillery forward observer with us and he was trying to adjust his fire on these tanks. I don't imagine a bunch of engineers ever said quite so many prayers as we did in those few minutes, when the German tanks were almost upon us before the artillery observer could get his fire on them. The tanks were less than 200 yards from us when our artillery finally began hitting all around them. Dad, remember about the terrific barrage that I told you about when I was at O.C.S. at Fort Sill, layed down by 109 artillery pieces. Well, that barrage was child's play compared to the barrage the good old American artillery put on those attacking German Tiger Tanks. I can't tell you how many tanks or Germans that were knocked out in front of our positions that night, but they were really stacked up. What few German tanks that weren't knocked out, turned tail and fled. All night long we could hear the wounded Germans out in front of us hollering 'surrender.' This is one English word they all learn before they are sent on the line.

We were in these positions for about ten days. During that time, we drove off the spearhead of two major German thrusts and several smaller ones. Our boys fought like veterans. I have two .30 calibre machine guns in my platoon, and I'd wager that during those ten days each accounted for a company of German infantry piled up in front of it. My boys had never seen any actual combat before, but every one of them did a job that I'll never forget.

On Christmas Day we got out of our fox-holes, one squad at a time, and walked down into the valley behind us and had a hot turkey sandwich brought up to us by our cooks.

I certainly want to thank you for the nice fruit cake and two cans of nuts. People have been very nice to me this Christmas. I received packages from the Everitts, Entrikens, Dickie Bass, Juda Shipley in addition to all those I mentioned in my last letter.

Juda Jane sent me a swell identification bracelet with my name and serial number on it, and Elaine sent me a 'Saint Christopher, Protect Us' medal to wear around my neck.

It's about time I'm getting some sleep, so I shall write again soon.

I love you all dearly,

Bob

A month later Lieutenant Bass was killed in action.

The Allies crossed the Rhine at several points in March 1945. There was more hard fighting to come, however, before the fall of the Third Reich. Charles B. MacDonald was a company commander in US 2nd Infantry Division, slogging its way towards Karlstadt, some 50 miles southeast of Frankfurt.

F company joined us at the second hairpin curve in the highway. I formed my company in the woods on the left of the road, the 2d Platoon leading the assault with 3d and 1st Platoons echeloned to the left rear to protect the wooded flank. Colonel Smith radioed to ask if we were ready, and I looked at Captain Calhoun and he nodded. I signalled to Lieutenant

Whitman, and the lead scouts stepped boldly into the underbrush. *We will now take a short walk into the woods for the purpose of nature study. Please excuse our silly walking formation. We were raised in an army camp.*

My map showed that the first likely spot for an enemy defense was a north-south highway which met the road we were following at a crossroads in the woods almost a quarter of a mile distant. There might be enemy patrols between us and that point, but the crossroads seemed the only logical defensive position until we should emerge from the woods at a point overlooking the town of Ellershausen slightly less than a mile away. Our orders were to hold up at the far edge of the woods to await the completion of the bridge across the Weser and the subsequent arrival of tank support.

I tried, but I could not put the memory of the heavy motors that I had heard during the night from my mind. The harsh memory of riflemen against tanks in the gruelling Ardennes battle was stamped indelibly in my mind, and I could not avoid the overwhelming fear of meeting the Germans on such terms again.

The riflemen ploughed slowly through the woods, hindered by the dense underbrush. I followed close to the highway as it continued slightly south of east after making its last deliberate turn at our starting point.

I pushed around a thick bush. On the ground before me lay a tangle of bicycles and human bodies. The bodies were German and their faces were rapidly turning a sickly shade of green that seemed to blend with their uniforms.

'Must be the patrol the 1st Platoon hit,' someone said, impassively. 'Lieutenant Bagby's men sure got far enough up the hill.'

One of the dead German's lips were pulled back, baring irregular teeth in a sickening snarl; the eyes of another stared blankly at me; a thin trickle of blood from the temple of another appeared to be still warm. I wondered why the Germans turned green so quickly after death, and then I remembered that someone had once said that it was due to a diet deficiency.

A report came over the radio from the 2d Platoon. They were coming out of the underbrush now, but they were still in the woods. So far, no trouble.

So far – I thought. They should be reaching the crossroads soon.

Colonel Smith and Captain Byrd came abreast of me on the highway.

'Call your men out of the woods to the highway, Mac,' the Colonel said. 'There's nothing here. That's pretty obvious. Move them over to the road where they can make some time and let's get going.'

I looked at him dubiously. I wanted to scream and ask what in hell was all the all-fired rush about, but I turned to Citrone and told him to get the three rifle platoons on the radio.

'Hello, G two,' Citrone began. 'Hello, – '

A sudden burst of small-arms fire echoed through the woods ahead of us. Bullets whistled overhead. I dropped instinctively to the ditch beside the road. The small-arms fire was so intense that I could not distinguish between German and American fire, but I wondered why so few bullets whistled over our heads. Whitman and his men must be laying down quite a volume of fire. There was no need to ask him if he had reached the highway. It was obvious that he had hit the German defenses there.

I had fallen behind when I stopped to talk with the Colonel, so I motioned for the CP group to follow and we moved up the ditch toward the sound of the firing. I looked around for the battalion staff, but I could not see them.

'Hmpf, nothing in the woods,' I said to myself.

The road curved slightly to the left, and I could not see the crossroads, but I knew that we must be near. The ground had leveled out. We had at last reached the top of the hill.

The firing stopped almost as suddenly as it had begun. A few scattered rifle shots remained.

'Call Whitman,' I said to Citrone. 'Ask him what's happening.'

Citrone called for 'G two.'

'We've come up against a bunch of Kraut dug in beyond another highway,' Whitman said. 'Looks like they've got quite a trench system.'

'Do you think you can move forward?'

'We'll try it with marching fire,' Whitman answered. 'I think so. Cantwell has been hit. Not too bad, but you'd better get a litter, and we need some ammo.'

I said, 'Roger.'

Abad was carrying the battalion radio. He contacted Captain Byrd.

'We'll get a litter squad right up,' he said, 'and we'll try for ammunition. No transportation but F Company's auto, but I'll send it back.'

I sent two men to the Weapons Platoon to collect all M1[1] ammunition they could spare. It was not enough. I sent them back to get any spare ammunition from the 1st Platoon.

The barrage of small-arms fire began again. There was the same rapid crescendo as before, echoing back and forth through the woods.

The picture of what was happening in the woods a few yards from me was clearer now even though the low-hanging branches of the trees obscured the view. The Germans were being given very little opportunity to fire their weapons. The platoon was laying down such a terrific barrage of fire that they were forced to keep their heads down in their trenches. And the 2d Platoon riflemen would be jumping up and running forward one by one, hiding here behind one tree, hiding there behind another, while their comrades fired and awaited their turns to move forward.

The firing suddenly stopped again. I noticed the litter squad kneeling in the ditch behind me. Whitman sent a man to the highway to guide the litter bearers and bring the ammunition. Two of the aid men moved forward in a half-crouch and entered the woods, their red crosses against a white background on their helmets glistening as they moved.

A burst of small-arms fire came from the right of the highway. The enemy's line must extend to the right as well, and F Company had run into trouble.

Whitman's platoon started to fire again, and the woods crackled with the sound of the firing.

---

[1] The Garand rifle, the standard rifle of the US Army during the Second World War, a gas-operated semiautomatic of .30in caliber loaded by means of an eight-round clip.

The aid men emerged from the woods carrying Sergeant Cantwell on a stretcher between them. I stood up to talk to him.

'I'm sorry as hell, Cap'n,' the sergeant said, and I could see that he was making an effort to keep his face from showing the pain which he felt. 'Just got in the way, I guess.'

'Nice going, Cant,' I said. 'Hurry back to us.'

He had a painful wound in the side, but the aid men thought there was no danger.

Two men from battalion headquarters arrived with their arms full of bandoleers of .30-caliber M1 ammunition. I sent it back to be distributed among the 1st Platoon and told the men from battalion to bring us another load. At the rate Whitman's platoon was firing, we would need several loads before we reached Ellershausen.

'Send the litter squad back,' Whitman called. 'I've got two more men wounded.'

Fulton ran back to overtake the litter squad. The two men returned with him and re-entered the woods, emerging a moment later carrying Private First Class Carby J. Simpkins, who was wounded in the upper leg. Private First Class Herbert I. Flam walked with them. He had been hit in the left shoulder. Both men had been hastily bandaged in full view of the dug-in Germans by the courageous platoon aid man.

Captain Calhoun was just across the road with his forward CP group, and we decided it would be best to coordinate our next assault in order to reach the crossroads at the same time. Thus, neither company would be endangered by enemy fire from the flank after reaching their respective portion of the enemy position. He said he would order his platoons forward when they heard Whitman's men open fire again. I radioed the information to Whitman.

The sudden fusilade of fire from the woods came once again, and I knew that Whitman's men were endeavoring to make this their last assault. F Company answered with a small-arms barrage on the other side of the road. The rapid fire was sustained, and then slowed down gradually until I could hear only scattered shots.

'We've crossed the highway,' Whitman radioed. He was breathing heavily. 'Patton's on my left. We're going on.'

I signalled the CP group and the Weapons Platoon forward, and we moved the few remaining yards to the crossroads.

The woods beyond the north-south highway became a dense forest of big firs. German dead and equipment were scattered in and around a series of trenches which zig-zagged back and forth beneath the heavy branches of the fir trees. The damp red earth piled high in front of the trenches showed that they were freshly dug Five wounded Germans in immaculate uniforms except for blood stains here and there screamed and moaned for medics. A German officer, still wearing his officer's cap with its shiny, black visor, saw as we passed that I was an officer. He called to me for help and pointed alternately at a decoration on his blouse and a bleeding wound in one leg. The decoration must have meant something, but I did not understand, and I was revolted at his appeal to me as a member of the 'officer class.'

We passed on. There was no time to care for the stupid officer. The aid men in the rear would care for him in time.

Small-arms fire sounded again to the front. Whitman had run into trouble again, and the noisy chatter of small-arms fire told me he was pulling no punches.

'They're trying to hold up at a firebreak,' he radioed. 'Patton's platoon's up beside me now. We can handle it OK.'

I wanted desperately to go farther forward to where I could see what was going on, but I knew that it would be necessary for me to be almost atop the forward riflemen before I could see anything through the dense woods, and I remembered again the folly of moving too far forward the night I was wounded. I contented myself with cautioning the CP group to be alert for snipers that the lead platoons might by-pass.

The firing stopped to the front, and I knew that the 2d Platoon was pushing forward again.

Captain Calhoun called over the battalion radio. His men had come upon a two-hundred-yard clearing on the right of the road. The woods beyond would most probably be defended, and he wanted permission to move his company through my sector. It offered concealment all the way to his objective.

I said, 'Roger,' and saw his men move across the highway ahead of us. I radioed Lieutenant Whitman that they were coming through our area.

I reached the firebreak where the lead platoon had met its second resistance. Two dead Germans lay as they had fallen, but there were no foxholes or trenches.

We passed through a few more yards of dense trees before we came abreast of the clearing on the right of the road. The route in our sector offered only slightly more concealment, and I could see the last of F Company's assault platoons moving up and mingling with my forward elements where the woods became dense again. The intervening space was carpeted with high grass and ferns, but the majority of the trees had been felled. Scattered rifle shots and the occasional staccato chant of a BAR came from the woods beyond the clearing on F Company's side of the highway.

We moved across the thin stretch of woods and overtook the rear elements of Sergeant Patton's platoon resting wearily beneath the trees. An occasional enemy bullet whined over their heads, but it did not seem to disturb them. Several men from the platoon were assembling a group of prisoners which grew ever larger as more Germans stumbled across the highway from the dense woods beyond the clearing. There seemed to be no pattern to any of the action. The riflemen bringing in the prisoners were from Whitman's platoon, but an occasional F Company man brought in a group. The Germans began to form in a ragged platoon formation, their hands high above their heads while GIs frisked them for weapons and valuables.

I found Sergeant Patton and asked him what happened.

'We were coming across the open stretch there when these Kraut opened up from across the road,' he said. 'Whitman didn't want to wait on F Company, so he headed on in after 'em. The woods must be packed with the bastards.'

Colonel Smith radioed to find out the situation. When I told him, he urged me to get moving again. I shifted Patton's 3d Platoon into the attack with the 1st guarding their left flank and told them to hold up when they reached the far edge of the woods. I would drop the 2d Platoon back into the support role as soon as they finished clearing the sector beyond the road.

A shell burst suddenly in a tree high above my head. For one agonizing moment I thought about the enemy tanks, but I heard no sound of motors and no second round. I decided that it was a round from a *Panzerfaust* (the German version of the bazooka).

One by one and in groups the German prisoners straggled and ran from the woods across the road. Finally, Lieutenant Whitman emerged.

'Goddamnit!' he said. 'Goddamnit! Goddamnit! I had those Kraut in there talked into surrendering when F Company came in shootin'. Damned Kraut jumped back in their holes and started fighting again. Goddamnit!'

We had another quarter of a mile to go through the woods, but the 3d Platoon fired only a few shots at fleeing Germans who were trying to reach the town beyond the woods. I caught up with the 3d there when they stopped. The highway curved at the point it emerged from the woods and ran at an angle across our front as it entered Ellershausen, a cluster of stone houses and farm buildings nestled on either side of the highway in a valley surrounded on three sides by low fir-covered hills. A few frightened Germans were fleeing across the open fields toward the town, and the infantrymen sat calmly at the bases of trees and shot after them as if they might have been quail on the rise.

I realized for the first time that the sun was shining brightly. We had been in the woods since the attack began, and I had not thought once of the weather.

Battalion sent forward a platoon of heavy machine guns from H Company with instructions to place them along the forward edge of the woods with my own light guns in positions from which they could place overhead fire against Ellershausen. The gunners went into position quickly and began to fire. The woods echoed with the loud chatter of the six machine guns firing at occasional targets that presented themselves in the valley to our front. Six additional guns opened up from the woods on the south side of the town, and I knew that F

Company had been ordered to the south and had been given a platoon of heavy guns as well.

Colonel Smith called for me to meet him on the highway near the point where the highway emerged from the forest. He said that replenishment on ammunition would be up shortly, and the bridge across the Weser would be completed before three o'clock. Our tanks had top priority for getting across.

Our preparatory barrage against Ellershausen would begin at 3:15 and last for fifteen minutes. At the end of that time F Company and a platoon of tanks would advance under overhead machine gun fire against the objective from the south and hit the town broadside. G Company would attack astride the highway toward the east, also with a platoon of tanks and overhead machine-gun fire. After clearing the town, we should be prepared to continue the advance. Regiment had assigned another objective.

I cursed Regiment. They were always assigning 'one more objective.'

I returned and gave the platoon leaders the information. The centre platoon was facing a draw which the highway entered before reaching the town and then followed into town. We decided to move out from the woods down the draw and rendezvous with the tanks at the point where the highway entered the draw.

The machine gunners continued their sporadic bursts toward the town. A lone German was stranded in a shallow dip in the ground on the open hill to our left, and the machine gunners laughingly fired short bursts slightly above the German's head. He waved a white flag frantically after every burst of fire.

An enemy machine gunner opened up on our position from the edge of the woods on the north side of town, but my six machine guns gave him their attention. He fired one more burst and was silent, but he had already revealed his position and I assigned my two light guns the mission of spraying the north woods as the riflemen moved in the open toward the town.

I heard the roar of tanks on the highway to our rear, and I knew that the time for the attack was drawing near. I double-timed the two hundred yards to the highway and contacted the platoon leader of the five tanks that would be with us. He agreed to start two minutes before the preparatory barrage was scheduled to end, meeting us at the junction of the road and the draw and continuing into Ellershausen in time to reach the buildings just as the artillery barrage should lift.

The preparatory barrage began as I turned from the tanker to return to the company. Artillery shells whistled again and again over the trees to cascade in a cloud of dust and roaring explosion upon the hapless town beyond. Heavy mortar shells plunked into 81mm barrels and joined in the explosive tumult falling on the town. The sound of the twelve machine guns and an assortment of smaller weapons reverberated over the countryside.

I ran back to the company. The 2d and 3d Platoons were in position, ready for the double-time assault toward the objective.

Three sleek P-47s emerged from the clouds, the sunlight glistening against their silver wings. Down and down they dived above the town, which looked now as if it would completely disappear in the smoke and confusion of the preparatory barrage. Their machine guns and cannon began to chatter and assert themselves above the din of the battle whose privacy they had invaded. Up and up they climbed, higher into the sky; and then as if they had suddenly spotted their prey, down, down once more, their machine guns and cannon barking derisively. Then they flew away toward the east, and we could see them dive on the next town, and one of the planes dropped a bomb.

Abad tried to say something to me, but I could not hear him above the noisy demonstration before us. I made out the word 'battalion' and told him to say that we were ready.

The artillery continued to whistle and explode on the town. The mortar shells dropped unheralded upon the objective. The machine guns chattered. A freakish lull appeared in the louder noises for a second, and I heard the 'plunk' of a 60mm mortar shell being dropped into a mortar tube somewhere behind me. The 4th Platoon artillery could not resist getting in on the action.

The lone German on the hillside was waving his white flag more frantically than ever.

I was ecstatic with an elation born of excitement. The men around me were laughing and patting one another on the back. This preparation was something for the book, and the unexpected appearance of the planes had added the finishing touch.

I looked at my watch. Four minutes to go before the barrage would lift. The men in the two assault platoons knew that the time was near and stood in half-crouches like animals waiting for the moment to spring. The smiles were gone from their faces, and in their places had come expressions of determination. It seemed impossible that any human being could survive the pasting which Ellershausen had taken and was taking, but the Germans always came out again when they were not supposed to come out.

If only they get there just as the barrage lifts!

I heard the roar of the tanks tuning up their motors. *Any minute now.* Time stood still for an instant.

Almost time now ... almost time ... almost ... GO!

The machine guns stopped firing. The scouts plunged from the woods with their comrades close behind them. The artillery and mortars fired their final rounds. I saw the platoon of tanks race from the woods in single file down the highway toward the draw. To the south I could see the lead riflemen from F Company emerge from the woods. Their tanks followed. They formed an approach-march formation on the open, downward sloping hillside, and I thought of the diagrams in the Army manuals.

My own men met the tanks at the rendezvous point with split-second precision. The tankers infiltrated their steel monsters into the formation and adjusted their speed to the slower pace of the foot soldier.

The light machine gunners began to fire again, the tracers from the light guns creasing the edge of the north forest, the tracers from the heavy guns forming an umbrella of fiery steel over the heads of the advancing infantrymen. The lone German stranded on the hillside waved his white flag.

The timing, the formations were perfect. I looked at the men around me, and they looked at me and at each other. The last time we had seen an attack like this was in the training films back in the States. They didn't make attacks this way in actual battle. Something always went wrong. No, they didn't make them this way in actual battle. This was a mirage that was ridiculous because it was so wonderful and so true.

The last rounds from the artillery and mortars exploded with a roar upon the town. Orange tongues of flame licked up, up into the air from burning buildings. Black smoke billowed above the flame. The lead riflemen disappeared from sight in the first buildings of the town. The lead tank followed them. They had made it. They had crossed the open space unimpeded. The rest would be just mopping up.

Enter: the villain. A German machine gun from a haystack on the hillside to the north suddenly broke its silence and opened up on the rear elements of the assault platoons. My light gunners did not vary from their mission of neutralizing the woods to the north, but the four heavy guns turned their attention to the intruder without a moment's hesitation. I saw the tracer bullets plunging into the haystack, and the hay burst into flame. *Exit: the villain.*

I cautioned the machine gunners to hold their fire until we should get past them, and I signalled my CP group forward. We moved at a half-run down the slope to the draw and the road and on toward the town. The fields on either side of us were littered with German dead. The riflemen had caught more quail on the rise than I had thought.

I entered the town with my CP group. Already at least fifty German soldiers were assembled before the second house, their hands raised high above their heads and dazed, startled expressions of incredulity on their faces. Others poured from every building as eager GIs sought them out with curses and shouts of derision. Some hurried alone down the street toward the assemblage, terror written on their faces.

We moved on. I looked back and saw my support platoon move into the town and join in the mop-up operations.

The fifth house was a mass of flame. Two cows stood nearby, chewing their cuds and staring without expression at the scene of destruction. A grey-haired German farmer stood with his arm around his aged wife and stared at the burning house, tears streaming down both their faces.

'*Alles ist kaput! Alles ist kaput!*' they sobbed hysterically as we passed.

I was not impressed; instead, I was suddenly angry at them and surprised at my own anger. What right had they to stand their sobbing and blaming us for this terror? What right did they and their kind have to any emotions at all?

'Thank Adolf!' I shouted. 'Thank Hitler!' I pointed to the burning house and said, '*Der Führer!*' and laughed.

The mop-up continued and guards from the reserve company began to march over two hundred prisoners to the rear. I wondered if the flag-waving soldier on the hillside had ever succeeded in surrendering.

Colonel Smith arrived by jeep and gave me brief instructions for continuing the assault. Our next objective, and the final one for the day, was to be shared again with F Company, the town of Varlossen a quarter of a mile to the east. G Company would follow the left of the road as before.

I instructed my platoon leaders to meet me at the hill on the eastern edge of town as soon as they could assemble their men, and I moved forward to have a look at the objective.

I climbed the low hill and saw that the road sloped down again into Varlossen. A lone house stood atop the hill on the left. Three tank destroyers were grouped around the house, firing at fleeing German vehicles in the valley beyond. I climbed the stairs in the house. Two light machine guns from F Company were firing from the east windows. An artillery observer was calling for fire on enemy vehicles evacuating Varlossen along a tree-lined road to the east. The noise of the TDs and the machine guns was deafening in the close room.

The plaster walls of the house began to crack from the concussion of the big guns on the TDs.

The men from the platoons arrived and lined up along a wooden fence beyond the house to watch the target practice, showing utter disregard for the basic military principles of cover and concealment.

But a German tank fired in the distance and the screech of an 88 mm shell whistled over our heads and exploded in the town behind us. The gallery quickly dispersed. The enemy tank fired again and again. The artillery observer said he picked him up with his glasses. He was firing from the edge of another village to the northeast, but by the time a soldier had gone downstairs to give the information to the TDs, the tank had pulled behind the cover of buildings in the town.

'No use now,' the artillery observer said. 'Sonofabitch will sure give us hell when he catches us on that open hill to the next town.'

I was suddenly afraid of crossing the exposed forward slope of the hill leading to Varlossen. It had been an easy day as far as casualties were concerned. I wondered why regiment did not let well enough alone and forget this next objective until the next day. The Germans would pull out during the night, if we would only give them time.

I went downstairs and found that my company had assembled. F Company was forming across the road. The tanks that would support us were lined up on the road.

The Colonel called Captain Calhoun and me together for final instructions. Another round of enemy shellfire suddenly whistled overhead and crashed behind us, followed by another and another.

'They're giving them hell back there in Ellershausen,' the Colonel said. 'Easy Company lost a jeep and trailer in the first barrage.'

The Colonel said the instructions were the same as before.

'Let me know when you're ready,' he said.

I walked to the crest of the hill with Captain Byrd while the company was forming. We stood looking at the terrain before us when the next barrage came in. We could tell by the *swish* instead of whistle that it was intended for us instead of the town behind us.

The Germans had evidently found the range of the confusion of men and tanks on the hill. The shells burst all around us, and shrapnel whistled low overhead. I could hear the sound of the gun being fired in the distance, followed by the noise of the shell in flight that grew in intensity and found me holding my breath when it finally exploded on the hilltop. Fragments whined above the shallow ditch. Another burst sounded in the distance, and we knew another was on the way.

'Two bits on where she'll land, Mac,' Byrd laughed falsely.

'No takers,' I answered.

I winced as the shell exploded on the hilltop.

With the end of the war in sight, POW camps were being overrun by the Allies. One of them was Stalag XI B at Fallingbostel, which was liberated by Eighth Hussars on 16 April 1945. The commander of the Hussars' reconnaissance troops, Tim Pierson, recalls the events of that day.

Nosing its way cautiously along sandy tracks that skirted or went through the many pine-woods that were the main feature of this country, the leading section of Honeys started off slowly. Though there was no sign of any enemy, similar woods had produced quite a few the day before, and the leading tank occasionally raked the edges of the trees and suspicious hollows or clumps of grass to discourage any panzer-faust expert that might be waiting hopefully for us to get within range of his very useful weapon. The afternoon before, when he had been missed three times, Lieutenant Anstey, the leading tank commander, confessed to feeling like a goalkeeper in a football match, but this particular sunny morning there was, much to our relief, no sign of them.

A wide clearing confronted us, obviously man-made, cut at right angles through the woods, its sandy surface covered with tufts of grass, stretching dead straight to the right as far as we could see, and to the left turning out of sight through two small mountains of earth. This must be the autobahn, though scarcely what we had expected, the maps have given no hint of this rudimentary stage in its construction.

We turned left, came to the huge heaps of earth and halted while the leading commander, Corporal Spencer, dismounted to have a look at what lay round them out of sight. No more woods, but a flat open expanse of grass bounded, some thousand yards away, by a long uneven line of low buildings, out of which, further to our left, rose what looked like half a dozen tall warehouses. Binoculars showed that the main mass of low buildings lay behind a high wire fence – and people, at first we saw one or two moving about, then made out groups of a dozen, and finally realised that the thickening of the bottom half of the fence was in fact a solid mass of them. At this moment the leading tanks of 'C' Squadron, approaching on a different route, came up behind us, and without waiting to see any more we jumped into our tanks and shot out into the open. In high spirits we crossed the grass as quickly as the ground would allow, but as the distance between us and the fence grew less we noticed that the predominant colour of the mass that was streaming out of the gates towards us was grey, dark grey. At the same moment we saw a French flag – or was it Dutch – which in our excitement we had not noticed before, fluttering behind the main gate. Our hopes sank; these were not British prisoners, but another of the camps full of all nationalities of Europe that we had come across so many times before. Perhaps there were some British amongst them, then again perhaps there was no British camp at all, and the Germans have moved XI B as they had moved so many others out of the way of the armies advancing from east to west.

The leading tank came to a stop as the first of the breathless, shouting stream of humanity surrounded it, and Corporal Spencer, still clinging to a faint hope, lent down and yelled 'English soldaten?' He repeated himself in a moment's hush and then a hundred hands pointed to his left, and the clamour of the excited crowd broke out with increased intensity. As he looked round for someone out of whom he could get some sense it seemed that every nation was represented, women as well as men, the majority in civilian clothes, with but two things in common; they were all happy, and all indescribably dirty.

Noticing one persistent man who seemed to have a smattering of English he hauled him up on to the tank and asked which way. The fellow pointed, and as the tank moved slowly forward the crowd melted away in front. He glanced over his shoulder and noticed that he was still leading, the Cromwells of 'C' Squadron were as uncertain as he had been as to the route, but were now following hot on his heels. It was going to be a close thing who reached the Camp first.

Parallel to the fence, which he had now reached, ran a concrete road, and turning left along this, to the accompaniment of cheers from the waving smiling crowd of prisoners and DPs that thronged its entire length, he soon passed the tall warehouses that had first been noticed in the distance. The fellow on the turret pointed excitedly forward, but Corporal Spencer could see nothing, except a road, tree-lined on both sides, that met ours at right angles. We halted at the junction; to our left the road went under a stone bridge built to carry the autobahn, but with no autobahn to carry looking comically like a piece from a child's set of toy bricks. A quick glance to the right revealed nothing more than an empty road. But the guide was tugging at Spencer's sleeve and jabbering away – and following with our eyes the direction of his pointing arm we saw across the road through a gap between two trees a khaki-clad figure wearing a maroon coloured beret, clinging to a wire fence beyond and jumping up and down, obviously shouting his head off, though not a word reached us over the noise of the engines and earphones.

And then all the way down to the right we could see between the tree-trunks more figures racing along the wire. We'd got there, and before the Cromwells, which came up behind just as we moved off down the road giving the glad news over the air. Three or four hundred yards down the road was the main gate to the camp and as we approached the sound of welcome from the crowd that lined the wire and covered the roofs of the camp buildings grew to a roar that penetrated our earphones above the noise of our engines. Inside the main gates was an open space packed with British prisoners, and beyond another wire fence, what looked like an inner enclosure was black with figures. This was Stalag XI B.

Quite staggering was the contrast between this scene and that which we had seen at other camps containing prisoners of the Allied nations. Despite the enthusiasm of the men inside you could see at a glance that here was order and discipline. The remarkable RSM Lord, Grenadier Guards, of the 1st Airborne Division had already taken charge and was busily engaged in his office giving peace-time orders to his Orderly Warrant Officers. Camp MPs, each with a red armband, policed the gates, and as the crowd came out to meet us there was no ugly rush but a steady controlled stream that surrounded each tank as it stopped, a stream wearing the headgear of what looked like every unit in the Army. The Airborne beret predominated – men of D-Day, Arnhem, even the Rhine crossing who had only been inside for a few weeks – but you could pick out the hats, caps, berets and bonnets of a score of others. And under each one was such a look of happiness and thankfulness that made us as happy to be the cause of it. It was a quiet crowd that thronged round us; they had had their cheer, and now when the moment came for words, few words came. Mostly they were too moved to speak, men who could only grin broadly and clasp your hand as the tears ran down their cheeks. You couldn't speak yourself, only shake as many as possible of the hands that stretched towards you, and grin back, trying to take it all in, and marvel. For these men didn't look like prisoners; the battle-dresses were pressed and clean, here and there web belts and gaiters were scrubbed white and the brasses gleaming, they might have been off duty in a town at home instead of just walking out of prison wire behind which they had been for anything from five weeks to five years.

Memories of that scene leave a picture of a healthy and, if not overfed, certainly not starving crowd, of apologetic requests for cigarettes and one man turning green with his first puff, having given up the habit for his three years inside; of the creases in the tartan trews and the shining buttons on the jacket of a CSM[1] in the 51st Highland Division, who admitted having marched five or six hundred kilometres from East Prussia and who didn't look as if he had been more than five or six hundred yards from his own front door; of the Camp MO indignantly denying cases of typhus; of the German Commandant and a few of the camp guards standing apart in a small group watching unmoved the reversal of his role, and handing over his automatic with an offer to show us over the nearby storehouses; scraps of conversation 'I've been waiting five years for this day' – 'Three days ago we expected you', and in contrast, 'You've come too soon, my jacket's still wet', this from one who had washed his battledress specially for the occasion: and from one as impressed by our appearance (we hadn't washed or shaved for nearly forty-eight hours) as were we by theirs. 'You look like real soldiers'. There were several requests to see a Jeep, which we could not unfortunately produce at that moment; much signing of autographs on both sides and nearly always the first question 'What's your mob?' and finding several members of the Regiment in the camp, taken at Sidi Rezegh in 1941; and finally, on asking news of their erstwhile captors, being told that they were not long gone and were carrying panzerfausts. This was more serious, with all these fellows about, and on asking the police to clear the road we got the first startling proof of the state of the camp discipline. For at a word from a tall figure wearing the Airborne beret, RSM Lord, the Camp MPs went round, and in a very few

---

[1] Company Sergeant Major.

moments and without a murmur these scores of men, some of whom were tasting freedom for the first time in more than five years, made their way back behind that same barbed wire and netting that to them must have been a symbol of all that was hateful and depressing of this life.

We left as the vanguard of visitors was arriving, the VIPs and the not so VIPs, the Press and the frankly curious, all wishing to get a first-hand glimpse of the first large predominantly British camp to find itself in the path of the British Army of Liberation. And we left taking with us an impression that will never fade; of men whose courage and hope had been kept alive through long years of boredom and privation by their faith in their comrades and their country; and whose behaviour in their moment of triumph when faith had been rewarded was an example of the highest traditions of the Army to which they belonged.

And that might have been the end of our part in the proceedings of what was for all of us a great occasion. But later on that day we happened to pass that way again when things were more normal; erstwhile prisoners strolling about in groups, or sitting in the sun enjoying a smoke and waving contentedly at the passing traffic. But all was not quite normal, for as we came up to the main gates where we had received such a reception a few hours earlier, we saw a troop of armoured cars obliging some movie-cameramen by driving slowly past a group of wildly waving and shouting ex-prisoners; and for a brief moment, as we beheld the scene as spectators and not actors, we felt again all the emotions of that most memorable day.

As the Third Reich was relentlessly squeezed between the Western Allies and the Red Army the Germans retreated, taking their human booty with them. James Sims missed liberation by the Eighth Hussars.

Early in March '45 about a hundred of us were herded to one side after roll call and marched down to Fallingbostel Station and loaded into cattle trucks. We had no idea why this was done and where we were going, and this terrible uncertainty every day of a prisoner's life is something he has to adapt himself to or go mad. As it happened we were being taken just a few miles down the line to a small wayside station. British rocket-firing Typhoons had caught a train there which was a mixture of civilian wagons and petrol tankers. The train had been completely destroyed and the Germans were using a Tiger tank to pull the engine off the line. On a nearby ditch lay the charred remains of about 100 people piled on top of one another. We were forced to clear the bent and twisted track in order that German railwaymen could lay some new. It was raw, cold, wet weather and our only meal was half a pint of swede soup daily at noon. We had to walk down the line to get it and eat it walking back in order that we didn't waste any time getting the line cleared.

The guards for this job, which lasted about a week, gave us a hard time. They were old, sick and fed up both with the war and us. Some of them had lost sons on the Russian front and whole families in air raids and one day a chance remark by a Belgian prisoner sent one old guard berserk. He beat the Belgian unmercifully until restrained by one of the German NCOs. I was beaten up myself on this job by a Pole, one of the many who joined the German Army. I had tried to shelter for a minute or two from the rain and cold to eat my 'skilly'.

No sooner was this job completed than the German formed a larger working party of 300 men, they called these slave labour details *Kommandos*. Despite still open wounds and being by now down to 7 stone through a bad attack of dysentery, I was picked as one of the 'fit' ones to go. Many of us were not sorry to see the back of Stalag XI B for it was a truly terrible place. A former concentration camp with, so rumour had it, 30,000 dead buried in mass graves.

The *Kommando* offered fresh sights and sounds and perhaps the chance of escape. We were searched by SS men in the camp theatre before leaving and then marched out to Fallingbostel Station.

On the way we passed a party of British prisoners just captured and they gave us the heartening news that the Allies were across the Rhine.

This was about the first definite news we had received since capture and we cheered and even sang. Once again we climbed into cattle trucks and after an uneventful journey arrived at a fairly large station at dead of night. It was interesting to see the almost familiar activity but we were soon marched out of the goods yard and through the town. We shouted 'Wakey-Wakey' at intervals to annoy the townsfolk. We were billeted in a very large building which was a sort of barn. We slept on straw on either side of a cobbled road which led through the middle of it, and it wasn't long before we discovered that the straw was lousy. There was one cold-water tap for washing between 300 men and one latrine which was a large wooden box with carrying handles. This was situated in a small windowless room at the end of a passage and it was lit by one faint bulb. I never dream of Arnhem but I sometimes dream of that terrible toilet and the smell and general weird atmosphere, it was a real nightmare.

We discovered the town was Uelzen, a large market town and also an important rail junction. From 7 am to 7 pm we slogged to work in all weathers, shifting wreckage on a cup of acorn coffee for breakfast, half a pint of swede soup for lunch and one slice of black bread and a cup of rose-leaf tea every evening. Despite the work, the brutality and lack of food, it was better than the Stalag because there was so much to see. The activity of a large German town during wartime, the constant arrivals and departures of trains, the many strange uniforms, the German civilians, some friendly, some fearful and some who showed their hate by throwing stones at us.

One or two attempts to escape were made but these were very dicey affairs and the chances of success were practically nil. All the men who made such attempts were recaptured and rigorously dealt with and lucky not to be shot. There was no chance to hoard even a small food supply necessary for an attempt and most of us were so emaciated we found it all we could do to get through the day.

Every day the USAAF droned over in blocks of thirty or more Fortresses. Never was the complete supremacy of the Allies in the air so apparent.

There was ample evidence that Uelzen had already been bombed quite heavily especially near the station area and there was the fuselage of a B-17 lying on one of the goods platforms. Whilst actually at work, although constantly under German Army guards, we were directed by civilian foremen and we found them quite decent, also the engine-driver who would give us hot water if we wanted it.

The civilian in charge was only interested in keeping his beloved railway running and his son was glad to be back helping him, having been invalided out of the Luftwaffe. He had been shot down near Leningrad and his empty sleeve was a mute testament to the accuracy of Russian AA fire.

Within two weeks all the main lines through Uelzen were clear and one particular day there were no less than four military trains in all at the same time. Two were bound for the Eastern front, one carrying tanks and the other Dutch and Belgian SS volunteers. The SS jeered us and as the train moved off we pelted them with bricks.

Going west were two other trains, one composed of youths being hurried from the training camps to the front line. The other train was full of wounded from the Russian front. From my observations it would appear that Uelzen was some sort of clearing area for badly wounded, as one saw many soldiers and sailors who had amputations. What a target and not a bomber in sight, only late in the day a lone Mosquito circling three times before making off home.

Another dreary day started and we had a quick sluice, gulped down our acorn coffee and marched to the station where we drew our picks or shovels and were spread out along various sections of the track to work. At 9 am a lone Fortress appeared from the west which was very unusual and we dived for cover as it suddenly dropped a bomb. At least we thought it was a bomb because of the familiar whistle but when it hit the ground there was only a muffled report.

Its path was a trail of white smoke which hung like a beckoning finger over Uelzen Station. From the west came a dull drone of many aircraft engines and when we looked our hearts stood still, for the sun glinted on block upon block of

Flying Fortresses. As if a signal had been given we all started to put as much distance between us and the station as we could. SS, German Army guards, old people, prisoners, women and children, all heading for the open country as fast as possible. Some of us, because of old wounds and general poor health, found it difficult to maintain the pace and the guards were nearly frantic. We finally reached the shelter of some woods as the first bombs came down. Beside me an SS officer cringed in fear as a stick of bombs fell near and a German mother tried to soothe a frightened child. The ground shook as explosion after explosion rocked the whole junction and a huge pall of yellow dust arose and blotted out the sun. One B-17 was hit by AA fire and the pilot put it on automatic control so that it circled lower and lower. At each revolution a crew member 'hit the silk' and all the crew escaped, before it finally plunged to earth and exploded.

The raid continued all morning and we got no 'skilly' that day at all and over 100 prisoners were killed in the bombing, for at 15,000 feet one cannot distinguish friend from foe. We had to pick our way through a lunar landscape when the raid was over....

After the devastation of the town the Germans moved a Flaktrain in and it was commanded by a stocky, good-natured German warrant officer. Red-faced, with a chest full of decorations and a cigar always in his mouth, he was a complete realist.

When we asked him how long the war would last he replied, 'It all depends on the speed of your tanks.' He was not upset about the idea of losing in 1945 and said something I, for one, have never forgotten. 'Ten years from now you'll be paying me to help you keep out the Russians' – prophetic words.

Edgar Randolph was an Australian field ambulance private who had been taken prisoner in Crete. In January 1945 he began a march from his POW camp in Silesia which ended in Stalag XVIIIB B, 25 miles southeast of Vienna. This was a mixed camp of Russians, Hungarians, French and Eastern European partisans. The Red Army was closing on Vienna, and another 'march-out' was staged which gave Randolph a grandstand view of the Third Ukrainian Front's assault on the Austrian capital.

On April 4, 1945 we woke at 7 a.m. or so and moved out of the barracks into a queer hush. Not a sound anywhere – the Germans had taken off. One of the guard towers had been blitzed after sundown by aircraft – the guards up there were dead and the camp gate by the German barracks was unlocked. No-one wanted breakfast, so a dozen of us moved past the Russian compounds (they were sticking close to home) to the north fence. We had a good view for three to four miles over the plain, which was one to two miles wide. At 8 a.m. Russian infantry started across the plain to attack the river on the other side of it. It was an awesome sight and, even now, I get a slight 'sinking feeling' as I visualise it. They came into view round the end of the ridge against which the Stalag was built. It was very rough indeed for a couple of miles. They were in arrowhead formations of about twenty man platoons, fifty yards apart, and about the same behind one another. They just kept coming, line after line, and filled the whole plain, the further ones heading for the town of Bruch and the nearer gradually fanning out to cover the ground in front of us. There were literally thousands of men, who just moved at a walking pace inexorably on towards their objective. They made no attempt to take advantage of 'dead ground' – they just kept going ahead.

The Germans in the position on the river opened up and threw everything but the kitchen sink at them and we could see them dropping in ones, twos and threes as they advanced. As the men dropped, the arrowheads closed up and when they became too few for a formation they just joined on to the nearest one. They kept on like this till, after about twenty to thirty minutes, the leading lines were 200 yards or so from the trees along the river. The front formations then dropped down and opened their first fire on the Germans. The next lines went through them, dropped and opened fire, and so on. Then they reached the river and the sound of the battle intensified if anything. The troops to our front had, by this time, got half way across. They then took cover and moved on more slowly. Just then a German 30-cwt truck, with four or five men in the back, came roaring down the road from the ridge behind us (probably from an Observation Post on high ground). It rounded the Stalag and went flat-out down the straight towards the bridge, firing as it went, at the Russians, who had not yet reached the road. They got through okay and roared on to the bridge. As the truck raced on to the hump-back the bridge was blown (by their comrades), flinging the truck forty to fifty feet into the air, to drop apparently down into the river. Shortly afterwards two mounted Russians, each carrying a huge Red flag, galloped through the Stalag gates (opened wide for them by Russian P.O.W.s) and up the roads between the compounds, to show that at last we were FREE! ! (or were we?)

In mid-morning the next day we were ordered to parade with all our gear in our compound. At noon a Russian officer came and told us to move out and east. When asked what transport was available he just told us, in German, to use our feet – Budapest was 250 kilometres east – get going! 'Food?' we queried. The answer was sharp and clear: 'Do as we do, get it where you can.' So, out on the road, over the ridge eastward and on to Hungary – past Neusiedler See, a large lake on our left. On the flat land ahead we caught up with a column of refugees, mostly old men and women. As we closed with their rear, two Messerschmidt 109s ripped across on their way home and, as usual with M.E.s loosed off a burst each as they passed. Luckily, the planes crossed at right-angles – the place would have been a shambles had they flown along the road. There was one casualty. A very old woman received a leg wound. The civilians angrily refused our offer of help, so we pushed on ahead. Twelve hours and twenty-two kilometres from the start, we were allowed (at midnight) to camp in a burning and deserted village. Evidence everywhere of looting. A real mess. We moved on next day about five kilometres to Haltbahn, where we were deloused (how lovely to shower in *hot* water) and grouped for a day or so, then sent on our way toward Budapest. Myself and ten patients were left – a couple of sergeants (my friends in the last minute row in Stalag with the R.A.M.C. bod) and the rest privates.

It was then that we decided that when in Rome we'd do as the Romans i.e. the Russians. We were passing a farm and saw a wagon and horses standing in the yard, so just walked in and commandeered them. There was no-one about – so no bother. A little way on, another farm. We divided into two groups. One group went round the back, then signalled that some chooks were in a chicken-run. At the front, we knocked at the door and the farmer came out We asked him if he had any eggs or chickens. 'Keine Hühner' he said, so we gave the nod to the foraging party and a racket started among the chickens. The farmer rushed out shouting 'Meine Hühner, meine Hühner,' and started to put on a show. Our linguist told him he'd said he had none – but now we had two (with their necks wrung too!!) and if he made any more fuss we would call in the Russkies to arbitrate. Knowing very well this would mean the rest of his chooks would go off, he capitulated and we went on our way, rejoicing in the possession of 'chicken' – last tasted by me in Alexandria some four years earlier.

Being an ex-farmer, I was elected wagon boss and drove as long as we had the wagon and also looked after the horses. I got their shoes tightened up after a couple of days on the bitumen road and for nothing too, after casually mentioning the Russian Commandant of the village was interested in ex-P.O.W.s. My moral sense had taken a dive as far as the Austrians and Hungarians were concerned. Eighteen kilometres from Haltbahn we crossed the Hungarian border with Austria and on past Altenberg. We stopped a couple of nights in farm villages. The farmers in the villages worked land outside and had their stock, haysheds, etc. at the back of their houses. The farmers' wives cooked the chooks and provided bread for sandwiches for the next day's travel. We all slept around the big porcelain stoves they had in their kitchens. Very warm and comfy – if hard. They also gave us milk (bliss) to drink after I had helped with the milking in the evening. I had a mutual farming conference with half-a-dozen of the neighbours at each evening's stop. They had fair German and I had very little, but cockies everywhere can communicate regarding their methods and lifestyle.

Between Altenberg and Gÿor we came to a tributary of the Danube. The Germans had blown the bridge, so the Russians had made a long dirt causeway and then a pontoon bridge over it. It was about 100 yards wide and flowing fairly strongly. The pontoons were just wide enough to take a truck, so my party elected to walk over while I drove. So much for the patient's trust in their nurse! I negotiated the crossing safely and all rapidly clambered aboard again. Sixty or so kilometres past Gÿor the Russians had set up posts to pick up all ex-P.O.W.s and truck them by rail the remaining twenty kilometres to Budapest. It took two days to get there, engines being put on and taken off with great rapidity as different Russians came along and had different priorities (just like any other Army).

On April 13, 1945, we arrived at Budapest, four years to the day since we landed in Greece. It seemed a life-time. The Germans had blown all the bridges over the Danube (which, far from being blue, was a dirty greyish-green, no doubt due to the hundreds of miles of thawed snow-water pouring into it). The mangled remains of about five or six bridges were all we could see. The Russians had built a trestle bridge across to take rail traffic, so we crossed to the east bank and were marched out six kilometres, to camp behind barbed wire once more. Armed guards were at the entrance gate, and we found ourselves among hundreds of refugees of all nationalities. Next day a young Englishman and I decided we couldn't pass Budapest and not even see any of the city, so we found a small hole in the fence out of the view of the guards, enlarged it, slipped out and made our way by side streets into the city proper. Every building we saw had bullet and shell marks all over it – the result of the fierce six month house to house battle for the area – when the Russians finally took it. It was a back-to-normal Budapest we saw that day. The city was alive with people. There were Russian soldiers everywhere, but none took the slightest notice of us.

We came across a big posh hairdressing salon, so I decided to have my hair cut. Not having had the pleasure of this for well over a year I was *really* shaggy! My offsider said: 'What about money, we haven't a bean?' I replied that we were not 'Kriegies' (P.O.W.s) any more and we were 'on top', so who wanted money? We marched in. There were six chairs – five occupied – and women getting hair do's at the back. A barber came up, bowing and smiling (could it be my Aussie hat, again impressing people?). I intimated, in the Stalag German I spoke, what I required, sat down and he started. What a hair cut! He did everything but throw out the fleece. When he had finished I stood up and picked up my hat. He spoke in Hungarian. I shrugged. He spoke again and I said in German that I had no money. He screeched and out came the manager and three or four of his confreres. Just then my friend said: 'Try them with soap. You have a piece.' So I fished out a treasured cake of Yardleys Lavender, still in its paper ('twas from an early Red Cross Parcel and was saved for some future momentous occasion). I said in German: 'English soap?' The manager gingerly took it and smelt it. An ecstatic smile spread over his face. He held it round to all and sundry to savour this delightful scent, then said: '*Ja, Ja.*', handed it to my barber, spoke in Hungarian and the barber rang up the till, put the soap in and gave me ten pengos change! A graceful withdrawal by the troops and bang went the ten pengos on ten Hungarian cigarettes – black ones that made our heads swim and our eyes water.

On the way back to camp we came across a cinema with queues waiting to get in. We pushed in with some Russian soldiers (we were getting a bit uppish then) and selected two lovely seats in the centre of the theatre. They had a ticket of sorts on them, which we flicked away. All round were Russians, who greeted us most affably. They seemed to think we were 'Americanos' who were supplying them with the latest in trucks, guns and so forth. All the Russian we knew was 'Dobry dien' (good day) but this was enough for them and they appeared very matey. Just before the show was due to start there was a commotion near the door. A big Hungarian 'spiv', in ultra-expensive clothes and wearing three or four flash rings, was standing with his woman (also nearly dropping with the weight of jewellery) near the usher. He was gesticulating wildly and shouting at the top of his voice, pointing now and then to us. We ignored such low goings on, which seemed to make him madder. Then he and the usher started to work along our row toward us, still performing and, no doubt, with evil intent. All around us people were watching this free show, then, as the villains of the piece got close to us, about fifty of our brave and noble allies – the Russians – rose to their feet with a great shaking of fists and cries of '*Nyet, nyet.*' The enemy withdrew in disorder and took his girl friend back to the crowded rear seats, where I think they stood, and as peace and innocence prevailed, we settled down. And (would you believe it) were once again highly entertained by Spencer Tracy, Claudette Colbert and Co. in *Boom Town*, followed by Mickey Rooney in one of the Hardey Family series. We returned to camp through the front gate, uplifted by films and our adventures, much to the envy of the rest.

The long, hard British campaign to regain Burma, lost to the Japanese in humiliating circumstances early in 1942, was nearing its climax in February 1945. General William Slim, commander of the Fourteenth Army, had crossed the Chindwin in November 1944 and on 13 February took the Japanese by surprise, slipping IV Corps across the Irawaddy, 100 miles south of Mandalay. The aim was to seize the strategic railroad junction at Meiktila. By 28 February, Indian 17th Division and 255th Tank Brigade had broken into Meiktila. Slim takes up the story.

That day I had been on the Mandalay front where the break-out of 33 Corps, led by the 19th Division, was beginning in earnest, and I was anxious that it should be well timed with the 4 Corps operation. On my return in the evening to my headquarters at Monywa, I studied reports from Meiktila. These gave the impression that the attack was held up, and I decided I ought to go there. We could not risk a second Myitkyina.[1] I would fly in next morning. I was very angry when the R.A.F. informed me, with the utmost politeness but equal firmness, that they would not fly me to Meiktila – it was too dangerous! The airstrips had not yet been properly repaired, they were frequently under fire, and Japanese fighters were reported. It was no use pointing out that a whole brigade had been landed on these same airstrips, that they were being used every hour of daylight by unarmed R.A.F. and U.S.A.A.F. transports and that if they were being shot up that was not an R.A.F. responsibility as it was my soldiers who should protect them from ground attack. I was told that the R.A.F. would be delighted to fly any of my staff anywhere at any time, but not me, not to Meiktila, not now. This idea of my value was flattering, but extremely annoying. I was about to have it out with Vincent, when luckily, for the sake of our friendship which I valued, I had another idea.

---

[1] A town in northern Burma, close to the Yunan border, which was the objective of a combined British, Chinese and American offensive in the summer of 1944; it took much longer to capture than expected.

There had just arrived at my headquarters a visiting American general with his own Mitchell bomber. I asked him if he would like to come with me and see something of the Meiktila battle. As I hoped, with characteristic American generosity, he suggested we made the trip in his aircraft. I gratefully accepted and early on the morning of the 1st March we set out – I feeling rather like a schoolboy who had dodged his masters and was playing truant for the day. We flew to 4 Corps Headquarters on the river bank opposite Pagan, picked up Messervy,[2] and went on to one of the airstrips now in operation near Thabutkon. It was quite peaceful, though there was a little popping not far away and a few dead Japanese on the edge of the field. We were offered a second breakfast, and I ate my first Japanese-provided meal – biscuits and tinned food from a captured store. It was not very good. I gained more mental gratification from it than nourishment. Punch Cowan had sent a couple of jeeps to meet us, and we bounced merrily along the road to his battle headquarters just outside Meiktila. He soon put Messervy, me, and our American friend in the picture of the fight, which judging by the noise, smoke, and constant zooming of aircraft diving on their targets, was no skirmish. Indeed, this day, the 1st March, saw the bitterest fighting of the battle. Cowan's[3] troops were slowly biting into Kasuya's defences, tough though they were. 63 Brigade had begun an attack on Meiktila from the west, and, in spite of restricted approaches, were into the outskirts of the town. 48 Brigade with some tanks had resumed their assault on Meiktila East from the north, and were making progress against the most resolute opposition. 255 Tank

---

[2] General Sir Frank Messervy, commander of IV Corps.
[3] Major-General David 'Punch' Cowan, commander of Indian 17th Division.

Brigade and its infantry had seized a steep, heavily defended hill, which rose abruptly to five hundred feet on the edge of the South Lake, near the south-east corner of Meiktila, and gave observation over the whole area. Here bitter fighting was going on, as tanks and infantry clawed into the defences of the town itself.

Cowan's conduct of this difficult and divided battle was impressive. With his main attention fixed on the various assaulting brigades, he had at frequent intervals to glance over his shoulder as ground and air reports of Japanese movements in the surrounding country were brought to him. He had, too, all the anxieties of an air supply line, which rested on precariously held landing strips, at a time when ammunition and petrol expenditure was at its highest. Not least, he was very short of sleep and remained so for several days. Yet throughout he was alert to every change in the situation on any sector, and swung his air and artillery support to meet and take advantage of it. His firm grip on his own formations and on the enemy never faltered. To watch a highly skilled, experienced, and resolute commander controlling a hard-fought battle is to see, not only a man triumphing over the highest mental and physical stresses, but an artist producing his effects in the most complicated and difficult of all the arts. I thought as I watched what very good divisional commanders I had.

After speaking on the 'blower' to a brigade commander and listening in on the tank net – always an interesting and often a worthwhile thing to do in an action – I left Cowan conducting his grim orchestra. Assured that the battle was in competent hands at the top, I thought I would go a little closer and see how it was being handled lower down. I chose 48 Brigade as, at the moment, they seemed to be cracking a particularly tough nut. We went by jeep round the north of the town and then moved forward on foot somewhat more cautiously. We had a word with various subordinate commanders on the way; all very busy with their own little battles and all in great heart. One of them told us the best place from which to see anything was a massive pagoda that crowned a near-by rise. We reached it along a path screened from the enemy by bushes, and crouching below the surrounding wall, crossed a wide terrace, where already in occupation were some Indian signallers and observation parties. Peering cautiously over the wall, we found on our right the end of the North Lake, placid and unruffled. To our left front, about a thousand yards away, the main road entered Meiktila between close-built houses, now crumbling in the dust, smoke, and flame of a bombardment. We were, I knew, about to assault here, but it was the scene immediately below and in front of us which gripped the attention.

The southern shore of the lake, for nearly a mile, ran roughly parallel to the northern edge of the town. Between them was a strip about half a mile wide, of rough, undulating country, cut up by ditches and banks, with here and there clumps of trees and bushes. Three hundred yards from us, scattered along water cuts, peering round mounds, and lying behind bushes, were twenty or thirty Gurkhas, all very close to the ground and evidently, from the spurts around them, under fairly heavy fire. Well to the left of these Gurkhas and a little farther forward, there was a small spinney. From its edge more Gurkhas were firing Bren-gun bursts. A single Sherman tank, in a scrub-topped hollow, lay between us and the spinney, concealed from the enemy but visible to us. In the intervals of firing, we could hear its engine muttering and grumbling. The dispositions of our forces, two platoons and a tank, were plain enough to us, but I could see no enemy.

Then the tank revved up its engine to a stuttering roar, edged forward a few yards, fired a couple of shots in quick succession, and discreetly withdrew into cover again. I watched the strike of the shot. Through my glasses I could see, about five hundred yards away, three low grassy hummocks. Innocent enough they looked, and little different from half a dozen others. Yet straining my eyes I spotted a dark loophole in one, around which hung the misty smoke of a hot machine-gun; I could hear the *knock-knock-knock*, slower than our own, of its firing. Searching carefully, I picked up loopholes in the other mounds. Here were three typical Japanese bunkers, impervious to any but the heaviest shells, sited for all-round defence, and bristling with automatics – tough nuts indeed. The tank intervened again. Without shifting position it lobbed two or three grenades and a white screen of smoke drifted across the front of the bunkers. One of the Gurkhas below us sprang to his feet, waved an arm, and the whole party, crouching as they went, ran forward. When the smoke blew clear a minute or two later, they were all down under cover again, but a hundred yards nearer those bunkers. A few small shells burst in the water at the lake's edge. Whether they were meant for the tank or the Gurkhas, they got neither, and the enemy gunners made no further contribution.

When I looked for it again, the tank had disappeared, but a smoke-screen, this time, I think, from infantry mortars, blinded the bunkers again. The Gurkhas scrambled forward, dodging and twisting over the rough ground, until some of them must have been hardly thirty yards from the enemy. Somewhere behind the spinney, the tank was slowly and methodically firing solid shot at the loopholes. Spurts of dust and debris leapt up at every impact.

As the fight drew to its climax, we moved out of the pagoda enclosure to a spot a little forward and to the right where, from behind a thick cactus hedge, we had a clearer view. The tank reappeared round the spinney's flank and advanced still shooting. Gradually it worked round to the rear of the bunkers, and suddenly we were in the line of its fire with overs ricochetting and plunging straight at us.

One army commander, one corps commander, an American general, and several less distinguished individuals adopted the prone position with remarkable unanimity. The only casualty was an unfortunate American airman of our crew, who had hitch-hiked with us to see the fun. As the metal whistled over his head he flung himself for cover into the cactus hedge. He was already stripped to the waist and he emerged a blood-stained pin cushion. However, he took his misfortune very well and submitted to what must have been a painful plucking with fortitude.

After this little excitement, the tank having, to our relief, moved again to a flank, we watched the final stages of the action. The fire of Brens and rifles swelled in volume; the tank's gun thudded away. Suddenly three Gurkhas sprang up simultaneously and dashed forward. One fell, but the other two covered the few yards to the bunkers and thrust Tommy-guns through loopholes. Behind them surged an uneven line of their comrades; another broke from the spinney, bayonets glinting. They swarmed around the bunkers and for a moment all firing ceased. Then from behind one of the hummocks, appeared a ragged group of half a dozen khaki-clad figures, running for safety. They were led, I noticed, by a man exceptionally tall for a Japanese. Twenty Gurkha rifles came up and crashed a volley. Alas for Gurkha marksmanship! Not a Japanese fell; zigzagging, they ran on. But in a few seconds, as the Gurkhas fired again, they were all down, the last to fall being the tall man. The tank lumbered up, dipped its gun and, with perhaps unnecessary emphasis, finished him off. Within ten minutes, having made sure no Japanese remained alive in the bunkers, the two platoons of Gurkhas and their Indian-manned tank moved on to their next assignment which would not be far away. A rear party appeared, attended to their own casualties, and dragged out the enemy bodies to search them for papers and identifications. It was all very business-like.

If I have given more space to this one incident, that was being repeated in twenty places in the battle, than I have to much more important actions, I plead some indulgence. It was the closest I had been to real fighting since I had been an army commander, and it was one of the neatest, most workmanlike bits of infantry and armoured minor tactics I had ever seen. There is a third reason. The men who carried it out were from a Gurkha regiment of which I have the honour to be Colonel.

Back at Cowan's headquarters, we followed the general progress of the assault on Meiktila. It had not everywhere gone as smoothly as the fight we had watched. The enemy had not wasted the few days allowed him for preparation. Every house was a strong-point, every water channel had its concealed bunkers, every heap of rubble its hidden machine-gun or anti-tank gun. Snipers lurked in every ruin. It was costly fighting, and jeep ambulances shuttled between the battle and the airstrips carrying the wounded to quick and merciful evacuation. Progress if slow was, however, steady.

Throughout the 1st March and the following night, there was hand-to-hand fighting as savage as any yet experienced in a theatre where close combat was the rule rather than the exception. By evening, when we left for Monywa, our troops were well into the town, but the Japanese resistance showed no signs of breaking. They died where they fought, and as darkness fell, even in the sectors we had gained, survivors emerged from cellars and holes to renew the battle.

On the 2nd March in Meiktila East, 48 Brigade with artillery, tank, and air support slowly forced the enemy from house to house, until they were penned in the southern end of the town with their backs to the South Lake. 63 Brigade, in two strong attacks, cleared the whole of Meiktila West with great loss to the enemy. During the 3rd, after intense fighting, Meiktila East was finally cleared by a series of converging attacks. Enemy 75-mm guns engaged our tanks and infantry at point-blank range, but were gradually eliminated, one by one, until the last fifty Japanese jumped into the lake and were drowned or killed. The slaughter had been great. In one small area of the town alone, which measured only two hundred by one hundred yards, eight hundred and seventy-six Japanese bodies were collected. Meiktila was a shambles, but, by six o'clock on the evening of the 3rd, it was ours.

On 19 February 1945 two divisions of the US Marine Corps stormed ashore on the small island of Iwo Jima, only two-and-a-half hours' flying time from Japan, which was defended by 22,000 Japanese troops. Organized resistance ended on 16 March, at the cost of 6,891 Americans killed and 18,700 wounded. Only 212 of the Japanese garrison chose to surrender. The fighting on Iwo Jima produced one of the imperishable images of the war, the raising of the flag on the island's dominating physical feature, Mount Suribachi. T. Grady Gallant, a sergeant in the 4th Marines who took part in the assault on Iwo Jima, provides the background to the picture.

After breakfast the next morning, James Forrestal, Secretary of the Navy, who had been aboard a warship off Iwo Jima since D-day, climbed into a landing craft and headed for the island to make an on-the-spot inspection of the beach in the vicinity of Mount Suribachi before his departure for the United States by way of Guam late that same day.

As he was being transported to Red Beach, where he would inspect captured Japanese pillboxes and watch Marine engineers at work, Secretary Forrestal witnessed from his landing craft the raising of the American flag on the heights of Mount Suribachi.

The night before, February 22, 1945, the Fifth Marine Division had decided to send a patrol up the north face of the volcano. Enemy defenses at the base of the mountain in this area had been destroyed, and the entrance to the high ground stood ajar like a garden gate. And though the Japanese were still holed up in mountainside caves – and in prepared defense positions on the west side of Suribachi – it was urgent that a route to the top be discovered and the high ground seized.

When daylight came on February 23, a patrol of forty men began the historic climb and moved rapidly to the highest point of Mount Suribachi, where they raised a small flag tied to a stick at 10:37 A.M.

The *Special Action Report of the Fifth Marine Division* describes the achievement in icy professional language:

It was decided to send a patrol up the north face of Suribachi on the following morning. By choosing its route, a patrol from 'E' Company was able to climb to the lip of the crater without the use of special scaling equipment. By 1035, D/4, this patrol was on the lip of the crater. Upon signal from the patrol the remainder of 'E' Company climbed up to the top of Suribachi. No enemy fire was received during this movement as the bulk of the remaining Japanese in that area were located in cave positions near the base of the volcano on the west coast. At 1037 our Colors were hoisted atop Suribachi. By 1200 the mountain was completely surrounded and mopping up operations were commenced.

At that time CT-28 reported that over 1000 enemy installations of all types had been counted. The reduction of the remaining positions and the sealing off of caves in the Suribachi area continued throughout the day. CT-28 was maintained in the Suribachi area until D/10 mopping up and picking off Japs who succeeded in digging themselves out of caves during darkness.[1]

The *Special Action Report Iwo Jima Campaign* (G-3) *V Amphibious Corps Landing Force* is even more terse:

On the Southern front, RCT 28 continued the attack. A patrol of 40 men scaled the slopes and reached the highest point on the lip of MT SURIBACHI, where at 1037 they

---

[1] The report uses several abbreviations that may not be clear to the general reader: D/4 means D-day plus 4 days, or February 23, 1945; 1035 is 10:35 a.m.; 1037 is 10:37 a.m. and 1200 is Noon. CT-28 is Regimental Combat Team 28, Fifth Marine Division. D/10 is D-day plus 10 days, or March 1, 1945.

hoisted the American Colors. The encirclement of MT SURIBACHI was completed at 1200, though many of the enemy remained in the extensive cave system of the mountain.

Later in the day, the small flag used by the patrol in the initial raising of the colors was taken down and replaced by a larger flag attached to a taller and more sturdy pole. It was the erection of this flag that produced the inspiring photograph of the flag raising on Mount Suribachi.

One of the treasures of history – for without this photograph the triumph of Iwo Jima, which was to come twenty-two days later, would not have been so well understood by Americans – the picture was one of several made by Joe Rosenthal of the Associated Press. The photograph was awarded the 1945 Pulitzer Prize for News Photography, and became a symbol of the American fighting spirit not only in the Pacific, but throughout the world. But more important, it caught the essence, the primitive nature of the Iwo Jima struggle, and was a fitting tribute to the thousands of Marines who made such great sacrifices on that battlefield.

Though the first and smaller flag was seen by some Marines on the lowlands – and the word of the conquest was passed quickly from mouth to mouth on the front lines – it was not visible to the majority. The flag was taken down before many Marines knew of its presence. When they looked for it, after having been told a flag had been raised, it was gone.

When the larger flag went up, it was easily seen from the isthmus. Its presence was a great boost to morale in a military situation which was still extremely grim. Contrary to the belief of most Americans that the flag raising on Mount Suribachi marked the end of the struggle, the appearance of the colors on the heights underlined the continued intensification of the conflict on the island.

At the moment the flag was raised, Marines on the eastern front were just making contact with the edge of the major Japanese defense line that barred the important half of the island – the half that contained all the towns, miserable as they were, the majority of the Japanese troops, and one of the most complex combinations of broken terrain and defensive strength to be encountered in modern war.

But the fall of the mountain allowed full attention to be turned to the reduction of these enemy defenses. The Fifth Marine Division moved northward along the west coast and inland, the Third Marine Division, landing the day after the flag went up, hit the center of the line, and the Fourth Marine Division began to grind itself to pieces against the northeastern and eastern wall.

The direction of the battle was now toward the far end of Iwo Jima: the north, northeast, and east, while in the south Regimental Combat Team 28 continued the slow mopping up process in order to secure the Marine rear against infiltration, night raids, and counterattacks by groups of bypassed Japanese.

Suribachi's fall did not halt the heavy artillery and mortar fire on the beaches and across the isthmus, or the hum of small-arms fire in the air of the lowlands. There was no noticeable decrease in the intensity of battle, or was there any slackening in the work at the Marine cemeteries, or in the operating rooms of the field hospitals – or in the foxholes, gunpits, and tanks of the line.

The flag waved above it all, rippled above the battlefield and snapped in the breeze. Marines crawled on dirty bellies far below, pushed against crumbling, yellow rock, moved against the Japanese – and against time.

They advanced against the Japanese in the faith that the sacrifice their country demanded of them was worth just as much at that moment, and in that foul place, as it ever had been anytime in American history – and they died in the belief that it was.

Yamauchi Takeo was a Japanese soldier who surrendered on New Guinea in August 1945. Here he recalls some of the horrors of that campaign.

After the main force had passed over the gorge, they blew up the suspension bridge. The thousands who trailed behind were left to die. We were at the end of the line. Soldiers who had struggled along before us littered the sides of the trail. It was a dreadful sight. Some were already skeletons – it was so hot that they soon rotted – or their bodies were swollen and purple. What little they wore was removed by those who had less. Wearable boots were instantly taken, so most of the dead lay bare-foot. The worms crawling over the more recently dead gave them a silver sheen. The whole mountain range was wreathed in the stench of death. That was what it was like.

Our own forces blew up the bridge before we could cross it! We marched for another month because we were one day late. We'd already been marching for nearly two months by then, ever since the many battles at Finschhafen, and we'd almost gotten through the mountains to the coast. It was about the tenth day of February 1944. Behind me there were more thousands, completely dispersed, scattered. Many had gone mad. I couldn't get over the fact that, delirious as they were, they still continued to march in the same direction. Nobody, no matter how insane, walked the wrong way. The dead bodies became road markers. They beckoned to us: 'This is the way. Just follow us corpses and you'll get there.' That was true until we came to the gorge where the bridge had been. Now, we had to find the way for ourselves.

New Guinea was green, full of greenness, all year long. If it had been any other colour, you couldn't have stood it. The green provided some relief, but it was a desert of green. The advance units had quickly eaten all available food. The rest of the column had to survive on what little was left after they'd passed. The soldiers who fell by the side of the mountain trail increased rapidly, so mixed together that you ceased to be able to distinguish their units. When we left Finschhafen, we had already passed the limits of our energy, and yet we had to crawl along the very tops of ridges and cross mountain ranges. It was a death march for us.

It had rained for more than half a year straight. Our guns rusted. Iron just rotted away. Wounds wouldn't heal. Marching in the rain was horrible. Drops fell from my cap into my mouth mixing with my sweat. You slipped and fell, got up, went sprawling, stood up, like an army of marching mud dolls. It went on without end, just trudging through the muddy water, following the legs of somebody in front of you.

As you marched, you lost comrades from your unit. Usually, you just flopped down by the road, rested together, then moved on. But sometimes the one you were with would say, 'I'll just rest a little longer.' You'd lose the will to stand up if you sat too long. 'Let's get going. Come on!' I said to one. He was sitting at the edge of a cliff. He only lifted his glasses and wiped his face. I never saw him again.

The worst was the jungle at night. Even if you attached a white cloth to your pack, it couldn't be seen. You'd have to follow the person in front of you by pushing lightly up against his pack. You had to keep your mind focused only on that. Sometimes you'd move swiftly. At other times you slowed to nothing at all. Then you'd shout, 'Get going!' and find yourself pushing against a tree. If you tried to rush, you'd stumble, as if your feet were grabbed or clutched at by something. You weren't supposed to call out. The enemy might hear. Each step, you had no way of knowing if there was going to be ground under foot when it next came down.

At times the rain was heavy in the mountains, not like in Japan. It was more like a waterfall. You'd have to cover your nose or it would choke you. A valley stream could turn into a big river instantly. If you got caught there washing your face, away you went. People could die of drowning while crossing the mountains. I climbed mountains four thousand meters high. Dark black clouds swirled around us. I had the feeling the heavens were glowering down at me. Beyond the clouds, you could see stars even in daylight. It was like being in the eye of a typhoon, suddenly seeing those stars shining behind the dark clouds. It was a weird experience.

For a time after the bridge was blown up, military police, the Kempei, were stationed here and there along the trail, ostensibly to protect the security of villages along the way, and to direct stragglers. Soldiers often grumbled about them. One day I encountered a Kempei. He demanded that I salute him, even though he was a noncom. 'I'm a sergeant too,' I insisted, 'even though I don't have any stripes.' 'You must salute the Kempei forces!' was his only response. We didn't even salute officers in those conditions. 'You're alone?' he asked. I replied that I had a companion, but he was a little behind. 'Why didn't you kill him, then?' he demanded. 'You can't get out of these mountains if you wait for stragglers. It's all right to kill them. One or two of you doesn't mean anything.' He looked two or three years younger than me. The dark shadow of the Kempei disappeared from the mountains about half a month after the bridge went down.

In the army, anyone over thirty was an old man. Twenty-six or twenty-seven, that was your peak. The young soldiers, serving for the first time, didn't know how to pace themselves and died quickly, though there were many strong men, fishermen and farmers, among them. If you were older, you knew what you could do and what you couldn't. I was in what was called the regimental 'labor company,' but it was really a special unit organized for all kinds of difficult missions. We blew up enemy tanks with saucer-shaped mines. We'd approach moving tanks from their blind side and attach the charge directly to their hull. We'd trap them in tank pits. We were sometimes called the Special Attack Raiders. The heaviest casualties were in our labor unit. We were like a small engineering unit, building bridges and destroying enemy strongpoints, but we took pride in being like tiger cubs, the most valuable unit in the division. Our primary weapon was a flame-thrower.

One thing that surprised me when I went into the military was that the majority of the long-service soldiers had only gotten through elementary school. Many of the conscripts were well educated, many beyond middle school. You could recognize conscripts by their glasses. Regular soldiers often said, 'draftees have glib tongues, but are useless in action.' When I was a corporal, I once got into a fistfight with a sergeant for saying that there wasn't any difference between a regular soldier and a conscript when both are on the same battlefield risking their lives.

I turned down the chance to become an officer candidate. When they told me I had permission to apply, I said 'I don't like the army. If I liked the military I'd have gone to the military academy in the first place.' They beat me mercilessly for my impudence that time, I can tell you. You see, I didn't want to kill subordinates with my orders. I could watch out for myself, but I didn't want to determine what others should do. Eventually I reached the rank of sergeant, but it didn't mean much in New Guinea Nobody ever seemed to rank below me, since reinforcements never reached us. I was always near the bottom.

I heard later that our high command considered the battle at Finschhafen a turning point of the Pacific War. It seems they had an expectation that a victory there could have reversed the tide of war. In fact, we did rout the enemy easily – at first. I was amazed how weak the Australian soldiers seemed. Their infantrymen ran before us when we attacked. The next day, though, their artillery and airplanes bombarded us from all sides. Only when we were totally exhausted did their infantry return to mop up at their leisure. Our side had no fighting capability left.

The bigger the scale of the battle, the less we riflemen had to do with it. Cannons and machine guns dominated then. As you can imagine in infantry battles, machine guns were the stars. Five machine guns blaze away, spewing out six hundred rounds a minute. The bullets just come '*Ba-ba-ba-ba, dah-dah-dah-dah!*' You want to dig into the earth even just five or ten centimeters more. You can't raise your head. You know how well they know your position by the height of their fire. When the bullets come low you can't move. Your back is heated by the bullets. You can't fire your single-shot, bolt-action Type-38 infantry rifle. You'd feel too absurd. It's like a kind of symphony coming from both sides. You'd get intoxicated by it. An hour of firing like that and my whole way of looking at the world around me was different. I was transformed, along with Nature itself.

I came to feel the Australian military was very strong indeed. They didn't want to have infantry battles. They wanted to leave the fighting to mechanized power. The Japanese military only had infantry. Our artillery had almost no ammunition. If we fired even one shell, hundreds came back at us. 'Please don't fire at them,' we'd pray to our guns from our trenches. I had a sense then that one day war would be fought without humans. Just airplanes and artillery. War in which human beings actually shot at each other, where we could see each other's faces, that was over. What were we infantrymen there for? Only, it often seemed to me, to increase the number of victims.

The 'enemy'? I often wondered what that meant. We didn't hate the enemy. We seemed to fight them only because they showed up. I sometimes wondered why either side was there. It was like a plot by both sides to fight in this place. In China, at least, when our soldiers were killed I sensed they had been killed by a real enemy. There, two sides, similarly armed, grappled fiercely with each other, man-to-man.

In New Guinea, we didn't know what was killing us. Who killed that one? Was it death from insanity? A suicide? A mercy killing? Maybe he just couldn't endure the pain of living. I remember that war as mainly one of suicides and mercy killings. Once, as I was trudging along, a soldier by the road caught my eye. He'd lost his voice. He just pointed at my rifle and with a bent finger signaled that he wanted me to pull the trigger. I couldn't. My mind was still mired in some kind of lukewarm sentimentalism. I knew he had no hope, but I couldn't shoot him. Another time, I saw a man kill his younger brother. Love is such a cruel thing. That's what I felt then. The younger brother had gone insane, although he was the physically stronger of the two. They were in different units, and met by chance in a shack in the mountains. The younger brother was cackling madly when we came upon him. The elder one slapped him across the face and shook him, calling out his name. He just kept laughing. Finally, the elder brother shot him dead. I didn't even raise my voice. The brother and I dug a grave for him.

I knew an army doctor, about thirty-five years old, who volunteered to shoot all those who knew they couldn't survive. This I consider 'sacred murder.' Often subordinates asked their superiors to kill them when the main force was about to depart. If you were left behind, that was the end. A man who had the strength left to pull the pin could always blow himself up, so everyone tried to keep one hand grenade until the last moment. Even those who tossed away their rifles never threw away their last grenade.

My three years in New Guinea were a succession of such horrors. Everything was beyond my control. Planes roared directly overhead. We could smell their thirst for blood. No matter how many flew over, you knew the one that was after you. Once, I was just aiming my rifle when an enemy bullet actually got stuck in my barrel. If it had been a touch off line, the umpire's call would have been 'You're out!' A bullet went through a man's helmet, spun around inside and exited through the same hole. Around his head was inscribed a bald line where the bullet had gone. How can you explain something like that? You move your body just a little and immediately the place where you've been lying is hit directly. Luck? Accident? That just won't do it. I was forced to learn the limits of human intelligence. Things you'd think would logically be best for you often proved to be the worst. 'If you're going to die anyway, die gloriously,' I'd think. I often volunteered for special missions. Yet again and again I'd come back and find it was the main unit that had been wiped out while I was off on a dangerous assignment. I felt something was controlling us.

I never really killed anyone directly. I shot my rifle, so I might have hit somebody, but I never ran anyone through with my bayonet. In China, soldiers were forced to practice on prisoners, slashing and stabbing, as soon as they arrived for training. 'Stab him!' they'd order, indicating an unresisting prisoner. I didn't move. I just stood there. The platoon leader became enraged, but I just looked away, ignoring the order. I was beaten. I was the only one who didn't do it. The platoon leader showed them how, with vigor. 'This is how you stab a person!' he said. He hit the man's skull and knocked him into a pit. 'Now stab him!' They all rushed over and did it. I'm not saying I determined it good or bad through reason. I just couldn't take the thought of how it would feel, running a man through with my bayonet.

The New Guineans seemed immaculate. To get help from the natives in the mountains was the only means left to us. I was so happy to see that they accepted words without twisting them all around. We could communicate directly. When I first caught a glimpse of black people, I thought we'd never be able to communicate, but one of them spoke Pidgin English. That saved me. Because of Pidgin, I was not afraid. I understood

288

German, French, and English, but I was amazed how useful a few simple words could be. I was impressed by how beautiful human beings could be, too. An old native once left a mixture of roots and water and a little salt by my head when I'd collapsed flat on my back in the trail. And a village headman went himself to tell other Japanese two kilometers away that I had fallen ill, even though his people thought I was already dead.

I think the natives and the Japanese got along well. They'd dance in a circle when the moon was full. Those of us who were from farming or fishing villages would casually join in and dance, too, as if they were dancing in the Japanese countryside. They'd borrow drums and do it pretty well. The natives seemed really pleased by this. The whites never approached them; they merely frightened them with their guns. With the Japanese, they shared living. Sometimes I wonder why they cooperated with an army that was disintegrating. The Australians would win them over with goods, things like canned corned beef. We never had anything to return to them. All we could say was, 'Thank you.' Yet their kindness lasted to the very end of the war. Some village chiefs were executed after the war because they provided us with food. They were accused of 'hostile action' by the Allies. The enemy organized them to work as irregular guerrillas against us. Indeed, the thing I most regret about New Guinea is the incidents I learned of later where New Guineans were killed by Japanese. It makes me despondent to think that we could have killed people like that chief who saved me.

In the world we lived in on New Guinea, you had no use for the language or knowledge you had accumulated before you went there. Literature, which I'd studied at Keijō Imperial

University, meant nothing. I sensed that the extremes of existence could be reduced to the human stomach. Lack of protein, in particular, fostered a kind of madness in us. We ate anything. Flying insects, worms in rotten palm trees. We fought over the distribution of those worms. If you managed to knock down a lizard with a stick, you'd pop it into your mouth while its tail was still wriggling. Yet, under these conditions, a soldier offered me his final rice and a soldier I met for the first time gave me half of a taro root he'd dug up.

We had other fears on New Guinea. Near the end we were told not to go out alone to get water, even in daytime. We could trust the men we knew, but there were rumors that you could never be sure what would happen if another of our own soldiers came upon you. We took precautions against attack. I once saw a soldier's body with the thigh flesh gouged out, lying by the path. The stories I heard made me shiver and left me chilled to the bone. Not all the men in New Guinea were cannibals, but it wasn't just once or twice. I saw this kind of thing. One time, when we were rushing along a mountain trail, we were stopped by four or five soldiers from another unit. They told us they had meat from a big snake that they were willing to share with us. Their almost sneering faces unnerved me. Maybe we were thinking too much, but my companion and I didn't stop. 'Thank you, maybe next time,' we said, and left. I knew that if it were really snake, they'd never have shared it. They were trying to pull us in to share their guilt. We never talked about it afterwards, but when we reached the coast other soldiers warned us that there were demons in the jungle. Maybe this was just wild fear, but I can still visualize it clearly.

I didn't really have a future while I was trudging along in those mountains. There was no tomorrow, no next day. All I could think about was falling asleep, or following pleasant memories back into the past. Still, when a staff officer showed up, gathered maybe fifteen of us together, and told us to prepare for our final battle and issued us our final rations, I felt that the future had been foreclosed. I was now completely uncoupled from anything to come, in a closed universe. I thought if I could just drag myself a few steps further, I might actually grasp the situation a little better, know where I was, but I couldn't even climb the slightest incline without crawling on my hands and knees. Near the end, everything was called *gyokusai*. In the end, I never did it, but whole regiments were used up in those attacks, protecting us as we trudged through the mountains on our fighting withdrawal. This can be interpreted as a comradeship of which we were unaware.

Human beings can be divided into two extremes. I collapsed from fever many times. Sometimes a soldier who happened to pass by carried me on his back to the next village. One time a soldier I didn't know told me he had two *gō*, just a handful, of rice in his pack. 'It's no good to me now,' he said. 'You take it.' Some people are like that. They become extraordinarily lucid in the face of death. I was deeply moved, in a sense, but I couldn't say, 'All right, I'll take it.' After all, each of us kept that two *gō* of rice for the time of our own death, so we could say, 'Now I'll eat my last meal.'

Another time, when we were climbing from Kali into the mountains, I was hailed by a soldier unable to move. He asked me to cook some rice porridge for him with the rice in his mess kit. I got water but asked one of our men to make it for him, since I was such a bad cook. By the time the rice was ready, darkness had descended on the jungle. At last somebody guided me back to where he was. 'Your porridge is ready!' I said as I shook him by the shoulder. He simply fell over. Already dead. I wonder what on earth he must have been thinking while that rice porridge was cooking. Maybe 'That guy ran away with my last rice!' I did my best and it was no good. I felt wretched. The soldier who'd guided me there opened the dead man's mouth and put some of the porridge in. All he kept muttering was 'What a pity, what a pity.' I saw the two extremes of humanity. I don't know what divides men that way. There's something murky and filthy in human beings. If you've seen this, you might find yourself at one or the other of the poles.

One day natives brought in a soldier on a stretcher. I couldn't tell who he was at first, but he was from our special unit. He told us his name. We'd last seen him when we were going over the ridge line more than a year earlier. On the very day they carried him in, he was shot at a deserter. The man who shot him still regrets doing it. But if you were ordered to do it, you had to. If they had gone strictly by rank, it would have been my job. I was officer of the day, so in one way, I'm the one most responsible, but the warrant officer didn't pick me. I'm grateful for that and I feel guilt and responsibility toward Yoshimura, my friend, who had to shoot him. 'Forgive me, Nagayama,' Yoshimura said twice in Osaka dialect, and then shot him. This took place after the end of the war, but just before we became prisoners.

I understand there were many such deaths by execution. For example, you'd get an order to 'take the message and report back in three days no matter how difficult.' You might have to travel a distance as far as from Osaka to Kobe in that time. But malaria was like a time bomb. If it went off you just collapsed and couldn't move. That happened to me. So a week later, you return and you're charged as a deserter. Even many officers were ordered to kill themselves for the crime of desertion. They'd go out on scouting missions, find themselves unable to get back in time, and so leave death poems behind. What a bitter feeling they must have had before being shot. The military was a place where only results were weighed, not reasons.

We didn't know anything about the war situation outside our bit of jungle. One day at the enemy camp we saw two flags go up, the Union Jack and the Japanese flag. We heard '*Banzai! Banzai!*' in Japanese. We'd never seen anything like this before. We then had three days of silence. Planes flew over and dropped leaflets proclaiming, 'Peace has come to the Orient.' Even the regimental commander didn't know about the end of the war. This must have been about August 15, but even that I don't know exactly. It would be a lie if I said I felt sad, or happy. I can't analyze my feelings at that time. I just felt, 'Well, so it is over.'

ACKNOWLEDGMENTS

The publisher has made every effort to contact the copyright holders of material reproduced in this book, and wishes to apologize to those he has been unable to trace. Grateful acknowledgment is made for permission to reprint the following from:

Wake Island Command by W. Scott Cunningham. Copyright © 1961 by Lydel Sims and W. Scott Cunningham. By permission of Little, Brown and Company.

Popski's Private Army by Vladimir Peniakoff (OUP 1991). Copyright © Vladimir Peniakoff. First published by Jonathan Cape.

A Ribbon and a Star: The Third Marines at Bougainville by John Monks Jr. Copyright 1945, © 1973 by Henry Holt &. Company, Inc.

Goodbye Darkness: A Memoir of the Pacific War by William Manchester. Copyright © William Manchester, 1981. Reproduced by permission of Michael Joseph Ltd.

Tank! 40 Hours of Battle by Ken Iout (Robert Hale Ltd 1985). Copyright © Ken Tout 1985. By permission of Robert Hale Limited.

Men of the Red Beret by Max Arthur published by Hutchinson 1990. Printed by permission of David Higham Associates.

Nothing Less than Victory: The Oral History of D-Day by Russell Miller. Reprinted by permission of the Peters Fraser & Dunlop Group Ltd.

The editor and publisher would also like to thank the Imperial War Museum for access to their collection and the staff of the Reading Rooms for all their help.

Printed in Great Britain
by Amazon

18546025R00169